"*The Magna Carta of Humanity* cries out like a voice in the desert calling for a bold rediscovery of the vision of freedom that once helped to shape the English-speaking world. The imperative to respond with humility and rediscover the ancient paths rings out on every page."

Philippa Stroud, CEO, Legatum Institute, London

"The survival of the Jewish people in history is a miracle in itself, but Guinness goes beyond that. He argues that the Sinai revolution provides both a precedent and a pattern for the future of humanity. This is a bold argument and a must-read for anyone seeking to understand our present global crisis."

Tomas Sandell, European Coalition for Israel

"Clichés aside, America is at a crossroads. Will the spirit of 1776 (the American Revolution) or the spirit of 1789 (the French Revolution) inspire us through the upheavals and crises of recent years? Os Guinness takes us back even further, to the original revolution of freedom, the Exodus. Os sees the big picture through the right lens, that of the Bible and the Bible's constructive influence on America's founding ideals (1776). He is our Tocqueville, an outsider who knows us better than we know ourselves."

Douglas Groothuis, professor of philosophy, Denver Seminary

"This book should be read by anyone who is concerned about the future of America and of Western civilization. In warning that Western freedoms are under threat, Os Guinness is not issuing an angry culture-war call to arms but a rational, cogently argued case for looking again at what made America and the West so successful in the first place. Guinness is a masterful writer. He pulls no punches in his critique of what ails the postmodern West. His arguments will and should be hotly debated, but they should not be ignored."

Rob Gifford, senior editor, *The Economist*

"In Os Guinness's penetrating analysis, the Jews' exodus from Egyptian bondage towers above all human revolutions, dramatically revealing the nature and power of freedom's divine author. He draws from the deep well of Scripture, and in particular rabbinical wisdom, to reflect on the very nature of God, who affirms the extraordinary uniqueness and ineradicable dignity of every single individual. With his vast learning and dazzling insights, Guinness leads us through a compelling critique of worldviews and philosophies lurking the global landscape over the centuries and eloquently urges humanity's return to the fountainhead, the 'Sinai revolution' that gave life and breath to the mighty vision of freedom rightly ordered under the voice of God."

Ken Starr, former president of Baylor University

THE
MAGNA CARTA
OF HUMANITY

SINAI'S REVOLUTIONARY FAITH
AND THE FUTURE OF FREEDOM

OS GUINNESS

An imprint of InterVarsity Press
Downers Grove, Illinois

InterVarsity Press
P.O. Box 1400, Downers Grove, IL 60515-1426
ivpress.com
email@ivpress.com

InterVarsity Press® is the book-publishing division of InterVarsity Christian Fellowship/USA®, a movement of students and faculty active on campus at hundreds of universities, colleges, and schools of nursing in the United States of America, and a member movement of the International Fellowship of Evangelical Students. For information about local and regional activities, visit intervarsity.org.

All Scripture quotations, unless otherwise indicated, are taken from the New American Standard Bible®, copyright 1960, 1962, 1963, 1968, 1971, 1972, 1973, 1975, 1977, 1995 by The Lockman Foundation. Used by permission.

Chapter 5 contains material adapted from Last Call for Liberty by Os Guinness. Copyright ©2018 by Os Guinness. Used by permission of InterVarsity Press, Downers Grove, IL, USA. www.ivpress.com.

While any stories in this book are true, some names and identifying information may have been changed to protect the privacy of individuals.

The publisher cannot verify the accuracy or functionality of website URLs used in this book beyond the date of publication.

Published in association with the literary agency of Wolgemuth & Associates.

Cover design and image composite: David Fassett
Interior design: Jeanna Wiggins
Images: cover painting: © Eugène_Delacroix_-_Le_28_Juillet._La_Liberté_guidant_le_peuple. (wikimedia)
    Washington painting: © Washington_Crossing_the_Delaware_by_Emanuel_Leutze,_MMA-NYC,_1851
    old ripped torn paper: © NikolaVukojevic / iStock / Getty Images Plus
    black brush stroke: © MirageC / Moment Collection / Getty Images
    white crumpled paper: © Kwangmoozaa / iStock / Getty Images Plus

ISBN 978-0-8308-4715-0 (print)
ISBN 978-0-8308-4716-7 (digital)

Printed in the United States of America ∞

InterVarsity Press is committed to ecological stewardship and to the conservation of natural resources in all our operations. This book was printed using sustainably sourced paper.

Library of Congress Cataloging-in-Publication Data
A catalog record for this book is available from the Library of Congress.

| P | 25 | 24 | 23 | 22 | 21 | 20 | 19 | 18 | 17 | 16 | 15 | 14 | 13 | 12 | 11 | 10 | 9 | 8 | 7 | 6 | 5 | 4 | 3 | 2 | 1 |
| Y | 42 | 41 | 40 | 39 | 38 | 37 | 36 | 35 | 34 | 33 | 32 | 31 | 30 | 29 | 28 | 27 | 26 | 25 | 24 | 23 | 22 | 21 |

DOM

And to Jenny,

My beloved, my friend, and my heart's delight.

And with heartfelt gratitude to Rabbi Lord Jonathan Sacks,

whose brilliant, creative, and fruitful wisdom is

a compass and a guiding light in the present chaos.

And to all who long and strive for a

brighter human future in our time.

Let my people go!

MOSES TO THE PHARAOH OF EGYPT, EXODUS

You will know the truth, and the truth will set you free.

JESUS OF NAZARETH, *GOSPEL OF JOHN*

Should any of our nation be asked about our laws, he will repeat them as readily as his own name. The result of our thorough education in our laws from the very dawn of intelligence is that they are, as it were, engraved on our souls.

JOSEPHUS, *CONTRA APIONEM*

A good man, though a slave, is free; but a wicked man, though a king, is a slave. For he serves, not one man alone, but, what is worse, as many masters as he has vices.

AUGUSTINE OF HIPPO, *THE CITY OF GOD*

Freedom is the man that will turn the world upside down, therefore, no wonder, he hath enemies.

GERRARD WINSTANLEY, *A WATCHWORD TO THE CITY OF LONDON*

I doubt much, very much indeed, whether France is at all ripe for liberty on any standard. Men are qualified for civil liberty, in exact proportion to their disposition too put moral chains upon their appetites; in proportion as their love to justice is above their rapacity; in proportion as their soundness and sobriety of understanding is above their vanity and presumption; in proportion as they are more disposed to listen to the counsels of the wise and good, in preference to the flattery of knaves. Society cannot exist unless a controlling power upon will and appetite be placed somewhere, and the less of it there is within, the more there must be without. It is ordained in the eternal constitution of things, that men of intemperate minds cannot be free. Their passions form their fetters.

EDMUND BURKE, LETTER TO A MEMBER OF THE NATIONAL ASSEMBLY

I will insist that the Hebrews have contributed more to civilize men than any other nation. If I were an atheist, and believed in blind eternal fate, I should still believe that fate had ordained the Jews to be the most essential instrument for civilizing the nations. . . . They are the most glorious nation that ever inhabited this earth. The Romans and their empire were but a bubble in comparison to the Jews.

JOHN ADAMS, LETTER TO F. A. VAN DER KEMP, 1808

None are more hopelessly enslaved than those who falsely believe they are free.

JOHANN WOLFGANG VON GOETHE, *ELECTIVE AFFINITIES*

The absolute monarchies have dishonored despotism; let us be careful that the democratic republics do not rehabilitate it.

ALEXIS DE TOCQUEVILLE, *DEMOCRACY IN AMERICA*

Since the Exodus, freedom has spoken with a Hebrew accent.

HEINRICH HEINE, *GERMANY TO LUTHER*

What will one not give up for freedom?

FYODOR DOSTOEVSKY, *NOTES FROM THE DEAD HOUSE*

The time is coming when we shall have to pay for having been Christians for two thousand years.

FRIEDRICH NIETZSCHE, *THE WILL TO POWER*

Liberty lies in the hearts of men and women; when it dies there, no constitution, no law, no court can save it; no constitution, no law, no court can do much to help it.

JUDGE LEARNED HAND, 1944

We are impressed by the towering buildings of New York City.
Yet not the rock of Manhattan nor the steel of Pittsburgh but
the law that came from Sinai is their ultimate foundation.
The true foundation upon which our cities stand
is a handful of spiritual ideas.

ABRAHAM JOSHUA HESCHEL,
MORAL GRANDEUR AND SPIRITUAL AUDACITY

If we fail in our promises to each other, and lose the principles
of the covenant, then we lose everything, for they are we.

JOHN SCHARR, _LEGITIMACY AND THE MODERN STATE_

The Western world has arrived at a decisive moment. Over the next few years, it
will gamble the existence of the civilization that created it. I think that
it is not aware of it. Time has eroded your notion of liberty.
You have kept the word and devised a different notion.
You have forgotten the meaning of liberty.

ALEXANDER SOLZHENITSYN, _WARNING TO THE WEST_

To defend a country you need an army. But to defend a free society you need
schools. You need families and an educational system in which ideals are passed
on from one generation to the next, and never lost, or despaired of, or obscured.
There has never been a more profound understanding of freedom. It is not difficult,
Moses was saying, to gain liberty, but to sustain it is the work of a hundred
generations. Forget it and you lose it.

RABBI JONATHAN SACKS, _COVENANT & CONVERSATION: EXODUS_

CONTENTS

INTRODUCTION

UPSIDE DOWN OR RIGHT WAY UP?

"SON, WE'RE IN TROUBLE. Chiang Kai-shek has just abandoned the city. We are at the mercy of the Red Army." My father's words to me early in 1949 are indelibly printed on my mind. I was seven and a half years old, and we were living in Nanking (Nanjing), the capital of the Western-backed Kuomintang, or the Nationalist government of China. We had met the Generalissimo and Madame Chiang, we had witnessed the hasty packing of the Western embassies, and we had felt the pressure of the noose slowly tightening around the city. Soon, the People's Liberation Army, led by the ruthless Lin Biao, was to march in and take over the fearful population that the Japanese had so brutalized twelve years earlier in the horrendous rape of Nanking.

The Chinese civil war was over. The People's Republic was victorious. History's fifth great modern revolution had succeeded. Communism had taken over the world's most populous country. Loudspeakers were set up. Trials began. Executions took place. Fear and terror reigned. Friends who knew us well could no longer acknowledge us for fear of their lives, and locals who only a week earlier had seemed so friendly were baying for our blood. "Death to the blue-eyed foreign devils!" would greet us if we ventured out of the house. The horror of Mao Zedong's Chinese revolution, in which tens of millions of his fellow countrymen were to meet their end, was underway. My father was denounced and publicly accused of trumped-up charges, and many of my parents' friends were executed, imprisoned, or persecuted. The violence of the reign of terror was terror enough, but as the communists knew, the real terror they held over the head of the city was the unspoken fear of who or what might be next.

Years later as a graduate student at Oxford, I came to know the eminent Jewish philosopher Isaiah Berlin at All Souls College. Curiously, he had witnessed the Russian Revolution at the very same age in 1917. He had been horrified by one memory above all as he was walking through Saint Petersburg, then Petrograd, with his governess—the spectacle of a police officer dragged off by a mob and lynched. It had left him with a horror of mobs and physical violence for the rest of his life.

When we compared the memories of two seven-year-old boys witnessing a part of the two great revolutions of the twentieth century three decades apart, 1917 and 1949, there was no disagreement at the high table at All Souls. We had both been marked for life by twentieth-century Marxism and certain conclusions were beyond question: First, the communist revolutions, with their totalitarian repression, were an evil rivaled in modern history only by Adolf Hitler's national socialism (Stalin, Hitler, and Mao setting the bar for modern dictatorship); second, the two English-speaking revolutions, though different because the English failed and the American succeeded, were united in their distinctive views of ordered freedom, so they would always stand firm against the revolutionary totalitarianisms of the right and left, as they had done in World War II; and third, socialism was un-thinkable in America anyway because Americanism and the American dream were powerful surrogate ideas that rendered the appeal of socialism redundant.

Little wonder that fifty years later I stand aghast as an admirer of America's great experiment in freedom as I witness the unfolding of recent events in the United States. Meddlers are never welcome in a family quarrel, but there are times when silence is impossible. As I write, leading voices have called for a root-and-branch revolution of a different sort. Legitimate protests against racism have erupted into violence, looting, arson, and anarchy, and large swathes of American society appear to be unable or unwilling to condemn the violence and defend their own revolution—and many are deeply ashamed and opposed to their own revolution. The destructive anger, of course, is merely the activist expression of the radical ideas that have rampaged through American schools, colleges, universities, and wider intellectual circles over the last fifty years. If 2020 was "the year of the Black Swans," it was a rerun of 1968, "the *annus ca-lamitous* of the Sixties," but now fermented for a full half-century.

The grapes of wrath have ripened again. The great American republic is as deeply divided today as at any moment since just before the Civil War. Yet this time no Abraham Lincoln has stepped forward to address the evils, appeal to the Declaration of Independence, defend the better angel of the American character, demonstrate the magnificence of "government of the people, by the people, for the people" in our time, and call for a "new birth of freedom." Strikingly too, the deepest roots of the present division lie in the ideas and ideals of a revolution that is flatly opposed to the American Revolution. In one generation America has been bewitched by ideas and ideals that owe nothing to 1776 and the American Revolution, and everything to 1789 and the French Revolution. In short, partly through design and partly through drift, America appears to be abandoning the ideals of the American Revolution for ideas that are disastrous not only to America but to freedom and to the future of humanity.

THE MAGNA CARTA OF HUMANITY

This book is a response to America's crisis by a firm and longtime admirer of the American experiment. Three major themes run through my argument. First, the American crisis is a crisis of freedom and must be understood as such. Following Augustine of Hippo's notion that nations must be understood and assessed by what they love supremely rather than by such factors as the size of their population and the strength of their armies, there is no question that America's supreme love is freedom. In particular, America's freedom is a unique concept of ordered freedom that is the legacy of the Hebrew Scriptures and of the Hebrew covenant in particular. The present crisis of freedom therefore goes to the very heart of the American republic and all that the American experiment stands for. It is a crisis whose outcome will prove as decisive as that of the Civil War. It is also a global crisis in the sense that its outcome will be crucial for the prospects of freedom in the human future.

Second, the present crisis stems from the fact that over the last fifty years, major spheres of American society have shifted their loyalties and now support ideas that are closer to the French Revolution and its heirs rather than the American Revolution. The two revolutions share the same name, *revolution*, and the same century, the eighteenth, but they are decisively different at almost every point—their sources, their assumptions, their policies, their narratives, and their outcomes. These differences mean that the choice between the two revolutions will prove decisive for America and for freedom. What Lincoln proclaimed in June 1858, when nominated to run as a Republican candidate for the US Senate, is true all over again. He echoed Jesus of Nazareth and applied the point to his time, but it is true again in ours. "A house divided against itself cannot stand."[1] *America cannot endure permanently half "1776" and half "1789."*

Third, the time has come for a new global thrust on behalf of freedom and justice for humanity. The inadequacies and failures of the last several centuries in politics have become plain, especially in terms of the hollowness of much traditional liberalism and the horror of much radical leftism. The best way forward for America and the world must be through rediscovery and a fresh examination of what I will call the Sinai Revolution. Historically, it was the Exodus Revolution, and not the French Revolution, that lay behind the genius of America's ordered freedom or covenantal and constitutional freedom. A rediscovery of the foundational principles of the Exodus Revolution is therefore the once and future secret of true revolutionary faith and a sure path to freedom, justice, equality, and peace.

These ideals are not clichés, and they must once again become solid realities in the coming generations. But while many radical and revolutionary claimants promise them, the urgent need is to deliver them, and the surest way to do so lies in the precedent, the principles, and the practices of the Exodus Revolution. Rightly understood, there is no rival to the Exodus Revolution in its realistic and constructive understanding of freedom. *Sinai*, and not *Paris*, represents such a beacon of freedom that it should be recognized as nothing less than the Magna Carta of humanity.

To anyone not deafened by the incessant noise of the current politicking and culture warring, and not mesmerized by the triple screen gazing of mobile phones, computers, and televisions, we are clearly at a most extraordinary moment in world affairs—for the human future, for the global world, for Western civilization, and for its lead society, the great American republic. This book therefore addresses the current crisis as part of the great human quest for freedom. And it goes beyond analysis to argue there should be a bold rediscovery of the vision of freedom that once helped to shape the English-speaking revolutions and that could now stand as a beacon for the peoples of the whole world.

1776 VERSUS 1789

But let me slow down. As the world emerges from the global coronavirus pandemic, two of the deepest questions raised are, Do Americans realize the contours of the world of the future that has been exposed? And will America now walk more humbly? Neither history nor human existence must ever be taken for granted. The passing of the angel of death devastated many of modernity's lesser gifts, such as comfort and convenience, but it also rocked the central citadel of the idol of mastery, control, and self-reliance. For all our reason, science, technology, management, and punditry, human existence is never fully under human control. What history has always taught in terms of time, globalization now teaches in terms of space. Self-congratulation should always be advised to take a longer view and a wider perspective. Unthinking claims to exceptionalism shrink to a more modest size for anyone who knows history and the wider world. Each of us has only a finite life, and every super-power is only one nation like other nations.

What then makes America distinctive, and how strong and healthy is that distinctiveness today? Let me enter the discussion from the perspective of America's past. The war that climaxed the American Revolution ended with the surrender of the British and Hessian forces at Yorktown, Virginia, on October 19, 1781. Perhaps apocryphally, tradition says that as the defeated troops marched out, the band was ordered to play a popular ballad from a century earlier, "The World Turned Upside Down." (The 2015 Broadway musical *Hamilton* included a new song with this title as an homage.) The original seventeenth-century ballad came out of the heart of the teeming ferment of radical questioning, debate, dreaming, travel, freedom, and conflict that made up the astonishing two decades of the English Revolution, a revolution sparked by the demands for freedom. ("Freedom is the man that will turn the world upside down," Gerrard Winstanley, the Diggers' leader declared to the city of London.)[2] Turning the world upside down was a leading theme of the English Revolution, and the English Revolution was the first of the five major revolutions that have shaped the modern era: the English, 1642; the American, 1776; the French, 1789; the Russian, 1917; and the Chinese, 1949.

The English Revolution witnessed the eruption of a colorful and rowdy cast of characters who burst onto the scene to disrupt the long-established status quo that, across all the different royal houses, had ruled England since time immemorial—the Agitators, the Levellers, the Diggers, the Ranters, the Quakers, the Shakers, the Seekers, the Masterless Men, and the Fifth Monarchy Men. Truly they and their republicanism turned the world upside down as they furiously set out to do—but only for the world to be turned right way up again, as their opponents and eventual conquerors saw the situation when Charles II returned and the monarchy was restored in 1660. At first sight the English Revolution was the failure of the five.[3]

But what is the right way up for a society? Who says so, and how are we to decide? Such questions raise issues that the global era would do well to debate today, for the unprecedented challenges of the global era raise the question as to which ultimate beliefs and which visions of political freedom can best lead the world forward. Those questions are not theoretical or academic. They lie at the heart of two immediate issues now troubling the American republic, but with huge longer-term implications for the West and the world at large.

First, what is the root of the current American crisis—the *great polarization*? As I said, the American republic is as deeply divided today as at any time since just before the Civil War, but why? Contrary to what many think, the division is not simply the result of growing inequities, the clash between the coastals (New York and California) and the heartlanders (in the Midwest and South), or between the populists (Hillary Clinton's "deplorables") and the globalists (one-world advocates of borderless nations). The deepest division is between two mutually exclusive views of America: those who understand America and freedom from the perspective of 1776 and the American Revolution, and those who understand America and freedom from the perspective of 1789 and the French Revolution and its ideological heirs.

Such current movements as postmodernism, political correctness, tribal and identity politics, the sexual revolution, critical theory (or grievance studies), and socialism all come down from 1789 and have nothing to do with the ideas of 1776. These movements and their ideas are far more important than the professors, the politicians, and the protesters who express them today. Indeed, these ideas and ideologies subvert the very foundations of Western civilization, and they are designed to do so. They are the real *dramatis personae* without which the drama of America's current crisis cannot be understood or resolved.

Second, why is there so far no American leader addressing the crisis from the vantage point of the American Revolution? That is the startling difference between the 1850s and today. There is currently no equivalent of Abraham Lincoln's leadership in the crisis. Lincoln not only addressed the evils of the hour, supremely slavery, but he did so by addressing them in the light of the Declaration of Independence and "the better angel" of the American experiment. For all today's talk of "making America great again," no American leader currently addresses what made America great *in the first place*. For a nation that is a republic by intention and by ideas, that deeper understanding is indispensable. No purely political, economic, managerial, or technocratic solution can compensate for the absence of foundational ideas.

To be sure, Americans still show a massive interest in the individual heroes of their founding generation—as evidenced by recent bestselling biographies of George Washington, John Adams, Thomas Jefferson, and others, as well as the Broadway musical *Hamilton*. But there is no equivalent interest in the character and workings of the American experiment itself, its distinctive understanding of freedom and the roots that made it what it is. And an entire generation has now been raised on the anti-American account of history promoted by writers such as Howard Zinn and the 1619 Project. The better books may still be read, but the founding leaders cannot be resurrected. If the great experiment in freedom is to continue, their ideas and the roots of their ideas must be recovered, and there must be leaders today who can set out those ideas and their relevance for our time.

IT WAS THE HEBREW REPUBLIC, STUPID!

Appreciation for history is scarce today, public debate is only rarely lit by foundational principles, and there is a further reason why the needed discussion fails to get off the ground—especially in the speech code, cancel culture of many American and European universities. Debate is often ended by prejudice and a fashionable consensus that chokes it off from the start. Modern freedom, toleration, and human rights, it is said, are all a result of the loosening of the restrictions and superstitions of religion, and therefore only any progressive narrative must remain adamantly secular. There is therefore a stifling consensus in many intellectual circles that trumpets its own canonical orthodoxy: freedom, toleration, and human rights owe everything to the blessings of the Continental Enlightenment in the eighteenth century and to the deep revulsion against the wars of religion in the seventeenth. In the great pursuit of freedom for the world of tomorrow, faith and freedom—Sinai and Paris—are said to be opponents, not allies. If America ever had any better angels, the critics add, they have been tarnished irreparably and can no longer be cited today. Full stop. End of discussion.

In fact, that view represents only one side of the debate we need to be having, and with any debate it takes two sides to make a genuine hearing. That first side is certainly powerful and fashionable. In *Nature's God*, for example, Matthew Stewart rejects the mainstream understanding of the American Revolution and traces back its genealogy to "heretical origins" and the less-known "revolutionary dimensions of the American revolution."[4] "The real story of America's philosophical origins," he claims, "properly begins in ancient Greece, and its first protagonist is the most famous atheist in history [Epicurus]."[5] Stewart highlights the ideas of Thomas Paine, Thomas Jefferson, Ben Franklin, Ethan Allen of the Green Mountain Boys, and Thomas Young, who set off the Boston Tea Party, and then shows how their ideas go back to the Greek philosopher Epicurus, the Roman poet Lucretius and the Dutch philosopher Spinoza. ("I too am an Epicurean," Jefferson wrote to William Short in 1819.)[6]

According to this view, the real roots of American freedom, the meaning of terms such as *nature's God* and *self-evident truths* and the very significance of America for the world's liberal order today do not lie where they have long been thought to lie. They lie in the ideas of radical thinkers dismissed in their time as "deists," "infidels," and "atheists," but whose thinking was well ahead of their time and has only now come into its own. Soon the time is coming, Stewart concludes, when those ideas will triumph completely. "Yet time changes all things," and soon we will be able to see into the future "a nation that will have liberated itself from all forms of tyranny over the human mind. Call it the land of the free."[7]

Such dreams of freedom are soothing and self-evident to many modern minds, which then raise the drawbridge and lower the portcullis against further debate. But in fact the other side deserves a hearing. Such arguments on the first side are skewed, and their main claim is flatly contradicted by a more accurate view of what followed the wars of religion. Freedom in the seventeenth century did not come from heretical origins, as claimed, but from principles out of the Hebrew Scriptures brought back into public discourse by Reformation thinkers and by public intellectuals such as John Locke and John Milton.

Debates over freedom flourished in Reformation countries such as Switzerland, the Netherlands, Scotland, and England. Even the so-called heretics based their appeals on biblical grounds. Thomas Hobbes, an atheist, cited the Bible more than any other book in *Leviathan* and far more than the classics. And whether or not Thomas Paine's atheism ultimately came from Epicurus or Lucretius, many of his arguments and appeals in his bestselling *Common Sense* came directly from the Bible. His attacks on the notion of monarchy, which were surely decisive in the American Revolution, appeal directly to the teaching of the Hebrew Scriptures.

The truth is that key ideas from the Hebrew and Christian Scriptures, rediscovered through the Reformation and disseminated through the invention of printing, were decisive in both the English and American Revolutions and especially in the rejection of monarchy and the rise of republicanism—and all this well before the French Enlightenment in the eighteenth century. In the case of the English Revolution, these biblical and Reformation ideas ended up on the losing side and are now viewed as part of "the lost cause." But in the case of the American Revolution they were central to what became the "winning cause." Their stamp on the American way of freedom is unique and consequential, even if rejected today because of the flaws and inconsistencies in the way the American Revolution lived out its understanding of Sinai.

Thus, as historians Eric Nelson and Michael Walzer point out, the seventeenth century was the "Biblical century," and the English revolution was "the war of the saints" because of the impact of the Reformation principle of *sola Scriptura* (Scripture alone). Its impetus was to point people back to the Hebrew Torah and above all to the revolutionary significance of the exodus, the "Hebrew Republic," and to the thinking of the "Christian Hebraists."[8] "For roughly 100 years," Nelson writes, "European Protestants made the Hebrew Bible the measure of their politics."[9] Needless to say, these biblical ideas contributed to freedom well before the Enlightenment, though they were then emphatically rejected by the Enlightenment, and also by the French, Russian, and Chinese revolutions that were the later heirs of the French Enlightenment.

In sum, Western liberalism is rooted in ideas that are undeniably Jewish and Christian, and the weakness of much liberalism as it confronts radicalism today is simply the result of the denial and dismissal of these roots. Cut flowers are rather less hardy than well-rooted trees.

THE VOLCANIC EXPLOSION OF 1789

That last point is critical for understanding the modern crisis of freedom. The English and American Revolutions are decisively different from the French Revolution, and the future of freedom depends on appreciating the differences and choosing between them. The uncomfortable truth for Americans is that the United States may still be the world's lead society, but the ideas of the American Revolution no longer inspire the world's pursuit of freedom—even for many of America's intelligentsia and the younger generation. The French Revolution towers over revolutionary thinking and action as "the great revolution" of the modern age. A spectacular Vesuvian explosion occurred in 1789. It lasted only ten years before Napoleon announced, "It is over" in December 1799, but its influence around the world is far from over. What flowed from it like red-hot lava was the notion of "the revolutionary" (created by 1789) and the "revolutionary faith" that has been powerful in the world ever since, which I will call "Paris" (even though it flourishes today in many places, but not in Paris).

The French Revolution has been described as "the central cause of the malformation of modern ideological thought."[10] Certainly, it ignited a host of revolutions and changes in its train. It became the precedent for other revolutions, it helped shape the rise of nationalism, it created the *left* versus *right* division in politics, and it raised the idea of the revolutionary as an activist whose ideology is as passionate as any religion and whose dream it is to transform humanity and change the world. Some of the later revolutions were successful, above all the Russian and the Chinese revolutions. Many were a failure—including the failed Paris revolutions of 1830 and 1848. The latter marked the end of the revolutionary era in Western Europe as well as the end of the Romantic movement. Victor Hugo immortalized the revolution of 1848 in his novel *Les Misérables*, later celebrated in its turn by the legendary musical of the same name.

But whether the later revolutions succeeded or failed, behind them all was 1789. When the French Revolution was over, the world had changed forever. "On a whole host of political, intellectual and structural planes," historian David Andress wrote, "the French Revolution is the fount and origin of our modern world."[11] Hannah Arendt judged that "it was the French, and not the American Revolution that set the world on fire."[12] Literary critic George Steiner summarized the watershed significance even more extravagantly: "The French Revolution is the pivotal historical-social date after that of the foundation of Christianity. . . . Time itself was deemed to have begun a second time."[13] This spirit of Paris resonated throughout the world long after Paris itself had ceased to be a center of revolution. The Jewish poet Heinrich Heine captured this spirit perfectly in the nineteenth century. "Freedom is the new religion, the religion of our time. . . . But the French are the chosen people of the new religion, their language records the first gospels and dogmas. Paris is the New Jerusalem, the Rhine is the Jordan that separates the consecrated land of freedom from the land of the Philistines."[14]

The eminent historian and the US Librarian of Congress James H. Billington has told the story in his magisterial *Fire in the Minds of Men*. Revolutionary faith is "perhaps the faith of our time," and "modern revolutionaries are believers, no less committed and intense than were the Christian or Muslims of an earlier era."[15] Revolution has always been compared to a spark and a flame. When anti-Napoleon conspirators in France were ridiculed for having no Archimedean lever and only a match, they replied, "With a match one has no need of a lever; one does not lift up the world, one burns it."[16] If traditional religion is to be described as the opium of the people, Billington remarks, "The new revolutionary faith might well be called the amphetamine of the intellectuals."[17]

Almost as if prefiguring the script of Fyodor Dostoevsky's novel *Demons*, France's *great revolution* and its *revolutionary faith* (Paris) poured out in three major directions, each one taking up one of the three great tricolor ideals of 1789: *liberté, fraternité*, and *egalité*. American radicals have somehow missed the point, but *liberty*, which was the passion of the American Revolution, has always been the weakest of the ideals to be taken forward by 1789. *Fraternity* became the inspiration and the watchword for *revolutionary nationalism* in the nineteenth century, and *equality* (or the classless society) became the Holy Grail for the *revolutionary socialism* that also developed in the nineteenth century—though it became truly powerful in the form of communism only in the twentieth century.

Thus, the French, the Russian, and the Chinese revolutions all broke decisively with the precedent and principles of the English and American Revolutions, and the differences between the first two and the last three have proved, and will continue to prove, fateful for freedom. The Russian and Chinese revolutions represented the first successful establishment of secularist regimes in history: the Russian doing so in Europe and the Chinese in Asia. Along with Hitler's Germany, the Russian and Chinese revolutions were also the first regimes to produce genuine totalitarianism. With the horrendous quartet of their total ideology, total mobilization, total surveillance, and total repression, these to-talitarian regimes became the epitome of oppressive evil and the complete denial of liberty. Lenin's triumph through the Bolsheviks was also, in Billington's words, the "first major break in the basic unity of European civilization since Luther."[18]

There is no surprise in the break between the American and the French Revolutions, for unlike the English and the American Revolutions that were rooted in the Bible, the French, the Russian, and the Chinese revolutions were rooted in the French Enlightenment (and less obviously in the world of Masonic Lodges and Adam Weishaupt's Illuminism, as Billington demonstrates). These last three revolutions were overtly antibiblical, antireligious, and anti-Christian, and their overall record on freedom has been dismal. Far from ushering in the final form of freedom and representing a second coming of Epicurus, their claims to be the true and reliable source of human freedom have been left in tatters by the history of their repressive secularist regimes in the twentieth century and the slaughter of millions of their own citizens.

SAYS WHO?

The "Biblical century" was revolutionary, but with an entirely different vision of revolution than the French Revolution. In fact, the idea of turning the world upside down came directly from the Bible, where the prime revolutionary, and therefore the subversive of the status quo, is said to be God himself. As the Hebrew Scriptures see it, God is the true revolutionary. God creates order, but humans create disorder. So if right is to prevail and humans are to flourish, the disordered order must itself be overturned and God's order reasserted. "You turn things upside down," the prophet Isaiah charges his generation (Is 29:16 NIV). *Turning the world upside down is therefore God's way of turning the world the right way up.*

For most of history, religion in a thousand forms may have been "the flowers on the chains," as Karl Marx charged, but not the faith of the Bible. "For the first time, God is associated with change, transformation, revolution."[19] Faith in God is therefore protest against any and every status quo and all abuse of power. Revolution, though with a vision that is radically different from the vision of the political left, is central to the repair and restoration of the world. A new vision, a new way, a new family, and a new people are at work in the world. This revolution is constructive, not destructive. In turning the world the right way up, the revolution is restoration.

Both the Hebrew psalmist (Ps 146:9) and the prophet Isaiah declare, in the words of the King James Version, "The Lord maketh the earth . . . waste, and turneth it upside down" (Is 24:1). The Jewish and Christian faiths were the original revolutionary faiths long before the French Revolution. Both were called to be countercultural protest faiths, though the Christian church too often abandoned its biblical calling and became the chaplain to the status quo and even the cheerleader to a series of oppressive establishments. Today, following the shaking of world events, this positive and constructive vision of Jewish-Christian transformation is being rediscovered around the world.

The better-known precedent for the term *revolution* came later in the Bible when certain agitators in the Greek city of Thessalonica stirred up a riot against the early Christian mission of Paul of Tarsus with the famous words: "These that have turned the world upside down are come here also" (Acts 17:6). Beginning with its powerful and distinctive way of peacemaking, which was the antidote to the false peace of Pax Romana, the early Christian movement was regarded as subversive and countercultural. Later still in the first century, the Romans attacked the Jews themselves for attempting to turn the world upside down. When the historian Tacitus explained Judaism to his fellow Romans as he told the story of the Jewish wars under Vespasian and Titus, he commented: "Moses introduced a new cult, which was the opposite of all other religions. All that we held sacred they held profane, and they allowed practices which we abominate."[20]

Plainly, "turning the world upside down" is a relative notion. It all depends on who says so, why, and what they mean by it. The mere claim to be revolutionary is not enough in a day when the idea is trivialized in common speech and co-opted by advertising and a thousand mini claimants. The question is, which revolution are we talking about, and where does it lead? To Paul's opponents the accusation was a highly dangerous charge of sedition, serious enough to cause a riot and threaten his life, and the ultimate crime in the Roman Empire. Consider the fate of Spartacus and his six thousand followers who were strung up on crosses along the Appian Way. Later, the emperor Julian again leveled the charge against the Christians as he tried to restore the world by turning it the right way up as he saw it from the vantage point of paganism ("For through the folly of the Galileans almost everything has been overturned").[21]

But of course, Paul of Tarsus, his Christian converts, eventually Julian's successors, and the Roman Empire at large saw things differently and he was eventually called "Julian the Apostate." The charge against the Christians had turned into a compliment. They believed that the good news they proclaimed was truly revolutionary, and the only way to set the world right again. Centuries later Karl Marx in his Young Hegelian days spoke of finding Hegel standing on his head and turned him the right way up, though doubtless Hegel would have protested at the indignity of such treatment of a master by a disciple.

And so it goes. One person's right way up is another person's wrong way up. One person's revolution is another person's rebellion, just as one person's fight for freedom is another's terrorism, one person's liberty is another's license, and one person's sanity is another's madness. (Think of Ken Kesey's countercultural novel and the film it spawned *One Flew over the Cuckoo's Nest*.) For the Jewish people the exodus is the "master story of freedom," whereas Friedrich Nietzsche argued in *The Anti-Christ* that exodus stood for the return of a "slave morality" that he attempted to overturn in its turn through his own "revaluation of all values."[22] Just so the Puritan vision that historians describe as the "lost cause" in England became the winning cause in New England and then in America as a whole. Or again, the years 1642, 1776, 1789, 1917, and 1948 were all years that heralded major revolutions in world history, but the differences between the aspirations and achievements of the first two, the English and the American, and the last three, the French, the Russian, and the Chinese, are still the stunning, sobering, and prime shapers of the modern world and the future. The central contest is still between Sinai and Paris.

Remembering relativity is an important reminder and especially so when it comes to freedom, for Sinai-style liberation is entirely different from the Paris-style liberation of the progressive left. This book is for all who care about freedom and all who dare to be on the wrong side of those considered the "right people," for it challenges the fashionable views of who is right and what is wrong. I am arguing here for what many supporters of Paris dismiss as the reactionary faith or, at best, as the other revolutionary faith. *But rightly understood, Paris and the progressive left lead to repression, whereas Sinai is in fact the true and the original revolutionary faith, the best and most inspiring vision of freedom—the right way up for humanity.* But with all the clichés, confusions, and conflicts surrounding contemporary freedom, and with all the relativity of different assumptions and perspectives of others offering their views, everything depends on what we mean by *freedom* and why. As Johann Wolfgang von Goethe noted in *Elective Affinities,* no one is more hopelessly enslaved than those who falsely believe they are free. (What, for example, does it say of America as "the land of the free" that more Americans are bound by addictions and in recovery groups than any other people in the world?)

In the tumultuous chaos of the present moment we must each be clear about where we stand, what sort of freedom we are advocating, and why. The fact that a given situation has existed in a certain way for a long time does not mean that it is the right way up. Even the most powerful, prosperous, and seemingly permanent status quo needs to be justified and not simply asserted. Custom, consensus, popularity, and fashion may all be wrong, and the upside-down world of the outsider and the minority may well be the right way up in the end.

What matters too is that we are raising the question of freedom today when the world faces unprecedented tensions between three of the most powerful modern claimants to human allegiance: the Jewish and Christian faiths, progressive secularism, and Islam. And once again, the world finds itself torn between the two great bookends of human history, *authoritarianism* and *anarchy.*

Authoritarianism is the world of order and stability without freedom (represented today by the governments of China, Russia, Turkey, Cuba, North Korea, and many other countries). It endangers humanity through what Billington calls the twin threats of "total war and totalitarian peace"—the latter being "a state of permanent war preparation without fighting."[23] Anarchy, on the other hand, is the world of freedom without order and stability (increasingly represented today by trends in the United States and much of the Western world). The present challenge is to establish genuine personal freedom and substantially free societies in a generation that pays lip service to freedom while all the time it is pulled toward one or other of the extremes—which, like all extremes, such as national socialism and communism, grow to resemble and reinforce each other at the point of their extremism.

THE QUEST FOR ORDERED FREEDOM

Why is the present moment so significant? The crisis for the West and the wider world lies in the fact that humanity now faces a simple but urgent question that must be answered in the coming generation: *Is it still possible in the advanced modern world to build societies with both freedom and order at the same time? To build and sustain communities and nations that demonstrate the highest values of human dignity, freedom, justice, equality, compassion, peace, and stability?* Can we solve the conundrum on which the French Revolution was impaled: guaranteeing both freedom for all and power for the people—without producing chaos and thus prompting the control of dictatorship? Or is that goal naive, a quixotic attempt to square the circle, and are such goals utopian under the conditions of advanced modernity? And do we have to settle, instead, for subservience to the proliferating rules and regulations of different political and managerial elites (aka Olympian oligarchies) whose expertise has trained them to know what they believe is right and good for the rest of us—if only we were as wise and good as they are?

This book takes these questions seriously. That is why the present moment is ripe with potential for a better way forward for humanity—if only there is leadership rather than passivity, reason rather than rage, hope rather than despair, and commitment to hard thinking and hard work rather than reliance on quick fixes and easy solutions. But of course there is no question about the diversity, relativity, and conflicts of today's perspectives, and it would be easy to predict the almost certain dismissals that any vision would spark from those who hold a different vision. The task, then, requires cheerful humility as well as clarity about what lies behind this attempt or any attempt. As humans we all stand and speak from somewhere—it is quite impossible to speak from either nowhere or everywhere. So whether we have to defend our positions publicly or not, we all need to make sure that we have answered two initial questions—at least to our own satisfaction.

First, we must be clear what we believe is *real*. And second, we must be equally clear about what we believe is the *right side up* and why. The competition and clash of proposals in today's world demand no less. This book itself is an answer to the second question. It sets out what I passionately believe should be the right side up for human societies, and it depends crucially on what I believe is real and is therefore an answer to the first question. For many people the issue of reality is irrelevant if not frivolous. Life is for living, and that is the end of the matter. Anything else is mere theory, and therefore only for the philosopher if not for the birds.

The question of *reality* has become important again because the Hindu and Buddhist view that the world is an illusion, *maya*, has been given fresh credibility in our time. Popular films such as *The Matrix* have raised the question once more, and speculations from the world of artificial intelligence have seconded the idea that what we think is reality is in fact only someone else's simulation we find ourselves living in. In the words of the ancient Chinese sage, "If when I am asleep, I am a man dreaming I am a butterfly, how do I know that when I am awake, I am not a butterfly dreaming I am a man?"

For reasons that will become clear as we proceed, I do not hold the view that reality is an illusion. As quantum theory shows, the reality in which we live our daily lives may not be as simple and straightforward as it appears, and according to many ultimate beliefs our daily reality may not even be the ultimate reality. It is, however, a reality we may trust for all the purposes of a full, rich human life on earth—including the joys of human relationships, the important pursuits of business, art, science, and all the countless issues raised by what Socrates called "the examined life."

FRATERNITÉ, EGALITÉ, BUT WHAT HAPPENED TO LIBERTÉ?

To all who survey the landscape of the last two centuries, it is clear that the French-style revolutionary faith and its fiery ideas have been major carriers of revolutionary action in recent centuries. Paris has ignited a myriad of revolutionary and would-be revolutionary leaders, writers, journals, debates, secret organizations, and conspiracies, with as many dead ends as successes. (Their descendants in America today are equally a potpourri of diverse and conflicting causes such as Planned Parenthood, Occupy Wall Street, Antifa, Black Lives Matter, and countless others—all superfunded to the tune of billions by progressives such as George Soros.) But the overall pattern is clear. In all the ferment of passion and radicalism one dominant stream of the revolutionary faith has made the major impact in each century. In the nineteenth century the mainstream was not, as many might have guessed, revolutionary socialism or communism. It was *revolutionary nationalism*. It comprised those who hailed 1789's ideal of *fraternité* (brotherhood) and used it to forge the revolutionary nationalism that launched successful independence nationalist movements in Italy and Greece. It also contributed to secular Zionism and the creation of the state of Israel and to what later morphed darkly into fascism and national socialism—Hitler: "This revolution of ours is the exact counterpart of the French Revolution."[24]

Oddly, those who stressed fraternity had such a blind admiration for the "brotherhood of man" that they forgot the realism of the Bible's reminder: the tensions between brothers (and between sisters) can be even more devastating than the oedipal tension between fathers and sons that was so loved by Sigmund Freud. Prince Metternich was so appalled by the French Revolution's hypocrisy toward its own ideals that he remarked, "When I saw what people did in the name of fraternity, I resolved, if I had a brother, to call him cousin."[25]

Needless to say, the second major stream, *revolutionary socialism*, was conceived and hatched in the nineteenth century, but it made its chief impact in the twentieth century when it burst through in the form of the two communist revolutions, in Russia in 1917 and China in 1949. The communists had no time for revolutionary nationalism or even for the French Revolution. The latter were incomplete revolutions, which had left too many stillborn dreams in their wake. Their own goal was the dream of an *unfinished revolution*, and they emphasized the ideal of *egalité* (equality) rather than fraternity. They used it to forge the beginnings of what they considered total revolution (exemplified by the intellectual labors of Karl Marx and Friedrich Engels). For them the failed revolution of 1848 was the watershed between earlier "petty-bourgeois" forms of social change and their own brutally hard-nosed realism about the authoritarian leadership and the violence and terror that successful mass revolution would require.

This revolutionary socialism became the dominant revolutionary faith of the twentieth century, which blazed out in the form of communism and still survives. It disdained Western liberalism and even most of the earlier forms of revolution. It was adamant that its science-and-economics-savvy revolution had shed all traces of utopian sentimentalism and could now fulfill the disappointed hopes of 1789 and 1848. It was the hardline Marxism, established by Vladimir Lenin in Russia in 1917 and Mao Zedong in China in 1949.

The third and until recently less-obvious form of revolutionary faith is *revolutionary liberationism*, often known as neo-Marxism, Western Marxism, cultural Marxism, and even as user-friendly Marxism. It grew from the work of Antonio Gramsci, the Frankfurt School, and postmodern thinkers such as Michel Foucault and Jacques Derrida. It has led to the revolutionary ideology that has become prominent in Western Europe and parts of the United States after the 1960s. Today, in the twenty-first century, communism is still powerful in China, but it is this third revolutionary faith that is advancing throughout the West, and in America it is beginning to overturn the influence of the American Revolution. If the vision of a Grand March was the old revolutionary dream of the progress of freedom and brotherhood led by the workers of the world, it took Mao's Long March in China in 1934 and Herbert Marcuse and Rudi Dutschke's 1960s call for a "long march through the institutions" to bring the revolution of Western Marxism to its present position of influence in intellectual circles in America.

Just as the Great Awakening of the 1730s led to the American Revolution of 1776, so the radicals hope that their "great awokening" today will lead to the second American Revolution and fulfill the unrealized dreams of 1789. A cultural revolution is well underway and America's "olds" ("old customs, old culture, old habits, and old ideas") are as threatened as China's were from Mao's Red Guards in 1966.

The harsh light thrown on the record of Lenin, Stalin, Hitler, Mao, and Pol Pot makes it impossible to see that either revolutionary nationalism or revolutionary socialism can usher in freedom and justice. Their record has been disastrous for humanity and freedom. They both led to terror and unprecedented repression and slaughter, and they still do. The West now faces the challenge of the third revolutionary faith. In the form of postmodernism, political correctness, tribal politics, and the extremes of the sexual revolution, the advocates of cultural Marxism and critical theory are now posing serious threats not just to freedom and democracy but to earlier understandings of humanity and to Western civilization itself.

The progressive left has already transformed America in striking ways. It has created one-party faculties (in many elite universities), one-party newsrooms (in much of the mainstream press), one-party tech media companies (in firms such as Google and Facebook), and one-party states (in California). Before the statue-toppling iconoclasts took to America's parks and squares, they had already been hard at work undermining the foundations of the republic in the classrooms. America's equivalent of France's "treason of the intellectuals" is far advanced, and the future of 1776 is called into question—not least because of the weakness of its defenders. The prospect of America sliding toward one-party national politics would sound the death knell of the American Republic.

It is time for the world to pause and make an accounting of all three streams of revolutionary faith and to assess the prospects for true freedom in contrast. There can be no doubt about the terrible cost of giving primacy to *fraternity* and *equality* as the guiding principles of freedom and justice. The price in human lives alone is more than one hundred million. Yet the challenge for the present generation is not simply to turn back to talk of *liberty* but to examine which vision of liberty best grounds the ordered liberty that brings with it justice, peace, stability, and the equality of dignity—and this time, liberty for all without exception. Is the way forward to be 1776 reformed? Or is it to be 1789, which to this point shows no capacity for reformation at all?

We already face a choice when it comes to considering liberty—between three different traditions of freedom in Western history. The first tradition has been called "the ancient liberties of the English," though its roots go back to Anglo-Saxon sources in German forests. Its guiding star was the Magna Carta and the cluster of freedoms, such as freedom of expression, trial by jury, the presumption of innocence, and *habeas corpus*, which were all strengthened by the celebrated stand against King John of England at Runnymede in 1215. The second tradition comes from the influence of the "Hebrew Republic," which represented the impact of the rediscovery of the book of Exodus through the Reformation, the affirmation of the exodus as the precedent and pattern of Western freedom, both for revolutionaries and slaves, and the decisive contribution of covenant to seventeenth- and eighteenth-century political thinking—especially to the rise of American constitutionalism and its distinctive view of ordered liberty. And the third tradition is the one that has come down from the French Enlightenment and the French Revolution, the "great Revolution," and their heirs, such as Karl Marx, Friedrich Nietzsche, Antonio Gramsci, Wilhelm Reich, Herbert Marcuse, Saul Alinsky, and Michel Foucault.

Plainly, the first two traditions of freedom overlap and complement each other, and the third is flatly opposed to them both at many points. Yet equally plainly, the third tradition now overshadows the other two in thinking circles across much of the world. It silences the first tradition as White privilege and shoulders aside the second as religious and therefore irrational and on the wrong side of history as secular progressives view it.

Behind these three traditions of freedom, of course, lies yet another series of choices with even greater consequences: the difference between the three major families of worldviews and ultimate beliefs in the world—the Eastern family of faiths, represented mainly by Hinduism, Buddhism, and various New Age movements; the Abrahamic family of faiths, represented by Judaism, the Christian faith, and Islam; and the secularist family of beliefs, represented by those with an atheistic, naturalistic, or materialist view of reality and life. The latter is the philosophy that goes back to ancients such as Epicurus and Lucretius as well as moderns such as Machiavelli, Spinoza, Hobbes, Marx, and Freud. It therefore stands once again as the enduring rival to the Bible's view of existence and life.

The choice between Sinai and Paris and their different views of freedom carries consequences that are monumental for the human future. As always, contrast is the mother of clarity. Let there then be a fair comparison and a wise assessment —assumption by assumption, principle by principle, and outcome by outcome. The significance of the choices between them is now magnified even further by the profound questions raised by the prospects of the rapidly approaching future. *What is a human being? Is there a future for humanity as we have known ourselves up till now? What will the conquest of nature mean when the final battle is the conquest of human nature? Will humanity survive human beings?* And as I said, in the midst of these titanic questions an enduring political question is unavoidable: Can we humans create a way of ordering our societies that fulfills the highest aspirations for human dignity, diversity, freedom, justice, compassion, peace, and stability—along with the highest responsibility for our fellow creatures and the earth? These are some of the questions that cry out to be addressed at this extraordinary moment in time.

THE MASTER STORY OF FREEDOM

This book argues for the Sinai Revolution—the highest, richest, and deepest vision of human freedom in history. After nearly two and a half centuries it is clear that Paris and the revolutionary faith that flowed from the great upheaval of 1789 has betrayed its promise again and again—in all three major forms. Shaped and bound by its assumptions, it cannot hope to do otherwise. It is flawed, it spells disaster for humanity, and it needs to be reexamined comprehensively and firmly rejected. Paris and 1789 in whatever form ends with revolutionaries who are wreckers and tyrants. The need today is for restorers and builders.

This book therefore calls for the repudiation of the revolutionary faith of 1789 and its contemporary offshoots, and for a major reconsideration of Sinai, the original revolutionary faith of the exodus and the Bible. As Rabbi Lord Jonathan Sacks argues in many ways through his many books, *Exodus is both the master story of human freedom and the opening of history's greatest and most sustained critique of the abuse of power.* Those two claims are of monumental significance at this present moment in history, the second being especially crucial for countering the vaunted power-based theories of the progressive left. The book of Exodus and the first five books of the Hebrew Scriptures as a whole are nothing less than the Magna Carta of humanity. Even more than the historic 1948 "Universal Declaration of Human Rights," Sinai offers a vision of the deepest and most comprehensive foundations for human freedom ever to ring out over the landscape of humanity—and it also provides the only solid foundation without which even the great ideals for the "Universal Declaration" itself are built on sand.

In stating that claim and citing Rabbi Sacks, I must promptly acknowledge my debt. The vision of freedom outlined here owes everything to the Hebrew and Christian Scriptures and the wise and brilliant understanding of Rabbi Sacks, the former chief rabbi of Great Britain. (This book is therefore dedicated to him along with my beloved wife, to whom I owe an unpayable debt of a different kind, for her love and fierce loyalty over many years.) Doubtless, Rabbi Sacks would say that he is only standing on the shoulders of the giants of the long, unbroken tradition of his people. That is true, and what a tradition it is. But he too is a giant, and the freshness and profundity of his thinking about freedom deserve far wider recognition and discussion.

This book is intended to serve that end. Rabbi Sacks is well known, but this is to introduce him and his thinking about freedom to circles where he deserves to be even better known. If I have captured his wisdom in any way, the credit is entirely his. If I fail to do justice to his brilliance, the responsibility is mine. I no more agree with every word he has written than, doubtless, he would agree with mine. In all cases, readers would do well to go directly to his writings, beginning with his magnificent series on the first five books of the Bible: Covenant and

Conversation. The depth and relevance of his teaching in our present moment would be impossible to overstate. From foundational human questions (How do we as human beings *relate* to each other at all and to God?) to equally foundational political questions (How do we as human beings *negotiate* life with each other when we are all so different and we all want our freedom?), his answers are profound and they carry profound consequences for life today.

The enduring legacy of Lord Sacks's work as a rabbi lies in his exposition of the riches of the Torah and his care for his community and people, but he is also keenly aware of the wider crisis facing Western civilization and the world today. People all over the world, he notes, are passionately concerned about climate change, but he addresses what is equally if not more urgent—the *cultural climate change* that is damaging the way we used to live and beginning to shape the way we need to live if humanity is to flourish. The Western world is the child of faith. At its best it is a moral and cultural achievement. To think that it can be kept alive by technocrats, pundits, and policy wonks is a folly beyond belief.[26] As Rabbi Sacks argues in a thousand ways, "You change the world, not by the idea of power, but by the power of ideas."

THEY KNOW IT SO WELL THAT THEY DON'T KNOW IT

Who is this book written for? I am writing primarily for Americans and for all who are interested in the "state of the union" of the world's lead society, though also for a far wider circle of readers. America's great experiment in freedom was once the closest to the Sinai vision because it was largely, though not consistently, based on it. Sadly, its initial and glaring inconsistency, slavery, is the chief reason why even Americans are rejecting their founding today. The hypocrisy of the contradiction between slavery and the Declaration of Independence was obvious to other countries from the beginning. William Wilberforce and other abolitionists pleaded with Thomas Jefferson and other American leaders to deal with the evil at the outset. Wilberforce even proposed that the English-speaking peoples form a "concert of benevolence" to advance the cause of global freedom, but he was rebuffed.[27] Yet the evil and hypocrisy were truly an evil and a hypocrisy, and if acknowledged and corrected the Declaration still stands clear and strong. Thus, as the world's lead society still, America's choice between the different visions of freedom will set a powerful precedent for the rest of the world. Americans should therefore reconsider the Exodus vision of freedom with great care.

For one thing, Exodus provides a benchmark to assess where their great experiment stands today, including its flaws and blind spots. For another, Exodus provides a blueprint for rededication and renewal if that is the American decision. To make America great again can only be done by taking seriously what made America great in the first place, and reconsidering Exodus is indispensable to that task. There are two orders to be considered in the rise and fall of nations— the physical order, including the economy and the military, and the moral order, including freedom and justice. To try to make America great through the economy and the military alone can only fail.

Yet sadly there are reasons why Americans may be the last to be interested in the Exodus vision. The United States is suffering from profound philosophical cynicism, moral corruption, and serious social collapse. Many of America's intellectuals have become tone-deaf and chronically unable to consider that anything might be real beyond the confines of Plato's cave. And too many Americans, especially those who are younger, have already been bewitched by ideas coming from the other revolution, 1789, and not 1776. Thanks to Howard Zinn and others, they now appear hell-bent on rejecting ideas from their past, which they have not tried to understand, even as they embrace ideas from the other revolution, which they have not examined as closely as they need to. Many in America see only their ancestors' errors and at once think that makes them wiser and better than their ancestors. Yet they do not try to understand what their ancestors thought and why, let alone ask where the alternative ideas will lead them. Almost daily, many Americans are throwing out the proverbial baby with the bathwater. The *woke* movement signals its hubris when it speaks and acts as if it is wiser than God and far superior to its ancestors. Perhaps saddest of all, in their confusion, anger, and uncertainty many Americans are not thinking about freedom and first principles at all.

Survey the stormy skies of the ideas currently swirling around America— including postmodernism, political correctness, identity politics, tribal politics, the sexual revolution, socialism, critical theory, and the politics of the progressive left. How are Americans to respond? Many Americans know their ancestors' ideas so well that they do not know them at all. Familiarity has bred inattention. Freedom taken for granted is freedom well on the way to being lost. In short, Americans today are both agonizingly close and limitlessly distant from their own deepest roots, so they condemn themselves to reap the alternative harvest of the very different ideas they have determined to sow. There is no need for such a disaster, but America waits for a leader worthy of its past and worthy of the crisis of our time.

The Sinai vision not only addresses freedom but sets out a way to renew and restore a free society when freedom breaks down, though at the moment Americans show no interest in taking it. They presently have neither the will nor the understanding needed to renew the American experiment. Thus the question Can America be restored? hangs over the nation as tantalizingly close but thus far not embraced. Through the vast carelessness of the powerful, America's crisis of cultural authority metastasizes apace.

This book is written with hope and in the interests of a major American renewal, but such is the conflict, chaos, and lack of leadership of today that it may be written only for a remnant who wish to live a better way regardless of the choice that Americans as a whole may make.

My audience is also wider than America. In my travels and speaking in different settings across several continents I meet people everywhere who are deeply dissatisfied with our present modern condition and who passionately long for a better world. They are eager to play their part among those who think more creatively about the human future and like George Washington are prepared to think of the world "a century hence."[28] This book is written for them too and for all who believe in human freedom, personal and political, and who believe that we have a responsibility to the world of tomorrow in which our children and children's children will live.

BOTH CONSERVATIVE AND PROGRESSIVE

The constructive vision outlined here is the freedom of a *commonwealth*—a morally responsible society of independent free people who are covenanted to each other and to justice, peace, stability, and the common good in their community. In the seventeenth century the vogue for such commonwealths was modeled on the "Hebrew Republic."[29] Today Rabbi Sacks writes of the same vision as a "republic of free and equal citizens held together not by hierarchy or power but by the moral bond of covenant."[30] In short, what is at stake in the reconsideration of Exodus is the vision of a good society—indeed, God's good society—and within it, a view of human life and a way of living that is unrivaled in history and rich with promise for our human future.

The chapters that follow outline seven of the great foundational Exodus truths for building a free and responsible society, many of which are neglected or rejected today. If there were more space, several other truths might be considered, but these seven are surely essential. Together, they demonstrate that Sinai offers far more than some interesting lessons from ancient history or a possible template to be applied mechanically to contemporary affairs. Rightly understood, Exodus shows us nothing less than the DNA of ordered human freedom, which should be an inspiration for citizens and political leaders alike. But what if America switches allegiance to 1789 decisively, as it is in the process of doing? Should that tragedy happen, the Sinai Revolution will still provide the basis for the alternative communities that will need to be built if freedom and justice are to be kept alive on the earth.

Together with Deuteronomy (the "second law" or renewed covenant), Exodus is quite simply a political classic and worthy to be studied on a level with Plato, Aristotle, Machiavelli, Hobbes, Tocqueville, Adam Smith, Marx, and John Stuart Mill. Exodus outshines these other classics for its combination of realism and idealism, its vision of freedom with justice, and its notion of freedom that is sustainable and collective. The first five books of the Bible, far more than Adam Smith's *The Wealth of Nations*, Karl Marx's *Communist Manifesto*, John Stuart Mill's *On Liberty*, or Adolf Hitler's *Mein Kampf*, are the indispensable guide to the quest for the growth and unfolding of human flourishing in the advanced modern world.

Let no one dismiss this vision as purely conservative simply because Exodus lies in the past. We cannot afford such prejudice. Our genius as human beings lies in our capacity to range over the past in terms of memory and history, and in our equal capacity to range over the future with our imagination and vision. Our best thinking must strive to conserve the best of the past, but it must also strive to progress toward the unrealized vision of the future. As with the Jewish and Christian faiths, the better we conserve, the better we progress, and the way to conserve well is always to change wisely. True conservatism and true liberalism are blood brothers, not enemies. Restoration and revolution go hand in hand. America always goes forward best by going back first.

Following Tertullian's famous question in the second century—"What has Jerusalem to do with Athens?"—Western civilization has often demonstrated the tensions between *Jerusalem* and *Athens*. Today, it is more precisely Sinai rather than Jerusalem that focuses the issues of freedom. The present global crisis of freedom does pivot partly on the tensions between Sinai and Athens, including ideas from Athens that were rediscovered during the Renaissance. But the truly critical clash of our time stems from the differences between Sinai and Paris and the ideas, from whichever stream, that were launched upon the world through the French Revolution in 1789.

WHOEVER HAS EARS TO HEAR

It only remains to give a warning that should accompany any discussion of freedom. The stakes for freedom in today's world are huge, and the choice between the Sinai vision and the Paris vision will settle the fate of the world in the near term. Choices always have consequences, but with the power of today's global interconnectedness and tomorrow's ultra intelligence, the speed and scale of the consequences of our choices about freedom will be magnified exponentially and without the cushion of any time lag. But quite apart from that essential choice, freedom is always subtler and more challenging than many people realize. The appeal and urgency of freedom are obvious: *if freedom is the capacity to express and exercise our wills, then we humans need freedom just to be ourselves and to be truly human.* Yet for all its obvious appeal, human freedom is never simple or straightforward. For one thing, freedom requires responsibility, which means that freedom can be challenging and a burden. For another, history shows that unless freedom is approached wisely, it can be mercurial and surprising. Freedom is often the greatest enemy of freedom, for freedom pursued in the wrong way all too often ends in serfdom rather than liberty.

The modern world is a far cry from the world addressed by the great Jewish leader Moses. It is advanced modern rather than traditional and urban rather than agrarian. Yet the principles set out in Exodus and the opening books of the Bible are as timely as they are timeless. The problem is not that the ideas are obsolete but that our generation is not noted for its careful consideration of first principles, its commitment to build determinedly and patiently, or for its civil debate over the challenges of going forward. An assertion today is something to be attacked first and assessed afterward—the social media's recipe for prejudice and folly.

But no matter. Our own times are never the sole standard for our thinking and our behavior. We are not responsible for being born in the times we live in but only for the responsibility and initiative with which we live in our time. As an even more famous Jewish teacher repeated pointedly to his generation when it was equally disinclined to listen, "He who has ears to hear, let him hear" (Mt 11:15). In a turbulent, contentious, and skeptical but exciting time like our own, no one can ask for more. Many people may suffer from what Max Weber called tone-deafness. Rabbi Abraham Joshua Heschel described the same condition as "hard of inner hearing."[31] Only the few, not the many, are ever open to listening, but it is always the few, and not the many, who will make the difference that will count in the end. Let there be a fair and wise consideration of a vision that is truly nothing short of the Magna Carta of humanity. Humanity and our children's children deserve no less.

America cannot endure permanently half 1776 and half 1789. The compromises, contradictions, hypocrisies, inequities, and evils have built up unaddressed. The grapes of wrath have ripened again, and the choice before America is plain. Either America goes forward best by going back first, or America is about to reap a future in which the worst will once again be the corruption of the best.

1

I WILL BE
WHO I WILL BE

PRINCIPLE 1: FREEDOM REQUIRES AUTHORITY

"In the beginning" is always the key. As the seed, so the flower. As the acorn, so the oak. As the sketch, so the portrait. As the embryo, so the human being who rises to play their part on the grand stage of life. But most of all, and in a manner that underlies all other beginnings and all other developments, as our ultimate belief, so our vision of humanity and the meaning of the universe and existence itself. Nothing short of that is how the Bible and the book of Exodus introduce the inescapable primacy, authority, and centrality of God for human life, for living—and for freedom. The Sinai Revolution in freedom begins with God, and this insistence is decisive. Where you stand and where you start is how you see what you see and whether you are likely to succeed or fail in your enterprise. That, at least, is where Sinai and critical theory agree, though the standpoint and the starting point for each one are completely different, and the differences make a world of difference.

Yet not so fast, for controversy flares up right there. Simply to mention the word *God* is to invite the most vehement objections today. The response of Paris and its heirs is instinctive and implacable. Unquestionably, they say, the Enlightenment has superseded any rational belief in God once and for all—unless anyone wants to entertain a private belief that has no relevance for public life. Voltaire, the epitome of the French Enlightenment, famously attacked the Catholic Church before the French Revolution with a slogan, *Écrasez l'infâme!* (Crush the loathsome thing!). His skepticism turned hatred flamed out into his signature watchword that he repeated hundreds of times. He was followed by others in their turn, such as the young English aristocrat, poet, and would-be revolutionary Percy Bysshe Shelley.

> Yet here I swear, and as I break my oath may Infinite Eternity blast me, here I swear that I will never forgive Christianity! Oh how I wish I *were* the antichrist, that it were mine to crush the Demon, to hurl him to his native hell, never to rise again.[1]

In the same way, the *philosophe* and encyclopedist Denis Diderot bluntly declared that the French would never be free until "they strangled the last king with the guts of the last priest."[2]

Such militant hostility flared out of the radical wing of the French Revolution from its beginning. Atheism, anticlericalism, de-Christianization, and open animosity to the church and God blazed out together in the fires of the insurrection, and in turn they reinforced the wider social and economic grievances and outrages and led to what became the *laïcité* or strict separation of church and state, which is now a characteristic feature of France's political system. Such militant animosity toward God (God is dead) and toward religion (the opiate of the people) is a recurring motif in the French, Russian, and Chinese revolutions. It has marked the revolutionary faith of left-wing political movements ever since and still does. But it is a choice that needs to be reexamined in the light of reason.

At the height of the ten years of the French Revolution, the Jacobin faction and their supporters laid waste to whole regions of France, such as the city of Lyon and the Vendée. They directed the brunt of their ruthless hate against the clergy no less than the long, pitiful procession of royals, nobles, and hapless others in the horrific denouement of the Great Terror of 1793. ("Terror is the order of the day," it was proclaimed, though ironically the period was also known as "the republic of virtue" because of the moralizing speeches of Robespierre as a "virtuous terrorist.")[3] Historians have described the terror as "social revenge in action."[4] Many of the victims were innocent, guilty only of being the heirs of their ancestors or members of their profession. But regardless, they were all manhandled roughly toward the steely embrace of the *razoir nationale* (the "national razor" of Madame Guillotine and her bloody "Mass for the masses").

To be sure, the French revolutionaries appealed to positive ideals such as reason, liberty, and nature, but it was always to serve their fight to the death against the church and God. The negative outbreaks of anti-Christian animosity were widespread and brutal. Churches were ransacked and priests butchered. Joseph Fouché, a Jacobin military commander, ordered the removal of all crosses and statues from graveyards across France, and to repress the hope of the resurrection he decreed that cemetery gates must have only one inscription, "Death is an eternal sleep." The climax of the revolutionary atheism was the famous "Cult of Reason" (*Culte de la Raison*) in November 1793. It was Europe's first state-sponsored established atheistic religion and the first attempt in human history to stamp out religion and religious practice altogether. Churches across France were commandeered and transformed into temples of Reason, the most important being Notre Dame in Paris. The inscription "To Philosophy" was carved over the door of the cathedral, a flame burned on the high altar to symbolize truth, and a provocatively dressed woman was enthroned as the goddess of Reason. The next year, in 1794, Citizen Robespierre replaced "the Cult of Reason" with another civic religion for the new secular republic, "the Cult of the Supreme Being."

Was such militant atheism accidental or central to the French Revolution and to the revolutionary faith that has exploded from it? Alexander Solzhenitsyn had no doubt that it was central to Marxism later (and we might add, to today's progressive left radicalism that is so close to it).

> The world has never before known a godlessness as organized, militarized, and tenaciously malevolent as that practiced by Marxism. Within the philosophical system of Marx and Lenin, and at the heart of their psychology, hatred of God is the principal driving force, more fundamental than all their political and economic pretensions. Militant atheism is not merely incidental or marginal to Communist policy; it is not a side effect, but the central pivot.[5]

Antifa protesters who burned Bibles in the Portland riots in 2020 and Black Lives Matter protesters who marched down the street in Charlotte, North Carolina, chanting "F--- your Jesus" were lining up with a long tradition. With such bitter animosity toward religion at the heart of the revolutionary left, is there any question that any reference to God, to Sinai, or to the importance of faith for freedom would be scorned if not dismissed from the start? Standpoint theory, however, rightly requires that we state where we come from.

A KEY TO THE PRESENT MOMENT

These old details from the story of the French Revolution are anything but dusty, and they need to be taken seriously. They provide an important key to understanding the present crisis in America, and they bear on the present story in several ways.

First, the anti-Christian and antireligious hostility of the French Revolution is a reminder that requires a candid confession from Christians. If Jews and Christians are called to be witnesses to God (Is 43:10), whether Christians behave as Christians affects whether others will believe what they say. All too often, Christian behavior has flatly contradicted Christian beliefs. The church has deserved many of the attacks made on it and its stands in public life. Christians have betrayed their Lord, dishonored their faith, and brought down the attacks on their own heads—and never more so than in their shameful treatment of God's people, the Jews. Far too often, through the centuries, the church has been the major casualty of its crimes and follies. It has asked for the way it has been rejected. Can anyone dispute, for example, that the European church in the medieval, the late medieval and the Renaissance ages was both horribly corrupt, egregiously oppressive, and a mainstay of the wider systems of injustice? It was stained indelibly by the excesses of the Inquisition, the evils of the persecution of the Jews, and such horrendous notions as "error has no rights." Almost all that was done wrong in these centuries was blessed in the church's name. Who could believe in God if he was the author of such monstrosities?

Lord Acton's dictum that "All power tends to corrupt, and absolute power corrupts absolutely" is justly famous, but people forget that it was written in the context of discussing his own church. Had the Hebrew prophets been alive during the Renaissance or in the reigns of Louis XIV and XV, they would doubtless have been the first and the most outraged to excoriate the many evils of Christendom, the shameless corruption of the clergy, or earlier on the brazen succession of secular princelings that were the ostensible "vicars of Christ" and purporting to walk in "the shoes of the fisherman." What was true in France and Russia, and thus the backdrop of the French and Russian revolutions, was also true in the American South, and thus the backdrop of today's anti-Christian antiracism in America.

The truth is that no one can understand today's militant animosity of secularists toward Christians without appreciating a stubborn fact that Christians must ponder deeply: *The phenomenon of Western secularism is unique in history, but its leading cause is its revulsion against corrupt and oppressive state churches in Europe. Secularism stands as a parasite on the best of Christian beliefs and a protest against the worst of Christian behavior.* That same implacable secularist hostility to the Christian faith is blazing again today, not least in America, where it was once considered foreign, and it crucially affects the way any Christian proposal will be heard. A church unworthy of its faith in God will always blight the appeal of its message and stand as the main roadblock to anyone open to considering her faith in God. Confession, the willingness to acknowledge our sins and go on record against ourselves, is essential to Christian advocacy—and humility—today.

OUR CUT-FLOWER CIVILIZATION

Second, the same anti-Christian and antireligious animosity is a window into the current crisis of Western civilization. In *The Will to Power*, the notes published by Nietzsche's sister after his death, Nietzsche argued that "the time is coming when we shall have to pay for having been *Christians* for two thousand years."[6] Nearly a century and a half later, many more would say the opposite— the West is paying for the loss of its Jewish and Christian roots. Until 1789 it was commonplace and historically accurate to describe the West as a "Christian civilization," regardless of whether any nation had a formally "established church" or not. After the First Amendment in 1791, for example, there was no established church in the United States at the federal level, but there is no question that America understood itself as part of Christian civilization and no less so than Europe.

Many who made such claims about Christian civilization were prominent Christian spokespersons, so their assertions can be heavily discounted for their bias. In 1920, for example, Hilaire Belloc wrote that "the Faith is Europe and Europe is the Faith" (by which he meant strictly Catholicism and not even Orthodoxy or Protestantism).[7] Others, such as US Presidents Howard Taft, Woodrow Wilson, and Franklin D. Roosevelt, and British Prime Minister Winston Churchill could hardly be described as Christian spokesmen, yet they routinely referred to "Christian civilization" on numerous occasions as a noncontroversial reference. Historically, Western civilization owes much to the Jews, the Greeks, and the Romans, but the West outgrew the Mediterranean world, and it was the Christian faith that was decisive in founding first Europe and then the wider West.

Today, such claims would be dismissed instantly. They are controversial at best and reactionary and prejudiced, if not worse—a "dog whistle," it is said, for "White privilege," "Eurocentrism," "racism" and "colonialism." The cultural revolution of the 1960s has triumphed, and the "long march through the institutions" has succeeded. Famously, the European Union refused to acknowledge its Christian roots at the fiftieth anniversary of the Treaty of Rome, and even in America ideas and attitudes that were at the heart of the French Revolution have ousted ideas and attitudes at the heart of the American Revolution. The infamous cry of the Stanford protesters in 1987 has become the mantra of many in the educated classes of the West. "Hey, hey, ho, ho. Western Civ has got to go!"

Needless to say, what matters is not the label "Christian civilization," but the substance of the beliefs behind it. What is to become of notions such as human dignity, human freedom, and human rights if the Jewish and Christian truths that once made them powerful are abandoned? What will happen as our world becomes not only post-truth but post-rights? Ever since the 1930s critics such as Malcolm Muggeridge have charged that left-wing intellectuals in Europe were cutting off the branch they were sitting on. Nowhere is that more consequential than over human rights. Human rights are the direct reflection of our views of humanity, but with no foundational basis for human dignity, we have moved from what was once considered the *natural rights* of the Universal Declaration to the *antinatural rights* of abortion and euthanasia, and are now moving to the *transnatural rights* of transgenderism and the eugenics of tomorrow. The folly of cutting off the branch is now true of the West as a whole. The West has become a cut-flower civilization. It is living off the whiff of an empty bottle, and the pretense that we can count on everything staying the same as before is wearing dangerously thin. For a culture that was once literally God-given, in the sense that its ideas flowed from its faith in God, to jettison that faith cannot but be consequential.[8]

There is no more important alliance at this hour than between Jews and Christians, for the strength or weakness of the Bible in the West is the key to the survival of the West. As Rabbi Heschel said to Christians after World War II, "Nazism has suffered a defeat, but the process of eliminating the Bible from the consciousness of the Western world goes on. . . . Both of us must realize that in our age anti-Semitism is anti-Christianity and that anti-Christianity is anti-Semitism."[9]

The tangled relationship between the West and the Jewish and Christian faiths has immense consequences. It currently poses as profound a question for America as it once did to Europe. In Europe the measure of the influence of the Jewish and Christian faiths was both the measure of the reactions to them in the nineteenth century and the measure of the scale of the ideologies that replaced them in the twentieth century—supremely the communist and Nazi totalitarianisms, which were in essence monotheism-sized antireligious ideologies. Yet because of the disastrous history that followed, Europe today is somewhat wary and to some extent immune to the return of such dangerous fanaticisms.

America, in contrast, had the good fortune to avoid such ideologies in the past, mainly because of the positive strength of the biblical faiths in its earlier history. But the more recent weakening of those same faiths leaves America exposed and without the benefit of any immunity from the lessons of history. Thus today, when American secularism is more militant and the progressive left is roundly repudiating the Jewish and Christian faiths as "the single god religion of White privilege," America has a weakened immunity to fanaticism and anti-Semitism. The paradoxical result is that "the land of the free" is now the Western nation most vulnerable to ideology, fanaticism, and authoritarianism.

WHEN WORDS BREAK DOWN

Third, the anti-Christian and antireligious animosity of the French Revolution is a warning as to how not to settle differences today. When inequities soar and words break down, violence is never far away, and the costs of violence are often out of all proportion to the original cause. The strongest claims can provoke the most furious responses, and the most important debates are often settled in the worst ways. With ideas there are always choices and consequences. But as history demonstrates and the modern world underscores again, it is a travesty for humanity when disputes between different visions are settled with bludgeons, bayonets, bullets, bombs, and bloodshed rather than through conversation and debate.

In their day it was the French revolutionaries, and today it is their socialist and Marxist heirs who are the leading source of the rise in hostility toward religious believers in today's world. The troubling record of the revolution is a solemn warning about the current breakdown in the use of words in public discourse. Unless there is a halt to the downward spiral, today's inflamed rhetoric will be the precursor of tomorrow's open violence and then scapegoating, and even assassination. (After all, the attitude of the left is clear: if elections go the wrong way and investigations and impeachments also fail, what is there left but assassination? "The scapegoat must always die.") Plainly, there has to be, and there is, a better way to live with our deepest differences and settle them peacefully.

GOING FOR THE JUGULAR

Fourth, and most importantly for the heart of this chapter, the vehemence of the animosity to faith in God is a backhanded compliment to the importance of faith in God. There is no question that God is central to Exodus and its story of liberation. But there is also no way around the equal fact that to start a discussion of freedom by referring to God is a bridge too far for many people today. Those who feel like that are free to skip to the next chapter, though at the very least thinking people should always be interested in what other thinking people see as supremely important for their thinking—especially if what others believe is considered crucial to the common quest for freedom and human flourishing. According to the Exodus account, there is no greater freedom than demonstrated in this story, and God is not simply part of the story but absolutely, inextricably, and indispensably essential to the freedom shown. The attack on God, or the complete refusal to consider what God means to those who believe in him, is therefore an assault on what is central to faith in God and to beliefs that have been among the most consequential in human history.

Sociologist Rodney Stark declares that radical or ethical monotheism—the belief in a single, sovereign God—is the "single most significant innovation in history."[10] "Had the Jews been polytheists," he continues,

> they would today be only another barely remembered people, less important but just as extinct as the Babylonians. Had Christians presented Jesus to the Greco-Roman world as "another" God, their faith would long since have gone the way of Mithraism. And surely Islam would never have made it out of the desert had Muhammad not removed Allah from the context of Arab paganism and proclaimed him as the only God.[11]

Having embraced monotheism, Stark concludes, "these faiths changed the world."[12]

Current secularist rejections of such a claim have been swift, savage, and sometimes just plain ludicrous—all of which is revealing. Not long ago, the US Department of Veterans Affairs put on a display in New Hampshire that included a small Bible carried by a soldier throughout World War II—the book that more than any other created Western civilization. It drew an instant response from secularists that displaying the Bible was nothing less than an "outrage." The book that made the Western world, they claimed, was "a repugnant example of fundamentalist Christian triumphalism, exceptionalism, superiority, and domination, and it must not stand."[13]

At a more serious intellectual level, Gore Vidal, in the Lowell Lecture at Harvard College in 1992, displayed the same animosity. He argued that monotheism is "the great unmentionable evil" at the heart of America.[14] In the same vein, Christopher Hitchens delivered a sharp response to President George W. Bush's claim that Iran, Iraq, and North Korea formed an axis of evil. The real axis of evil, Hitchens declared repeatedly was Judaism, Christianity, and Islam. But no one has been more hostile and more deliberately offensive than Richard Dawkins. In his celebrated opening attack on the God of Sinai in *The God Delusion*, he writes,

> The God of the Old Testament is arguably the most unpleasant character in all fiction: jealous and proud of it; a petty, unjust, unforgiving control-freak; a vindictive, bloodthirsty ethnic cleanser; a misogynistic, homophobic, racist, infanticidal, genocidal, filicidal, pestilential, megalomaniacal, sadomasochistic, capriciously malevolent bully.[15]

Make no mistake. These frontal attacks, designed and launched to be an unanswerable blitzkrieg on faith, are the greatest compliment and invaluable help to thinking through the examined life. They focus on the essential issue. There is no way around the truth that, according to the Abrahamic faiths, God is the final and foundational factor for faith. The ultimate issue is neither Israel nor the Christian church nor the failings of either. All humans fail. Hindus, Buddhists, Jews, Christians, Muslims, atheists, and agnostics would all have to confess betrayals of their beliefs and principles. But in taking aim at the person and character of God, critics are going for faith's jugular. They are right to do so. Jews and Christians are no more special than atheists and Buddhists; what is special and admirable is the faith of the Bible. Both the Jewish and Christian faiths stand or fall according to whether God is truly there, whether God is who he says he is, and whether God can be known the way Jews and Christians say they have encountered him from the beginning and throughout their respective histories.

LYING IN THE BED WE HAVE MADE

One way to underscore this point is to stand back and compare the three different families of faiths or ultimate beliefs. A gigantic fact shines through all the comparisons. The difference between the world's ultimate beliefs pivots on the difference between what they each believe is the ultimate source of reality. Is it the impersonal ground of being of the Hindus and Buddhists? Is it the eternal and ever-changing random universe of Epicurus, Lucretius, and their modern secularist heirs? Or is it the personal and infinite God who disclosed himself to Moses at the burning bush and to Israel at Mount Sinai, and then, Christians believe, through Jesus of Nazareth? It will not do to translate the notion of God into any other category—as if *God* is only another term for love, ethics, community, or any human ideal. No. If the claims of the biblical faiths are correct, God is God, the final and foundational Presence, the reality underlying all existence, including our own.

That, ultimately, decisively, and forever, is the question that decides our view of life, the world, existence itself—and of course freedom. It means simply that behind the Jewish and Christian claims to truth and the power and influence of the biblical faiths at their best, as well as the vehemence of the repudiation of either faith at its worst, lies the foundational belief in the God who discloses himself and speaks in the Bible. Utterly unique and profoundly consequential, the character of the God of the Bible must be taken with deep seriousness if anyone is to understand the singular view of life and humanity that the Bible introduces and empowers.

Jump ahead in the argument for a moment. There is no question that the God who reveals himself in the Bible has been the direct source of three striking features of human existence at its most attractive: first, the highest humanism in history—*humanism* in the sense of championing the supreme human dignity and worth of the human individual; second, the surest grounds for founding and developing human freedom, both personal and political; and the third, the greatest and most sustained critique of the abuse of power in history.

Those are strong claims. They are anything but trifling pieties, and they stand in sharp, polar contrast to critical theory and the ideas of the radical left. What makes them possible is the majesty and mystery of the difference of God and the difference he makes. By all means "crush the loathsome thing," as Voltaire proposed, or "murder God," as Nietzsche claimed had happened in his time. But such assailants are driving a stake through the heart of the highest and most awesome of human aspirations and thereby reducing life to a different and far more dismal affair. The very vehemence of the hostility toward faith in God betrays the significance of the meaning of God and heightens the importance of understanding how people encountered God in the first place.

Thomas Jefferson, America's third president and the author of the Declaration of Independence, is often attacked for his moral hypocrisy. At the very time that he wrote the famous words "We hold these truths to be self-evident, that all men are created equal," he was attended by two slaves in Philadelphia, and he owned sixty slaves at home in Monticello, and six hundred slaves over the course of his lifetime. He also rebuffed William Wilberforce's plea to form a "Concert of Benevolence" between Britain and America to lead the world in getting rid of slavery. But surprisingly for such a giant of the mind, Jefferson also displayed an intellectual inconsistency to match his hypocrisy. He referred to the slaves in a letter, "Nothing is more certainly written in the book of fate than that these people shall be free."[16]

Written in the book of fate? Fate has never freed anyone and never will free anyone. Fate is antithetical to freedom, and freedom has everything to do with faith, not fate. Slavery is the norm in history and abolition is the exception. The moral triumph of the abolition of slavery was promoted by Quakers such as John Woolman and evangelical Christians such as William Wilberforce, while Jefferson did nothing. It was a tribute to their passionate faith, and it was in direct and persistent opposition to the age-old fate of the slaves. Freedom and fate are irreconcilably opposed. It was no "book of fate" but Exodus, the book of faith and freedom, that made possible the liberation of the Israelite slaves, the later liberation of the African American slaves, and the emergence of Dr. Martin Luther King Jr. and the civil rights movement. Slavery, after all, is the long-held human tradition, while liberation and abolition are the novelty.

ABLAZE BUT NOT BURNED UP

The entire story of the great liberation of Exodus flows from three direct and immediate encounters with God at the very outset of the account. They are decisive for the whole story of the exodus. Importantly, God encounters human beings and addresses them. The initiative is his. Thus God, who is at the heart of the Abrahamic faiths, is utterly different from any other conception of God, starting with the fact that we humans meet God when he reveals himself to us. He is emphatically not the fruit of brilliant human reflection, the finding at the end of a patient philosophical quest, the QED (that which was to be demonstrated) written to conclude any line of reasoning or the proof established by any repeatable scientific experiment.

Encountering the God of the Bible is therefore completely and utterly different from all the fruits of human reflection. It is quite different from what Gautama Buddha claimed to have discovered beneath the Bodhi tree, what any philosopher has ever found at the end of a long and arduous search for the meaning of life, or what any scientist has concluded after looking through the most powerful telescope or microscope. The God of the Bible encounters and addresses humans in history and through events. He speaks to us as persons and breaks into our experience in life. It may be possible to think of God as an idea, a theory, or an abstraction, and some people may be content to speak about him as such, but no one meets God himself like that. We meet God as the Supreme Presence, the reality of a living presence who addresses us as persons with presence. He discloses himself. He reveals himself to us. In the famous words of Blaise Pascal's "Night of Fire" on November 23, 1654: "God of Abraham, God of Isaac, God of Jacob, not the god of philosophers and scholars."[17]

Faith is more about God's search for humanity than humanity's search for God. Just such an encounter, indeed no less than three such encounters, lie at the heart of Exodus. Together, they form the pivot on which the whole story turns and from which the Bible as a whole surges forward with power. Exodus is the story of God encountering and liberating his people. Exodus is nothing if it is not the story of God. The first of those encounters is so central and so famous that many people do not realize that there are two other equally decisive encounters. The first is when God addresses Moses at the burning bush on the slopes of Mount Sinai. Tending his father-in-law's flock, Moses is arrested by the remarkable sight of a bush that was somehow ablaze with fire but not burned up.

Sitting under his Bodhi tree in Varanasi, Buddha concluded that the reality of this world was all illusion and impermanence, and he led his millions of followers down the same sad path. Standing before the bush that was burning but not burned up, Moses came to the complete and utter opposite conclusion—he came face to face with a Presence that meant *permanence* and *ultimate reality*. We humans tire, grow old, and die. Civilizations decline and fall. Entropy touches the whole of nature. The second law of thermodynamics operates everywhere. What burns, burns up. What fire destroys stays destroyed. But here, in this nondescript desert bush, was something burning that did not burn up, something as dynamic and destructive as fire that did not run down and did not destroy. What on earth could it be, and what could it mean?

In our day Peter Berger has described such an experience as a "signal of transcendence," an experience that punctures our given sense of reality and points beyond, creating wonder and curiosity. Turning aside, Moses suddenly found himself addressed by God who introduced himself as the God of Moses' fathers, Abraham, Isaac, and Jacob, and announced that he was sending Moses back to Egypt to liberate his people from their slavery.

Probably nothing was further from Moses' mind at that moment than freeing his people. Hebrew born but raised a prince of Egypt, he had once thought he might make a stand on behalf of his people, but his rash attempt to do so had been a fiasco, and he had fled for his life. Now, with the passing of time and his position as a shepherd in a foreign country, any thought of a rescue operation in Egypt was ludicrous. Moses therefore ducks and weaves to evade the commanding pull of God's call. Who was he to do it, and how could he possibly do it? He was inarticulate. But then, if the sons of Israel were to ask him for his credentials and inquire as to who had sent him, what was he to say to them?

God's answer stopped Moses in his tracks, just as it has stopped every thoughtful person who ponders what God said. The answer is three words in Hebrew, and they are often translated as "I AM WHO I AM . . . I AM has sent me to you" (Ex 3:14). The words come out of the silent desert air like a thunderclap. There is no preparation and no elaboration. Understood that way, the God who calls and commissions Moses names himself as the one who simply, finally, and foundationally is God—HE WHO IS. That is the beginning and end of it. God is God. All that exists, all that is there throughout the vast universe is only there because it is created, and it stands before God as creation stands before its Creator. There is no one and nothing higher than God, and it makes no sense to think of anyone or anything before God or behind God. Moses has met the Supreme Presence, the ultimate reality, the source of permanence, or more accurately, the Supreme Presence has encountered Moses and humanity has never been the same.

GOD IN THE FUTURE TENSE

But that is not how Rabbi Sacks and many Jews understand the three words in Hebrew. They put the accent on the future tense, not the present, and translate them as "I will be who I will be." The danger in the first translation lies in taking the absoluteness of God in a Greek direction and making God into the "god of the philosophers," the "pure being," or the "ground of all being" who does not, cannot, and will not change or feel anything. But viewing God as static, changeless, and unfeeling is wrong. God, as he reveals himself at Sinai and afterward, is faithful and unchanging (and not the god of process theology), but he is passionate and he is always on the move. Faith in God is always a journey, not an achievement or a condition. God is active and moving toward the future of his will and his design. As Rabbi Sacks points out, in this very disclosure God announces that he is about to enter history and intervene in an unprecedented way to liberate his people. God as Lord is the God of surprise. He can never be put into a box. He is not confined by human expectations. He is sovereign over the future as over the present. "He will be who He will be."

Ponder just two of the titanic consequences of this disclosure. First, the absoluteness of God as the Supreme Presence means that *who God is* is ultimate in the universe and therefore determines how we can view the universe itself. The immensity of this truth is staggering. Is the universe indifferent to us, as Richard Dawkins, the new atheists, and most naturalistic scientists believe? (Chance and necessity are behind everything.) Is the universe hostile to us, as most pagan religions have believed? (Those whom the gods love die young.) No, the Bible declares. God simply and absolutely is the Supreme Presence. Back of everything is God, and God reveals himself as a God of love and mercy and compassion and truth and justice, so love, mercy, compassion, truth, and justice are ultimate in the universe. Yes, there is brokenness, and certainly there are contradictions in the universe as we know it now, but they are humanly caused, and they are not ultimate and will not be final. Life is neither absurd nor tragic, but essentially good (though gone wrong). Our trust in God is therefore anchored surely. God is greater than all. God may be trusted in all situations. Those who know God have faith in him and need have no fear.

Second, the absoluteness of God in the future tense means that faith in God is future-oriented, forward-looking, and truly revolutionary. God is sovereign and always moving toward his purposes. "He will be who He will be," and he cannot and will not be stopped. Sacks's comments soar. The freedom of God underwrites human freedom, it transforms history into an arena of change, it calls into question every status quo, and it gives faith its future-oriented thrust as hope, and it holds out its messianic vision of the golden age that does not recede into the past (like that of most religions and societies) but beckons always from ahead in the future.

Like Moses, even as we ponder the immensity of what we have heard, we are on holy ground. *God's name says it all.* From that momentous disclosure onwards Jews have revered the four-letter name of God and held it to be holy and unpronounceable. Only once a year was the name YHWH said out loud and then only by the high priest in the holy of holies at the climax of Yom

Kippur, the Day of Atonement. For the remainder of the year, and for everyone else, people referred only to "the Name" (*Hashem*), and the actual name YHWH was passed over in silence.

When the Jews refer to YHWH, Lord, only as *Hashem,* "the Name," they express their reverence for God and remain silent before the majesty and reality of God as God most fully is in himself. As Rabbi Sacks explains, there is a difference between proper names and descriptions. "*Things* have descriptions, but only *people* have proper names."[18] YHWH or *Hashem* is the proper name God revealed to Moses to tell him what he needed to know as to who he is. It is therefore the word used when we encounter God existentially in a personal relationship with him—as in Martin Buber's famous description of I-Thou relationships or C. S. Lewis's famous prayer before prayer: "May it be the real You that I speak to, and may it be the real Me who speaks."

YHWH, as God's own self-revelation, is revered as the name that is singular, unique, and used only of God. By contrast, the term *God—Elohim*—is generic and used in the Bible both of other gods besides God and of God when speaking to people who do not know God in himself. As the name we treasure because God revealed it to us himself, YHWH is the name reserved for God as we encounter him in revelation, whereas *Elohim* is the name for God as we meet him in creation.

Rabbi Heschel was a philosopher, but he constantly stressed the difference between the name of God and the notion of God. He told of the time he was asked to speak at a conference on "the Jewish notion of God." He rejected the title at once.

> The God of Israel is a name, not a notion. . . . A notion applies to all objects of similar properties. A name applies to an individual. "God of Israel" applies to the one and only God of all men. A notion describes, defines; a name evokes. A notion is derived from a generalization; a name is learned through acquaintance.

The more appropriate title, Heschel said, should have been, "The Jewish Experience of the Collapse of all Notions in Relation to God."[19] After the burning bush, YHWH is a name and not a notion.

For people of faith, the "great revelation" means that the first principle of freedom, as for all human thinking and living, can only be the absolute authority and centrality of God whom we meet and come to know. *Faith* and *nonfaith* are entirely different modes of being. To move to faith in God from whatever form of nonfaith or other faith we were once in is therefore a life-changing experience and an epochal boundary crossing. God in his sovereignty is free, and for those who know him as he is, all discussion and experience of freedom begin and end at that point. From then on both Moses and his successor, Joshua, speak of God, in contrast to idols and all the human projections of the forces of the universe, as "the living God." What starts as a description of God becomes the name of God as he speaks and acts freely in his universe (Deut 5:25; Josh 3:10). At the very heart of the Jewish and Christian faiths, at the very center of all that Jews and Christians think and do, and therefore at the very core of human freedom is "the living God." Freedom begins with God.

WHEN THE DARKNESS WAS WORST

This awe-filled revelation to Moses on Mount Sinai lies at the heart of the experience and understanding of radical monotheism, the belief in the Supreme Presence, the "one true God" who is central to the three Abrahamic faiths. Yet that is only the first of three such disclosures by God in Exodus. The second and less-mentioned revelation is to Moses in connection with his meeting with the elders of Israel at the very lowest point of their slavery. Moses, together with his brother Aaron, had announced that God had sent them to free the Israelites, only to find that his attempt had made things worse. Slavery and a slow genocide (extermination of the male babies) were bad enough, but Pharaoh responded to their request for freedom by piling extra demands on them that were humanly impossible—the same quota of bricks but no straw to make them with. The Israelite foremen complained bitterly to Moses. Not only had he made them odious in their overseers' eyes, but he had also put a sword in their hand to make their lives intolerable.

Naturally, Moses went back to God, anguished. Hadn't he done exactly what God told him to do? But the situation had become far worse, not better. And God had not done what he said he would do. In fact, he had done absolutely nothing. So why had God sent him and then left him to twist in the wind? But that is the moment, at this lowest point in the entire story, when God reveals himself for the second time—first to Moses and then for him to relay to the Hebrew elders. "Now you shall see what I will do," God says (Ex 6:1).

That declaration is followed by an extraordinary passage that is not as appreciated by most Christians as it deserves to be because we mostly do not know Hebrew. I am told that in Hebrew, the words "I am the LORD" are repeated three times, and they form a framework for the passage, coming at the beginning, in the middle, and at the end. The first mention of "I am the LORD" is followed by fifty words in Hebrew, and then "I am the LORD" is repeated, followed by a further fifty words, ending in "I am the LORD" a third time (Ex 6:2, 6, 8). Such a carefully crafted style of literary expression is called a *chiasmus*, and it follows the pattern of A-B-C-B-A, with the second half of the passage mirroring the first half. It serves to highlight the three "I AM" declarations that frame it. The first fifty words are in the past tense, referring back to God's promises to the patriarchs, and the second fifty words are in the future tense, detailing God's promises to Israel. Now, God declares, he will free Israel.

Curiously, the passage also includes a fourth mention of the name YHWH, which has caused much comment. "I appeared to Abraham, Isaac, and Jacob, as God Almighty, but *by* My name, LORD, I did not make Myself known to them" (Ex 6:3). Was the name YHWH entirely new, as many people interpret this verse—in contrast to *Elohim*, the generic word for God? Not at all. The name YHWH appears 165 times in Genesis, beginning with the story of creation, where both words are used. God addresses both Abraham and Jacob by his name YHWH (Gen 15:7; 28:13). The key to understanding the word probably lies in the meaning of the verb "to know." Knowing in Hebrew is anything but detached intellectual assent. The word is also used to mean sexual intercourse, and it contains the idea of "knowing in experience" or "experiencing in reality." Thus earlier generations may have known that God was YHWH, but they had not experienced God in living reality, in decisive and dramatic rescuing power, as the Israelites (and Pharaoh) were about to know him.

UNIQUE AND UNBEARABLE

The third great revelation in the story of the exodus is all-decisive for the Jewish people. God comes down to address the Israelites at Mount Sinai once they have escaped from Pharaoh and crossed the Red Sea. The titanic drama of the experience constitutes them as God's people and becomes the founding event in their long and celebrated history. Yet Christians commonly read the account (Ex 19) and miss its momentous import. Many fail to understand the third revelation because it tends to be overshadowed, first by the drama of the surrounding events—the giving of the Ten Commandments and the rebellion of the golden calf; and second, by their focusing on the dramatic example of God's call to individuals rather than to the Jewish people as a nation.

Yet therein lies the uniqueness of the third revelation. God's call to Moses at the burning bush was to an individual, his call to Moses and the Jewish elders at their low point was to an elite group, his call to Isaiah in the temple in Jerusalem has rarely, if ever, been duplicated, and his call to Saul on the road to Damascus was in a highly unusual manner. *But what happened at Mount Sinai is unique: God addresses an entire nation in one place and at one time—men, women, and children—for the first and only time in human history up till now—* which by itself deserves pondering. Moses describes what that day was like to the next generation but then highlights its immensity as unique and unprecedented. "Has anything as great as this ever happened, or has anything like it ever been heard of? Has any other people heard the voice of God speaking out of fire, as you have, and lived?" Moses' questions are rhetorical, of course, and he hurries on to call on the whole of history to be his witness. "Has any god tried to take for himself one nation out of another nation?" (Deut 4:32-34 NIV).

God's address to Israel at Mount Sinai beggars description. But as Rabbi Sacks points out, two things are clear from the accounts in both Exodus and Deuteronomy. First, the audience was unique. God spoke to the entire nation rather than to a single leader or a group of elders, as he did in the first two revelations. Second, the experience was unique. "The sound was of almost unbearable intensity. The Israelites clamored around Moses begging him to ask God to stop. 'You speak to us and we shall listen, but let God not speak to us, lest we die'" (Ex 20:19).[20] In the Middle Ages some writers interpreted the fact that the revelation was to the whole nation as a guarantee of its veracity. If nearly a million people heard the same voice at the same time, it must have been certain. Today, the stress is on the political significance. The politics of freedom was born at Sinai. Israel, not the United States, was history's *first new nation.* The people of Israel, rescued by God and addressed by God, were to be a new and free people for him.

In sum, God's revelations in Exodus are decisive in history and decisive for the politics of freedom. As Rabbi Sacks points out, Sinai preceded Athens. Sinai has outlasted Athens. And Sinai, not Athens, was decisive in the seventeenth and eighteenth centuries and the rise of modern freedom. And as I shall argue as we explore these issues further, Sinai's vision of freedom is vastly superior to that of Athens (and London, Philadelphia, Paris, Saint Petersburg, and Beijing)— *and all because of who God is.* According to the Bible's view, there can be no understanding of freedom apart from understanding God.

LET GOD BE GOD

In this chapter and those that follow we are exploring a series of seven foundational truths that are at the heart of Exodus and essential for maintaining freedom
today. Each truth contains numerous possible implications, and we can only be
selective. That is emphatically the case with the great revelation of God in the
Bible. The difference of God from all other gods and all other authorities and
allegiances is the ultimate difference that makes the most far-reaching difference
in countless areas. An entire book might be written on this point alone, but
certain implications are vital for the understanding of freedom and human rights.

*First, if God is who he reveals himself to be in the Bible, then God, and not
reason, nature, or science, must be central to the thinking and living of all who
come to know God—and certainly to their entire understanding of freedom.* Coming
to know God as he reveals himself is the ultimate Copernican Revolution in
human life and thinking. Other authorities such as reason, nature, science, and
tradition are highly important in their place but no longer central and all-
important. *Revelation*, in the sense of the way we have encountered God and
who God has revealed himself to be, is now central and essential to all thinking.
All other ways of thinking and living must be decisively reoriented to be ordered
and shaped by the truth and the experience of God's revelation. How we see
God must shape how we see and live life. The response of all who come to know
God, experience God, and trust God as he reveals himself must be unequivocal.
From the moment of coming to know God, all who have encountered God in
such undeniable reality must say to themselves, *Know before whom you live, and
think, and act, and see life.* In the magnificent phrase attributed to Martin Luther,
the heart and soul of faith is to "let God be God."

People of other faiths and worldviews and those who have not encountered
God like this will doubtless find these words strange or even repellent. The chasm
between Sinai and Paris, for example, is vast at this point. Sinai begins and ends
with the ultimate Presence, so that faith rests on conviction and assurance that
are rocklike. Paris and critical theory, on the other hand, build on sand. They
glory in their bid for revolutionary freedom by attempting to reject what they
see as the oppressive confines of categories, the words and labels that pin people
in place like butterflies on a board—binaries such as male and female, for example.
In the process they set out to dismantle all categories, blur all boundaries, dis-
solve all clarity, and erode all certainties, only to end in a skepticism, incoherence,
chaos, and anxiety that is not so much free as unlivable.

At the very least, people who claim complete disinterest in God should try to understand what Jews and Christians believe and how they view life—above all because the implications for notions such as human dignity and freedom are so crucial for our life together. But let there be no misunderstanding or caricature of this position. Those who have encountered God in this way prize the importance of reason highly (just as they prize the important place of nature, science, and tradition). They do not for a second think that faith is irrational. Reason is absolutely vital, but rationalism, the *ism* based on reason alone, is wrong and dangerous because it represents the overreach of reason. Reason by itself can neither justify itself nor explain or sustain the meaning of life. When it is asked to, it inevitably collapses into irrationality as modern philosophy demonstrates.

The same is true of other good things that, good as they are, cannot carry the full weight of life. Thus, those who have encountered God prize the place and importance of science and the scientific method, but science can never replace faith because it speaks to the *how* question and not the *why*. Technology can be an extraordinary force for good. As it advances it presents us with ever more power and countless blessings, but it cannot advise us on how to use it well. Market economics is history's most successful way of creating wealth, but by itself it falls short. It opens up unprecedented choices and lifts more people out of poverty than ever before in history, but it is mute as to which choices would be wisest and best. The liberal constitutional and democratic state may be vastly superior to its rivals, above all in offering us freedoms of one sort or another, but it cannot supply the basis on which to use them well.

To let God be God is the heart of revolutionary faith, and that is what makes faith revolutionary. God's presence calls into question every status quo. That is why true faith must never become reactionary, and why faith must never simply bolster the status quo or provide religious legitimacy for cultures under stress. Revolutionary faith begins with a call to break with the status quo of the time each generation lives in, a conversion from all other ways of thinking and living, a radical turning and a revolution at the very center of all our thinking and living. Conversion in this sense is the ultimate defection from all other ways of thinking and living, the ultimate about-face, and the micro revolution that is the natural beginning of the revolutionary faith that faith in God leads to. Those who come to know God have their lives turned upside down and become his junior partners in the great project of turning the world the right way up again.

Just as the earth goes around the sun rather than the sun around the earth, so all thinking must do justice to the primacy and centrality of God and displace the false centrality of humanity and reason by itself. Thinking that begins and ends with human reason may be brilliant in its coherence, but it will necessarily be limited and reductionist. All that such thinking is doing is confining the world to the small circle of its own understanding, and like people wrapped up in themselves, that makes for a very small parcel. Thus, contrary to Protagoras, "Man is not the measure of all things," and reason most certainly isn't. Utterly brilliant though Leonardo da Vinci was, his *Vitruvian Man* is wrong—not, as the feminists say, because he is a man and young, handsome, and European rather than a woman, but because he is a human at the center where God alone should be. Only God is the measure of all things. Man as the measure of all things reduces humans, and reason as the measure of all things reduces them further. (Just remember the role of the will, freedom, and the unconscious.) Only if God is the measure of all things is Man both reminded that he is small but raised to be truly great.

As we shall see in chapter two, Jewish and Christian understandings converge at this point to form the highest humanism, but the secret begins here. The ancient Greeks and the modern secular humanists agree over the starting counsel "Know yourself." But not knowing God, they always try to understand human beings in relation to nature or to themselves, and they always end in reducing humanity to the level of nature or an animal or a machine. The Bible in contrast understands humanity *upward*, not *downward*. The grand premise of biblical faith, as Rabbi Heschel insists, is that humans are able to surpass themselves. Faith begins with the call to "lift up your eyes and see" (Gen 13:14), "know your God" (1 Chron 28:9), and "the fear of the LORD is the beginning of wisdom" (Prov 9:10), and not surprisingly it ends with the highest view of humanity. Humanity understood solely on its own terms will always be smaller than humans know themselves to be in experience. Only as humans transcend themselves, as they are called or questioned by their cosmos and supremely by their Creator, can they rise above themselves and become the creatures they were created and called to be. "There is no self-understanding without God-understanding."[21] Only if God is at the center can reason and human thinking be liberated to be wide-ranging enough to engage the full reality of the universe and the rich wonder of life and existence.

The Greeks reported that after Plato defined man as "a two-legged animal without feathers," Diogenes plucked a rooster and brought it into the Academy.

A "featherless animal," a "naked ape," a "selfish gene," "a gene's way of making another gene," the "toolmaking animal"? Human attempts at defining humanity go on and on, and the failures mount. Created in the image of God, human beings must be defined upward. They will never be defined downward to their own satisfaction.

Ludwig Wittgenstein described his work as a philosopher as helping the fly get out of the bottle. The fly buzzes around the bottle and never looks up to the neck and the open air above it. Eventually, it falls exhausted from its futile efforts and dies. By themselves, reason, emotions, nature, science, and tradition can do no better for our thinking and living. Vital though they are, not one of them is sufficient by itself, in isolation. Only when we encounter God and understand them under God do they come into their own. Only when we "let God be God" can human thinking and living be true, satisfying, and provide the foundations for genuine human flourishing.

To understand the universe fully we have to look for meaning that is outside the universe, and to understand ourselves fully we have to surpass ourselves and rise to the call of our Creator. The alternative for our relationship to the universe is to understand things downward, to make all knowledge a matter of power and end in exploitation and the ruin of the earth. The downward alternative for humanity is to see ourselves only as toolmakers, to make all knowledge a matter of causation and expediency, and to end in reductionism, determinism, fate, and alienation.

Against all the many varieties of contemporary humanism, the Bible asserts that God is the measure of all things, not humans. Worshiping God, understanding God, and bearing witness to God must all be decisively different because of the difference of who God is and the difference in the way he reveals himself. The Copernican Revolution changes thinking and living forever, and in every way. Because of who God is, it is completely and absolutely impossible for "Man" alone to be the measure of all things. To be sure, of all the life forms on earth only humans measure the world and life as we do. But those very measuring rods—reason, nature, and the scientific method—need to be measured and justified themselves, and none of them can justify themselves by themselves.

The truth, rather, is that "humanity before God" is the measure of all things, the standard for human responsibility, and the secret to a life lived well. None of us will understand or live life well until we see ourselves as individual women and men in relation to the One who is our Father, our Creator, and our judge.

Such is the power of the sun that the earth goes around the sun, and not the sun around the earth. Faith in God is a revolutionary faith with a calling to turn the world the right way up.

FREEDOM'S FOUNDATION

Second, the centrality of God as he reveals himself means that the sovereign freedom of God must be central to thinking about human freedom. Freedom requires authority, a source that authorizes it, and for the Bible and the biblical family of faiths, the authority and the source for freedom is God. He who says, "I am who I am" and "I will be who I will be" is the Lord who is sovereign and free. All freedom therefore stems from him and needs to be understood in his way. In God's sovereign freedom he can express and exert his will despite all interference and resistance. The Supreme Presence and final reality is not fate, chance, or necessity. Thus, when God says, "Let my people go," God in his freedom is working to free his people to worship him freely and to live together in freedom before him as freely as he intended them to live, as people created in his image and likeness.

Other philosophies and ultimate beliefs will rely on other authorities, such as reason, nature, science, and tradition and make them primary in their thinking. But for the biblical family of faiths, such is the great revelation of God at Sinai that no other authority is needed or desired. Freedom is the beginning and the end, the summary and the soul of the entire book of Exodus. And that freedom flows directly from the character and will of the sovereign God, who expresses and exerts his will despite all resistance and interference.

It so happens that, in the case of human freedom, no other philosophy or authority has been able to provide the foundation needed for freedom. At the height of the French Revolution, Robespierre and his colleagues made a determined bid to ground freedom without God. They tried to replace the worship of God with the worship of Dame Nature. To do so symbolically, they replaced the high altar of Notre Dame with a "mountain" of earth from which an actress, dressed in white, delivered a "Hymn to Liberty"—"Descend, O Liberty, daughter of Nature."[22] Daughter of nature? That is absurd, and the attempt was futile. Liberty is not the daughter of nature and never can be, even if we spell nature with a capital N and personify nature as Gaia or Mother Nature. Neither nature alone, nor reason and science alone, has ever given us the grounding for human freedom. Each of them leads not to freedom but to determinism. Freedom is the gift of God. It does not, cannot, and will not come from reason, science, or nature alone.

The truth is that modern science underscores determinism and undermines freedom with relentless insistence. The human claim to be free is a fiction. The only surprise is that this bleak candor is not taken more seriously. B. F. Skinner stated it unambiguously in the title of his bestselling book *Beyond Freedom and Dignity*. ("What is being abolished is autonomous man . . . the man defended by the literature of freedom and dignity.")[23] He argued that while the traditional Jewish and Christian view of humanity supported Hamlet's exclamation "How like a god!" this new Pavlovian view supports the statement "How like a dog!" Skinner did not consider that statement a setback for humanity but an advance, because it is the truth that science tells us. More recently, new atheist philosopher Sam Harris came to the same conclusion. "Free will *is* an illusion. Our wills are simply not of our own making. . . . We do not have the freedom we think we have."[24] Yuval Harari summarizes how, according to this secularist view, science has driven nails into "freedom's coffin."

> To the best of our scientific understanding, determinism and randomness have divided the entire cake between them, leaving not even a crumb for "freedom." The sacred word "freedom" turns out to be, just like "soul," a hollow term empty of any discernible meaning. Free will exists only in the imaginary stories we humans have invented.

But of course this bleak judgment represents a challenge not only to freedom but to liberalism. The ungrounded freedom that liberalism affirms is a pretense and an illusion, which is why establishment liberalism in America and many Western countries has folded so weakly when confronted by the radical left. "However," Harari continues, "over the last few decades the life sciences have reached the conclusion that this liberal story is pure mythology. The single authentic self is as real as the eternal soul, Santa Claus, and the Easter Bunny."[25]

Rabbi Sacks counters this bleak conclusion decisively. The so-called scientific dismissal of human freedom says more about the limits of science than about the nonexistence of human freedom. The fact is that a fallacy has dominated the scientific study of humankind.

> Science searches for causes; a cause always precedes its effect; therefore science will always proceed to explain a phenomenon in the present by

reference to something that happened in the past—anything from the genome to early childhood experiences to brain chemistry to recent stimuli. It will follow that science will inevitably deny the existence of human free will. The denial may be soft or hard, gentle or brutal, but it will come. Freedom will be seen as an illusion.[26]

The fallacy, of course, is not the fault of science itself but of *scientism* or the purely naturalistic vision of science that presumes to be able to use the scientific method to explain everything. The fallacy is simple, Sacks notes.

> Human action is always oriented to the future. I put the kettle on because I want a cup of coffee. I work hard because I want to pass the exam. I act to bring about a future that is not yet. Science cannot account for the future because something that has not happened yet cannot be a cause. Therefore there will always be something about intentional human action that science cannot explain.[27]

Martin Seligman argues in *Homo Prospectus* that the great mistake of Sigmund Freud and many others has been to focus only on the past and the present—on an individual's history, genetic makeup, and present drives, emotions, and stimuli and so to overlook everything that is forward-looking. The future, of course, cannot be measured, so the inevitable result of the naturalistic way of thinking is that we are each determined, caught in a web of causes, "a prisoner of the past and present."[28]

Once again, faith in the God of Sinai—"I will be who I will be"—always includes a future tense and a strong sense of vision, hope, and anticipation. Faith in God is forward-looking, future-oriented, progressive, and truly transformative and revolutionary. It is not simply caused, it causes. Karl Marx famously charged that religion is the "flowers on the chains" that decks out and disguises human captivity. Certainly, religion can be and often has been reactionary. Over the centuries, it has been corrupted again and again in order to bolster the status quo. Secularist ideology is easily corrupted too. Ironically, Marx started with the claim that the beginning of all criticism was the criticism of religion, only to end with a political religion that has ended all criticism.

The revolutionary faith of Exodus is quite different. It is all about freedom, change, transformation, and the future—the very freedom that science by itself cannot justify and revolutionary socialism has never achieved. Sacks quotes the

nineteenth-century Jewish philosopher Herman Cohen: "What Greek intellec-
tualism could not create, prophetic monotheism succeeded in creating. . . . For
the Greek, history is oriented solely toward the past. The prophet, however, is a
seer, not a scholar. The prophets are the idealists of history. Their seerdom created
the concept of history as *the being of the future*."[29] Sacks concludes with the
hauntingly beautiful summary of Harold Fisch, a literary scholar, who referred
to "the unappeased memory of a future still to be fulfilled."[30]

Later we will see how forgiveness is linked inseparably to freedom, and how
together they open up a future that can be different from the past. In Exodus
the free and sovereign God frees his people to worship him freely and to live
freely together before him. Revolutionary faith is uniquely the foundation and
fulfillment of the highest human freedom and the dynamic for the deepest human
transformation. Rabbi Sacks states the Jewish view boldly: "Judaism is a religion
of freedom and responsibility. Against all the many determinisms in the history
of thought—astrological, philosophical, Spinozist, Marxist, Freudian, neo-
Darwinian—Judaism insists that we are masters of our fate. . . . We can choose."[31]

RESPECT FOR THE OTHER
REQUIRES SELF-LIMITATION

A third implication is one that raises one of the greatest challenges of freedom:
*Any and all recognition of freedom means recognizing the integrity of the equal
freedom of others.* The mutuality and reciprocity of freedom is easy to say and
commonly said. ("A right for one is a right for another, and a responsibility for
both." "Injustice anywhere is injustice everywhere," and so on.) Yet this reminder
is all too often reduced to a cliché and then quickly overridden in practice. From
one side, extreme individualism turns freedom into the unbridled self-assertion
of some individuals with no serious concern for the equal freedom of other
individuals. From another side, postmodernism recognizes only the principle
of power, so we are each encouraged to assert ourselves until we hit the natural
limits to our own power in the face of powers greater than our own. In short,
the victory once again goes to the strong, and the weak go to the wall.

For Jews and Christians that situation is the breeding ground of injustice and
abuse of power. For these two faiths too, the barrier against that temptation lies
in the character of God as just, and an essential principle protecting the mutuality of freedom lies in the way God himself treats others. It comes from understanding how God, in his sovereign freedom, relates to humans created in his

image, with their own significant freedom. *God so respects the integrity of humans created in his image that he limits his freedom in regard to the freedom of the human heart and conscience—and so should we.* This principle is rooted in the Jewish notion of *tzimtzum*, the idea of divine self-limitation. As Rabbi Sacks explains, "If God is everywhere, how can anything else exist?" The answer is that "the very act of creation involved a self-limitation on the part of God."[32] The one place God does not invade or override is the human heart and conscience. Rebbe Mendel of Kotzk, the Kotzker, replied to students who argued that God was everywhere. "You have not understood. God lives *where we let him in*."[33] Rabbi Sacks expresses the same point simply: "Though God can create universes, He cannot live within the human heart *unless we let Him in*."[34] Or again, "In miracles, God changes physical nature but never *human* nature. Were He to do so, the entire project of the Torah—the free worship of free human beings—would have been rendered null and void."[35]

This principle (the humility of God's respect for the integrity of his creation) has immense significance in both the Hebrew and the Christian Scriptures. It is vital too for political notions such as freedom of conscience and religious liberty. God respects the integrity of the human heart, so he will not make us believe in him, and he will not force us to be moral. That truth lies behind religious freedom and behind a reliance on persuasion rather than coercion. Both are based on respect for freedom of conscience. To believe or not to believe and to choose to be moral or not is our responsible choice.

But the same principle also carries profound practical implications for freedom and the politics of freedom. Freedom is the freedom to be our individual selves and therefore to be properly self-assertive in expressing and exercising our wills—freedom of religion and conscience, freedom of speech, and freedom of association. But the full right of such freedom should also be marked by humility, responsibility, the self-limitation that is respect for others—and a willingness to sacrifice. Sacrifice and self-limitation are closely linked, for *sacrifice is simply self-limitation at a price*. Respect for the freedom of others is the fruit of respect for the integrity of others in themselves. Self-assertion at the expense of others is an abuse of power, but self-limitation is an expression of respect for another, just as sacrifice is an expression of love for another, whether for a family or a country. To recognize this truth and limit oneself is the beginning of humility, responsibility, freedom, and love.

WORDS MAKE WORLDS

A fourth implication of the great revelation in Exodus concerns the importance of words, and the importance of words for freedom—*God created the world through a word, and God reveals himself in words. Words are therefore essential for creating bonds and building a world of freedom, so all who know God and love freedom must be champions and guardians of words.*

The lofty Sinai view of words bears on today's situation in two main ways. First, and more generally, Sinai's high view of words stands in strong contrast to the way the advanced modern world simultaneously inflates, trivializes, weaponizes, and demeans words. In the great age of the visual, words play second fiddle to photos, graphics, and icons. In the world of consumerism words are mere lackeys to products, and in the realm of the social media words are no more than weapons with which to blaze back with hasty opinions and emotional counter-retorts. Rarely have words been so grandiose and so belittled. The F-word is near universal, and adjectives such as *awesome, wonderful,* and *terrific* are now synonymous and interchangeable with *cool* and *neat.* In the Babel of our media and social media, words have been hyped, worn out, and left threadbare. In Rabbi Heschel's telling description, words "turn waif, elusive, a mouthful of dust. Words have ceased to be commitments."[36]

Second, the Sinai view of words agrees yet crucially disagrees with Paris and critical theory over the importance of words. As we shall see in chapter seven, critical theory takes words very seriously. It analyzes discourse and the way in which speech expresses what a society takes to be truth and knowledge. The aim is to expose the power relations in a society as expressed in words, and it does that to identify where there is oppression and who are the victims. The deconstruction of speech is therefore a prime tool for liberating the oppressed and the marginalized. But the problem is that in both its theory and its practice everything is negative and there is no positive. There is ceaseless deconstruction, but no reconstruction. The dismantling is never followed by rebuilding. The result is a generation of "ever-offendables," hypersensitive to microaggression and "trigger words," and a steady erosion of freedom of speech through speech codes and political correctness. The outcome is the culture of grievance, the "cancel culture," the silence of the cowed, the rage of the crowd, and an overall shift from one oppressor to another.

In strong contrast, the Bible's stress on the importance of words is on behalf of the positive—the true, the good, and the beautiful in the service of trust, freedom, and justice. The power, the beauty, and the grandeur of the cosmos were called into being by a word, the dignity of humans was created by a word and is respected in words, and the freedom, justice, and peace of human community are all sustained by words. Thus gossip and slander are "evil speech" destructive of community as a murderous assault on the name and character of a fellow human made in the image of God. Lying too is prohibited as a lynching of truth and a violation of the bonds of the community.

Words make worlds and words destroy worlds. How then are we to relate to each other, and how are we to relate to God if we only have words? Is it meaningful to speak to God or to speak of God in any way? What does it mean to say that God is awesome, majestic, sublime, mysterious? Each of the encounters in which God disclosed himself defies description. Together, the experiences threaten to strain the power of words to the breaking point. Even at their most superlative, all the words we could ever use of God would always only be an understatement. Yet that is also the wonder of words. Words can be cheapened into clichés. Words can be twisted into lies and used to defame and destroy. Words can falter when called on to capture sublime experiences, and words can be leapfrogged by music when there is a summons to say the unsayable. (The Jewish sages say that the ram's horn, *shofar,* has a strange and heart-piercing sound before which "even the angels tremble.")[37] But at the end of the day words well spoken regain their power in a second. There is no substitute for words, and words are essential for human freedom as they are for communication of any kind. Nothing compares with the power of words to convey truth, make promises, build trust, negotiate with integrity, demonstrate loyalty, and so to sustain the rich ecology of a world of truth and freedom—not just between humans and other humans, but between God and humans. Words make worlds. No words, no worlds. Bad words, bad worlds. True and respectful words, a free and a human world.

Rabbi Sacks raises two foundational questions about human life, the first of which is, How do we humans relate to each other and to God? ("What is the bond between human beings and God?")[38] That question lies behind an obvious question that confronts the reader exploring the opening books of the Bible. If God is truly transcendent as the story describes, how could such a God ever communicate with human beings? And how could humans ever grasp someone who is ultimately mysterious, completely beyond, and utterly other, let alone talk to him in response?

There is no such problem for other religions. What they call gods are merely the personification of the forces of nature, so they are visible and easily represented in images—the sun, the moon, the stars, the rain, the storm, and so on. But YHWH as creator of all these forces transcends them. He is above and beyond them all and therefore invisible. No visible representation is either adequate or right. All images, icons, statues, and paintings are idolatrous because they reduce God to the level of the other gods and the forces of nature. So *revelation* poses a problem that is not a problem for the pagan religions. The challenge, then, is not simply communication between humans and other humans. The ultimate challenge is communication between God and humans. How can we relate to someone so awesome and so utterly beyond us, and how does God relate to us?

The Bible's answer to both questions is simple and straightforward but mighty: *words*. God is invisible, but he is not inaudible. Without words God would be incomprehensible to us, and we to each other. But words express the inner and the invisible. They make the deepest bonding possible. In revelation, God speaks and we listen. In prayer, we speak and God listens. And in our words to each other, we say in words what they could otherwise never know. The answer to God's mystery, Rabbi Sacks says,

> astonishing in its beauty and its simplicity, is that the meeting between us and God is like the meeting between two persons, myself and another. I can see your body, but I cannot feel your pain. How then can I enter your world? Through words. You speak, I listen. I ask, you answer. We communicate. Language is the narrow bridge across the abyss between soul and human soul. So it is between us and the Soul of the universe. Revelation takes place through speech. That is what happened at Sinai. Infinity spoke and the world trembled. In the silence of the desert the Israelites heard the voice of God.[39]

"God is close, but encountered not in things seen, but in words heard."[40]

NO FORM, ONLY A VOICE

Words, not storm, thunder, and lightning, are the sound of Sinai. This high place of words is at the heart of all three revelations in Exodus, particularly the first and the third. The whole drama of Mount Sinai, Sacks says, lies in the fact that "there is only one man, Moses, and the divine voice, as if to say that this is how history is changed, by the inner dialogue between a single soul and the God of freedom and dignity."[41] But the same high place of words is absolutely unmistakable in the third encounter, when God spoke to all Israel at Sinai and then centuries later to the prophet Elijah at the same mountain.

The mountain burned with fire as the Israelites camped before it. There was darkness, cloud, and dense gloom everywhere. But that was not the communication they were assembled to hear—any more than God's message was in the wind, the earthquake, and the fire that Elijah witnessed years later after his great contest with the false prophets on Mount Carmel. Then God spoke, as Moses recounted the scene forty years after Sinai, and God spoke with words, only words—and speaking to Elijah, as a single person, rather than the entire nation, he spoke in "a still small voice" (1 Kings 19:12 KJV). Only in the silence of the desert, Sacks concludes, when the people were "hyper-sensitized to sound" could "the sound beneath sound be heard."[42]

There was absolutely no visible form and no image to be seen at Mount Sinai, Moses said—only a voice. And when he recounted the terrifying Sinai experience to the next generation, he underscored the point. "*Remember* the day you stood before the Lord at Horeb. . . . Then the Lord spoke to you from the midst of the fire; you heard the sound of words, but you saw no form—only a voice. . . . So watch yourselves carefully since you did not see any form on the day the Lord spoke to you at Horeb from the midst of the fire" (Deut 4:10, 12, 15).

No form, only a voice. From that day on, Jews, and later Christians, have been the people of the Word and words supremely so among all the peoples of the earth. As we shall see, *Shema* ("hear" or "listen") becomes Israel's central way of knowing and loving God, and Judaism becomes "a culture of listening rather than seeing, of the ear rather than the eye."[43] Words, reading, reading aloud, reciting, listening, paying attention, and remembering are at the heart of faith, whereas the Bible links sight, images, and appearances to temptation, sin, idolatry, and disloyalty. Not sight but sound. Not images but words, even in our grand modern age of images when the graphic is king and words have been humiliated to the rank of *verbiage* and *words, words, words.*

SOUND VERSUS SIGHT

The same truth is evident long before Sinai, starting with the world's first sin when Eve trusted the lure of her senses and overrode the clear voice of God. Or again, the patriarch Isaac went wrong when he trusted his other senses rather than hearing. Being almost blind, he could not see Jacob's face so he was vulnerable to Jacob's impersonation of Esau. The sound of Jacob's voice suggested Jacob, but the taste of the food, the feel of the goats' hair on his arms, and the smell of the outdoors world suggested it was Esau. Isaac ignored his hearing, went with the other senses, and he was taken in.

Here is an immense difference between Jerusalem and Athens, Sinai and Paris, or between Matthew Arnold's Hebraism and Hellenism. And here too is an immense difference between the Bible and the modern world. As Sacks comments, classical Greece and its rediscovery in Renaissance Italy represented unsurpassed excellence in the visual arts—art, sculpture, theater, and architecture. The Jews excelled in none of these things, but they gave rise to "a culture not of the eye but of the ear."[44] In our modern word world too, Sacks notes, understanding is commonly linked to sight. (We speak of "insight," "foresight," "hindsight, "observation," and we say "look" when we want someone to pay attention.) In the Bible, by contrast, "instead of saying that someone thinks, the verse will say that 'he said in his or her own heart'" (thought being a form of speech, not sight).[45]

The significance of the difference between a listening culture and a seeing culture is profound. In the words of another rabbi quoted by Sacks, "From a human perspective it often appears as if seeing is a more precise form of knowledge than hearing. However, hearing has greater power than seeing. Sight discloses the external aspect of things, but hearing reveals their inwardness."[46] In pagan cultures, Sacks continues, they *saw* the gods—the sun, the rain, the sea, the storm, and the earth. These forces were both visual and impersonal. They could be captured in ceremonies and rituals that were spectacles for the eye. YHWH, by contrast, could never be seen, but he could be heard.

Words, hearing, and listening were appropriate to the encounter between God and humans and between humans and humans because words are not the end in themselves. Words represent what is beyond them and point us toward the reality they represent, whereas images, symbols, and ceremonies have to do with the eye, so it is easy and natural to stop short and be content with them. What is heard points beyond what we hear; what is seen satisfies us by itself, and sends us no further. Sacks concludes, "That is why the key word of Judaism is *shema.* God is not something we see, but a voice we hear."[47] Judaism is "a person-centered civilization—and persons communicate by words."[48]

SOCIAL MEDIA AND EVIL SPEECH

This stress on the Word, and on all words, bears directly on freedom. It lies at the heart of the discourse of a free society, and it underscores the Bible's devastating judgment of "evil speech" (*lashon hara)*, which in the Bible covers gossip, ridicule, and slander, and in today's world such things as trolling. Such speech, Maimonides insists, is "the evil tongue, which refers to one who speaks disparagingly to his fellow, *even though he speaks the truth*."[49] This is a principle that we should reflect on in the age of social media when, from political leaders and Hollywood celebrities down, cyber insults and cyberbullying have become instinctive and utterly degrading. Are Americans too caught up in their own pride and power to recognize that American public discourse has degenerated to the level of a verbal slum ruled by the vicious gang lords of the Twitter world?

Gossip is prohibited in the Torah (Lev 19:16), and Proverbs tells us that life and death are in the power of the tongue (Prov 18:21). Astonishingly, Rabbi Heschel reminds us, the Hebrew word *bloodshed* means both murder and humiliation, and the Talmud insists that it is better "to throw oneself alive into a burning furnace than to humiliate a human being publicly."[50] Rabbi Sacks notes that the Jewish sages regarded "evil speech" about a person as the worst of the sins, "as bad as the three cardinal sins—idolatry, murder, and incest—combined."[51] The practical reason is that "it kills three people, the one who said it, the one it is said about, and the one who listens in."[52]

The underlying reason is the place of words in creation and human experience. Anthropologists have argued that the function of language is to allow humans to cooperate in larger groups than other animals can. Rabbi Sacks writes simply, "Language is life. Words are creative but also destructive. If good words are holy, then evil words are a desecration."[53] "*Speech is what holds society together.*"[54] Unchecked, evil speech "will destroy any group it attacks—a family, a team, a community, even a nation. Hence its uniquely malicious character; it uses the power of language to weaken the very thing language was brought into being to create, namely, the trust that sustains the social bond."[55] Can there be any doubt that the brutal incivility of American discourse is now tearing America apart? And that a massive cleansing of language is essential for both personal and political reform in America and throughout the West? Rabbi Heschel lost family members in Auschwitz, but he underscored the seriousness of shaming at other levels: "Holocausts are caused wherever a person is put to shame."[56]

THE WORLD'S FIRST SOCIAL CRITICS

More positively, the stress on words and the Word is behind the elevated place Jews and Christians give to prophets. Their trademark statement, "Thus says the LORD," said it all. They were spokesmen and spokeswomen of the Word from God (spokeswomen because there are many women prophets in the Hebrew Scriptures, although there are no women priests). This transcendent standpoint shaped the prophets' double contribution. First, it was the source of their long-term vision. As Sacks says, "A prophet is a watchman, one who climbs to a high vantage point and so can see the danger in the distance, before anyone at ground level is aware of it."[57] Or as the Jewish sages said, "Who is wise? One who sees the long-term consequences."

Second, the transcendent Word was the standard by which the prophets forged their social criticism. Prophets were prominent and critical in the nation of Israel as the champions and guardians of freedom and justice. They were "the voice of God and the conscience of society."[58] Their calling was to speak the word of God, given directly by God, and to stand up for the covenant with God and thus to hold the nation accountable for its covenantal pledge. As Michael Walzer insists, they did not invent standards or obligations for the people. They were the champions and guardians of the covenant, and they simply cited the standard and obligations of the covenant.[59]

Thus, Walzer argues, "The prophets were social critics, perhaps the first social critics in the recorded history of the West. It is their sense of divine calling that makes the criticism possible."[60] Rabbi Sacks concurs, "The prophets were the world's first social critics, mandated by God to speak truth to power and to challenge corrupt leaders. . . . Without them, a society quickly becomes demoralized."[61] Compared with the kings, the prophets had no power. "They commanded no armies. They levied no taxes. They spoke God's word, but had no means of enforcing it. All they had was influence."[62] So long as the prophets were alive and active, the choice between *voice* and *exit* (or protest and withdrawal) could always be answered in strength by protest and engagement, with a view to reform and not in weakness through separation and withdrawal.[63] More threatened than threatening, the prophet, Walzer says, was "the embodiment of charisma without power, which is always a threat to power without charisma."[64]

In sum, people of faith take the Word and all words with supreme seriousness. A lie is an intention to deceive, but as such a lie is much worse than a mere terminological inexactitude, as Winston Churchill famously quipped. Lies, deceptions, half-truths, clichés, propaganda, "fake news," and trolling all work to destroy the fabric of truth and trust that undergirds freedom and a free society. Truth, words, intentions, promises, promise keeping, trustworthiness, and trust are the essence of freedom in both private and public life. Champions of freedom must be champions and guardians of words, truth, and respectful civil speech. Thus, according to the Bible and its family of faiths, existence holds its meaning and life gains its purpose because behind them stands the wisdom and the meaning of the Word who is God himself. Above, behind, around, and beneath all that is and all that ever will be stand the wisdom and the power of the Word.

SEVEN TIMES WORSE

One last implication of the great revelation in Exodus is worth drawing out at the start of our exploration. Knowing God and rejecting God are both highly consequential. An inescapable challenge rears up in the face of anyone who believes in the God of the Bible. If God is "He who is"—"I am who I am," or "I will be who I will be," *Only, Other,* and *Over all,* the one whose presence and reality is central, foundational and final to life and to the cosmos and existence itself—then why does it seem so easy to reject God? Can God really be God if defying him seems so inconsequential? The "humility of God" bears on the "hiddenness of God," but does it also mean that it is easy to live as if God does not exist? The main part of the answer will come in chapter two, but one part of the answer is relevant here. The rejection of God is far from inconsequential. Those who displace God must shoulder the consequences. They must necessarily put someone or something in his place, which means substituting an idol, and doing that is never inconsequential, either for an individual or for entire societies.

Idolatry is unavoidable for those who will not believe. "Man believes in either God or in an idol. There is no third course open."[65] The German philosopher Max Scheler stated the point succinctly. Idolatry is a central truth of the Bible that is echoed by many thinkers outside the Bible, such as Fyodor Dostoevsky, Marcel Proust, and Albert Camus. It is also powerfully demonstrated in history. Yet unquestionably, it runs directly counter to all the major currents of Enlightenment and post-Enlightenment thought. As Enlightenment thinkers see it, a cardinal doctrine of progressivism is that as the world advances and grows ever more modern, it also grows ever more secular—and has no need of God or idols.

The progressive conclusion is that Judaism, the Christian faith, and indeed all religions are becoming more marginal and less meaningful in the advanced modern world. God, gods, and the supernatural matter less and less, regardless of who they claim to be, and how they are understood. God has become irrelevant, faith trivial, and advancing modernity is hailed as the graveyard of religion. This progressive secular view is epitomized supremely in Nietzsche's confident declaration that "God is dead," and in the two-hundred-year dominance of the secularization theory put forward by Auguste Comte, Max Weber, and many others—which argues, in essence, "The more modern the world, the less religious the world." Our age, they say, has been *disenchanted* forever.

But the truth is that this once-powerful theory has lost its dominance. First, it was countered theoretically by better analysis, such as the work of sociologist David Martin, and then it was undermined empirically by the global explosion of religion, beginning with the Iranian Revolution in 1979. It is now widely admitted that many of the Enlightenment forecasts have proved wrong and require radical adjusting as well as greater honesty and humility. It was once predicted that modernization would lead to secularization. Now we see that the advanced modern world is both intensely secular and intensely religious at the same time. It was once predicted that globalization would lead to Westernization and the triumph of Western modernity over the whole world. Now we see that globalization is waking up almost the entire world, and in the process it is clear that there are multiple modernities, different ways of becoming modern, the West being only one among many. Or again, it was once predicted that the pluralization of religions ("Everyone is now everywhere") would lead to the privatization of all religion. Now it is clear that religion in the advanced modern world is both more private and more public at the same time.

The much-touted *displacement of God* needs to be seen against this backdrop. The last two centuries highlight the power and danger of two dangers—the various idols that have been erected in God's place, as well as the "demons" that have rushed into the vacuum created by his ousting. Rabbi Heschel warns that no simple human return to being merely animals is possible. The developments of science and technology have closed that option. "Mankind has reached a point of no return to animality. Man turned beast becomes his opposite, a species *sui generis*. The opposite of the human is not the animal but the demonic."[66]

First, and often on the extreme political right, there is the idol of "religious nationalism," through which a nation literally comes to worship itself instead of

God. Dostoevsky warned against this idol in his novel *Demons* and described it brilliantly through the character of Shatov, an extreme religious nationalist.

> If a great nation does not believe that the truth is in it alone (precisely in it alone, and exclusively), if it does not believe that it alone is able and called to resurrect and save everyone with its truth, then it at once ceases to be a great nation. . . . A truly great nation can never be reconciled with a secondary role in mankind. . . . Any that loses this faith is no longer a nation.[67]

Dostoevsky raises his warning to a crescendo in *The Brothers Karamazov*, in the titanic utterance of the Grand Inquisitor as he brazenly defies Jesus. The human need to worship something—whether God, an idol, or humans themselves as gods—will persist until the "end of the world, even when all gods have disappeared from the earth: they will still fall down before idols."[68] *Either God or an idol* is the dirty secret of human nature that will forever be the fly in the ointment for naive secularists. Today, Dostoevsky's warning is amplified through reactions to the perceived menace of the process of globalization and the philosophy of globalism. Many people are now tempted to resort to religion, whether true or false, as the best and only way to bolster their own national culture and to guard the cultural differences that they see threatened by the ironed-out uniformity of globalization. The irony should be obvious. Globalization stands simultaneously as the godfather to both secularism and polytheism, though neither appreciates the favoring of the other.

Second, and on either the political right or the left, there are the grand *political ideologies that are essentially religious* and have a godlike authority, power, and embrace. It has often been noted that when Jews abandoned their faith in God and became atheists—for example, Spinoza, Marx and Freud—they not only rejected their own monotheism but raised in its place a secular ideology with god-sized pretentions that are equal. Ever since the 1930s, Eric Voegelin, Denis de Rougemont, Arthur Koestler, Albert Camus, and others have grappled with the power of large-scale political movements such as fascism, national socialism, and Marxism and have seen in them "the form of religion" or the "functional equivalent of religion." (When Koestler rejected communism, he used to describe it as the god that failed.) What is behind all these movements, Camus argued, is the modern metaphysical revolt against God. That is what placed "the sordid god" of Nietzsche's Superman at the center of Nazi ideology and inspired Rousseau's "new Gospel" of the social contract that led to the French Revolution and its Reign of Terror. There will be no freedom and no way forward for the world, Camus warns, unless we renounce the idolatry of humanity.[69]

Third, quite different and starting not in the political extremes but the middle, there is the surprising and mostly unnoticed rise of the idol of democracy, consensus, and "the other." René Girard argues that the death of God has led to the worship of our neighbor and democracy. We are living in the grand age of David Riesman's "other-directedness"—through television, consumerism, fashion, advertising, polling, statistics, the social media, the celebrity culture, political referendums, Facebook likes, and numerous greater and lesser forms of looking to the other for identity and approval. This, says Girard, leads to nothing less the "divinization of the other" and to "mimetic desire" (not just that we desire but that we desire what others desire).[70] With the full flush of Enlightenment confidence, Ludwig Feuerbach had predicted that *Homo homini deus* ("Men will become a god to each other").[71] On the contrary, Girard says, Hobbes's conclusion is more likely *Homo homini lupus* ("Men will become a wolf to each other"). The constant looking to the other and to democracy as the highest expression of the will of the other will only lead to desiring the desires of others and therefore to comparisons, rivalry, envy, jealousy, hate, sadism, masochism, gossip, slander, and to countless forms of tension and strife, domestic, national, and international. As Alexis de Tocqueville warned, "Equality is a slogan based on envy. It signifies in the heart of every republican: 'Nobody is going to occupy a place higher than I.'"[72] This third idol lies behind the cult of sameness that, as we shall see, is a major impulse behind the tribal politics of the progressive left.

The full harvest of these three kinds of idolatry is ripening across the secular world. But for those who ponder the present in the light of its Enlightenment heritage, the outcome points toward a conclusion that the Enlightenment would find inadmissible: *Reject God if you will, but religion remains ineradicable, idolatry will prove inescapable, and in the extremes, the demonic will become inevitable.*

Tocqueville was forced toward this conclusion in the aftermath of the terrifying volcano of the French Revolution: "Men cannot abandon their religious faith without a kind of aberration of intellect and a sort of violent distortion of their true nature; they are invincibly brought back to more pious sentiments. Unbelief is an accident, and faith is the only permanent state of mankind."[73]

Dostoevsky stated the same conclusion earlier in *The Adolescent*. Unlike the Grand Inquisitor, who thinks he knows better than Jesus, Makar is a devout believer, but his conclusion is the same as the Inquisitor's.

A man cannot live without worshipping something; without worshipping, he cannot bear the burden of himself. And that goes for every man. So that if a man rejects God, he will have to worship an idol that is made of wood, gold, or ideas. So those who think they don't need God are really just idol worshippers, and that's what we should call them.[74]

In sum, all human beings have faith. The question is whether their faith is in God or an idol. The deepest folly is those who imagine they can empty their house of God and then relax in the comfort of their newly-won autonomy. They will be shocked at the outcome. Only the true God can cleanse the house of false gods and demons. Only the true God has the power to prevail over the emerging spirit of the Antichrist in history. Those who think they can do it by themselves, and believe they can do it by clearing out God himself, will find themselves invaded by forces that are seven times worse than anything they imagined. The Lord who is "I am who I am" and "I will be who I will be" is not mocked. God respects our freedom—even to reject him. But God is no less central, essential, and inescapable when he is rejected than when he reveals himself in the full reality of his presence.

SUPREME PRESENCE, SUPREME POSITIVE

That warning, however, cannot be the last word. It would be a travesty to end a chapter on God on a negative note, for to both Jews and Christians, the God who reveals himself in the Bible is overwhelmingly positive in every way. In speaking for his own people, Rabbi Sacks speaks for all who come to know God.

Jews were and often still are God-intoxicated people. For the knowledge of God in Judaism is not a form of theology; it is a form of love. That is what the Hebrew word "to know" means. It is inescapably an *eros* word . . . only when we love do we become vehicles for God's love. . . . For to love God is to love the world He made and the humanity he fashioned in His image. . . . To be loved by God is the greatest gift, the only one we can never lose.[75]

Exodus, then, begins with first things first. *The Name says it all. The Lord is God, Only, Other, and Over all. God is greater than all. He may be trusted in all situations. Those who trust in God need have no fear, for he is love.* From Sinai on, that great revelation of God is decisive for every twist and turn of the story of the journey to freedom that follows. Freedom flows from the primacy, the sovereignty, the authority, and the centrality of God.

America cannot endure permanently half 1776 and half 1789. The compromises, contradictions, hypocrisies, inequities, and evils have built up unaddressed. The grapes of wrath have ripened again, and the choice before America is plain. Either America goes forward best by going back first, or America is about to reap a future in which the worst will once again be the corruption of the best.

2

LIKE THE ABSOLUTELY UNLIKE

PRINCIPLE 2: FREEDOM MUST BE GROUNDED AND AUTHORIZED

Survival in Auschwitz hung by a slender thread for Primo Levi, the Jewish-Italian scientist. To escape a death sentence to the gas ovens, he had to pass an exam to be selected for Kommando 98, a squad of supposedly skilled scientific workers. Shaven-headed, starving, shamefully clothed, sniveling with cold, and smelly, he found himself standing uncertainly in front of his tall, slim, blond examiner, Doktor Pannwitz, who was sitting writing at his neat and orderly desk.

"When he finished writing," Levi wrote in his famous account of Auschwitz, *If This Is a Man*,

> he raised his eyes and looked at me. Since that day, I have thought about Doktor Pannwitz many times and in many ways. . . . Because that look did not pass between two men; and if I knew how to explain fully the nature of that look, exchanged as if through the glass wall of an aquarium between two beings who inhabit different worlds, I would also be able to explain the essence of the great insanity of the Third Reich.[1]

The terrible lesson of the twentieth century is that whenever there was a sufficiently large gap between who humans were and how they were seen, or when they were not seen at all and counted only as statistics, humans found themselves in deep, deep trouble. There was a much-quoted statement in pre-Nazi Germany, "The human body contains a sufficient amount of fat to make seven cakes of soap, enough iron to make a medium-sized nail, a sufficient amount of phosphorous to equip two thousand match heads, and enough sulfur to rid oneself of fleas." "Perhaps," Rabbi Heschel mused, "there was a connection between this reductionist statement and what the Nazis actually did in the extermination camps: make soap of human flesh."[2]

There is a difference between a *human being* and *being human*. One is a reality and ineradicable, and the other is an ideal and attainable, or not. The horror of the radical evil of the twentieth century lay in its utter desecration of both. The death camps, the killing fields, and in other parts of the world racism and colonialism, simultaneously exterminated human beings and exterminated being human.

"I have a dream," it was sometimes said in the 1960s, "that the humanity of man will transcend all ideologies." But that dream is a pipe dream. People may behave better or worse than their beliefs, but beliefs will always be the prime shaper of behavior—and beliefs about humanity have been like a roller coaster over the last century. Is humanity "heaven's masterpiece," nature's "sole mistake," or something in between? Are we only dealing with "the stupidity of dignity," a "squishy, subjective notion," "slippery and ambiguous," and a "mess" as Harvard's Steven Pinker has claimed, or is human dignity something that is incalculably more?[3]

THE STRIPTEASE OF HUMANISM

The twentieth century, it is said, began in August 1914 with the outbreak of the Great War. When the century finished,

> Two hundred and thirty-one million men, women, and children had died violently in the twentieth century, shot over open pits, murdered in secret police cellars, asphyxiated in Nazi gas ovens, worked to death in Arctic mines or timber camps, the victims of deliberately contrived famines or lunatic industrial experiments, whole populations ravaged by alien armies, bombed to smithereens, or sent to wander in their exiled millions across all the violated borders of Europe and Asia.[4]

World War I, which set it all off, was absolutely shattering to the continent it was fought on. It stripped away the complacent pretense that was the veneer of European civilization. Brutal, horrifying, senseless, and unnecessary, the carnage of the bloody trench warfare was the precursor of the horrors of the century to come. It was the beginning of the end for both the European Enlightenment and Europe as the capital of world civilization. It was also the beginning of a century of mounting questions about humanity and the emergence of a maelstrom of clashing views over what it means to be human.

Albert Einstein captured the new uncertainty of the twentieth century when he tried to distance himself from the ghastly evidence of the grand human abattoir that total war had produced. "What a pity we don't live on Mars," he wrote in 1917, "so that we could observe the futile activities of human beings only through a telescope."[5] At the same time, others showed an iron determination to face the worst and to rebuild with a new and superhuman effort. Among the boldest was Stefan Zweig's essay "The Tower of Babel" (1916). The conclusion of the war was a "monstrous moment" with a harsh clarity for the pretensions of Enlightenment Europe. "The new Tower of Babel, the great monument to the spiritual unity of Europe, lies in decay, its workers have lost their way." But Europeans must not give up, he urged. They must return to the construction. And the call to rebuild should come from "the old ancestor, our spirit, which remains the same in all forms, all legends, that nameless builder of Babel, the genius of mankind, whose meaning and salvation it is to strive against his Creator."[6]

The scorn of the French Enlightenment and the defiance of the French Revolution toward God were both unmistakable in Zweig's manifesto. So it was no accident, though ironic, that the dismal decades of the 1930s and 1940s were characterized not by a return to faith but by dark forebodings about the rise of functional equivalents of God: the political religions of communism, national socialism, and fascism. The amplified horror of war, as World War I led remorselessly to World War II, was compounded by the equal horror of the evil of totalitarianism. A spate of impassioned warnings was issued in response—Aldous Huxley's *Brave New World* (1932), Jorge Luis Borges's *Library of Babel* (1941), C. S. Lewis's *Abolition of Man* (1943), and George Orwell's *Animal Farm* (1944) and *1984* (1949).

By the 1960s new postwar factors were crowding onto the global stage to exacerbate the pressures even further—above all the Cold War, the arms race, the rise of environmental concerns, and the specter of nuclear Armageddon. Coinciding with the emergence of the counterculture and "drugs, sex, and rock and roll," an insistent theme in the 1960s was the troubled status of humanity. In 1961 Bertrand Russell, the leading voice in the Campaign for Nuclear Disarmament, wrote *Has Man a Future?* Jean-Paul Sartre spoke of the impact of colonialism as "the striptease of our humanism" ("Leave this Europe where they are never done talking of Man, yet murder them everywhere they find them.")[7] And in Berkeley, Mario Savio set off the Free Speech movement at Cal Berkeley with a fiery protest against the dehumanization of machine-age bureaucracy. "There's a time when the operation of the machine becomes so odious, makes you so sick at heart that you can't take part! You can't even passively take part! And you got to put your bodies upon the gears and upon the wheels, upon the levers, upon all the apparatus—and you've got to make it stop!"[8]

Taken together, the avalanche of developments in the first three-quarters of the twentieth century had raised momentous questions to humanity about humanity, but the most challenging were still to come in the last quarter. Toward the end of the century the dawn of the computer age witnessed an acceleration of science and technology that ushered in visions of artificial intelligence, ultra intelligence, whole-brain emulation, cryonics and life extension, robotics, cyborgs, gene editing, and the endless talk of singularity—somehow always just a moment or two away from the front door. With the possible enhancement and transformation of human nature itself, we are on the verge of the greatest triumph over nature in all of history. Humanity now faces one of the most extraordinary moments in the long story of our existence on planet earth. For today, we humans stand post-Auschwitz, post-Hiroshima, and pre-singularity.

Post-Auschwitz means that we have to answer the question, What does it say of us that those who carried out these monstrous crimes against humanity were the same species we are? *Post-Hiroshima* and the later defense of the doctrine of Mutually Assured Destruction (MAD) mean that we have to ask ourselves, What does it say of us that our safest defense against the threats of a menacing *other* is a counterthreat to destroy them entirely and even to destroy many of our fellow humans and much of the earth that is our home? *And pre-singularity* means that we have to explore the question, What has brought us to the point where we pursue progress and seek salvation through technology, even though the price of this salvation and progress is a vision of humanity that would be unrecognizable, if not repellent, to almost all human beings up until now?

In sum, the questions now facing us as humans are inescapable. Who do we think we are as humans? What is a human being? Is there any future for humanity as we have known ourselves to this point? What will Francis Bacon's "conquest of nature" mean when the final battle, as C. S. Lewis warned, means that "Man's conquest of Nature turns out, in the moment of its consummation, to be Nature's conquest of Man."⁹ There are few greater tasks for humanity than reversing the trivialized and deflated view of humanity, but that task must begin by recognizing where we now are. Rabbi Heschel escaped Auschwitz by only a few weeks and lost almost all his family in the gas ovens, but he hammered home the lesson for Americans for whom it was culturally distant: "The overriding issue of this hour in the world and Western civilization is the *humanity of man*. Man is losing his true image and shaping his life in the image of anti-man."¹⁰

A full survey of the last century's debates about humanity lies beyond our concern, but the broad outline is plain. Secular thinking started from the optimistic, progressive confidence of the eighteenth-century Enlightenment. "Man" would replace God, reason would replace revelation, progress would replace providence, heaven on earth would replace heaven, and science would replace the blind forces of evolution. Some, especially those reacting against corrupt and oppressive state churches, cried that they did not *want* God. Others, most often those who benefited from economic prosperity and technological advance, cried that they did not *need* God. But together, they would and could move beyond God with the long, bold strides of secular humanism at its most confident. Humanity had come of age and would now direct its own future. The humanist could both understand and manage history. Nietzsche's Superman would be the heroic protagonist, and self-creation would be the motto for the progress to be pursued.

History shows the folly of this boast, for only a fool can claim to understand history well enough to manage and direct it. What happened was that under the relentless pressure of multiple contradictions secular humanism has been humbled and has been forced to develop in three different directions. First, optimistic humanism (with its full Enlightenment confidence, often symbolized by Leonardo's *Vitruvian Man* at the center of all things) gave way to its opposite, *antihumanism*. For the feminists and postcolonialists of the 1960s, the *Vitruvian Man* was arrogant, chauvinist, and oppressive. Leonardo's "man," after all, was plainly a man, young, able-bodied, and European to boot. Were they supposed to look like that?

Second, many more who abandoned optimistic humanism did not stop with antihumanism but went further to *posthumanism* or postanthropocentrism. It was wrong, they said, to see humanity at the center of life, whether male or female. The old humanist view—Protagoras, Leonardo, and all—was attacked as "speciescentrism." In its place a massive search was launched to explore and locate humanity in terms of nature and to appreciate human solidarity with all the creatures on the earth. We humans, they said, are not special. Human exceptionalism is arrogance, which leads to hubris. We are one with the rest of the universe, they say. And when we come to see things rightly, we will recognize that stars, rocks, waterfalls, chairs, and scraps of paper all have a mind like us. They too are part of the *smart matter* of the "living cosmos."

Third, optimistic humanism progressed toward what is said to be the most revolutionary humanism of all, *transhumanism*. Whereas posthumanism understands humanity in terms of nature, transhumanism attempts to understand and empower humanity in terms of technology. Technology is the engine and the steering wheel by which we can drive progress forward, not only for ourselves but for the entire cosmos. What is at stake if transhumanists succeed, they claim, is the single most momentous development on earth in a billion years.

HOMO DEUS

There are many striking features of the splintering of Enlightenment humanism, though most are beyond our interest here. Two, however, are important to our exploration. First, all the current humanisms share a striking dissatisfaction with the human lot, a desire for complete liberation, and open talk of the need for salvation. We are now living amid the wreckage of our earlier illusions when humanity had higher notions of itself, and this time, they say, we must reach further and higher—achieving our own salvation through harmony with the earth for posthumanists or through machines for transhumanists.

In the words of an ardent advocate for transhumanism, "Ask anyone who's transgender. They'll tell you they're trapped in the wrong body. But me, I'm trapped in the wrong body because I'm trapped in *a body*. *All* bodies are the wrong body."[11] The desired liberation is not only from sickness, aging, and the countless bodily problems, but total emancipation from biology and the body altogether, an "unfleshed future" that is free even from death. The vision is of "techno-salvation" and "morphological freedom"—the liberty to take any bodily form that technology will permit.[12]

Hannah Arendt noted the profundity of this dissatisfaction half a century ago. It was nothing less than rebellion against human existence as we have known it. "This future man, whom the scientists tell us they will produce in no more than a hundred years from now, seems to be possessed by a rebellion against human existence as it has been given, a gift from nowhere (secularly speaking), which he wishes to exchange, as it were, for something he has made himself."[13]

Second, it is important to note that religious aspects are prominent in all the different fragments of humanism. Posthumanism, for example, has fueled a renewal of pantheism, fresh discussions of *Gaia* theory, and talk of Mother Nature and the Earth goddess. Transhumanism, for its part, so harps on the infinite possibilities of the mind at the expense of the all-too-limited body that it becomes a hi-tech resuscitation of ancient Gnosticism. "At present," philosopher John Gray writes of the new dualism, "gnosticism is the faith of people who believe themselves to be machines."[14]

The third and by far the most prominent religious feature of the humanisms is the open drive to be as God, especially in transhumanism. The drive itself, of course, is almost as old as humanity, but in its Promethean modern form it owes everything to the Enlightenment, to revolution, and to technology. Beethoven inspired many when he wrote his *Sinfonia Eroica* and described his defiance of God and faith, "No, thou art not dust, but indeed the Master of the Earth."[15] Heinrich Heine described his "obdurate friend"; Karl Marx as one of the "godless self-gods."[16]

Once again Gray minces no words when he writes as an atheist critic of the current trend. Transhumanism, he charges, is "religion recycled as science," a form of "techno-monotheism," and a "modern project of human self-deification."[17] No one is clearer and more brazen in affirming this humanist stance than Yuval Harari, a Jew writing from Jerusalem but as an atheist. If the great advances of the twentieth century triumphed over famine, plague, and war, we are now on the verge of even greater victories: achieving immortality, happiness, and divinity. What this shows, he writes in his bestselling book *Homo Deus* is that we are "godlings" and the "Gods of Planet Earth." In fact, we are about to "upgrade to Homo Deus," we have reached the place where we can see the "last days of death," and our successes are so extraordinary that we can claim with justification, "Scientists today can do much better than the Old Testament God."[18]

POST-TRUTH AND NOW POST-RIGHTS?

It is time to stand back and ask, Where has our progress progressed to? Nineteenth- and twentieth-century humanism claimed to be able to understand and master history, and it failed miserably. Twenty-first-century transhumanism claims to be able to understand and manage science and technology to master human nature. It will fail equally miserably. But the questions confront us. Where does humanity stand after this tsunami of developments over the last century? "Man has come of age," but what has become of him (or her)? The world has been declared to be post-truth, but there are signs that it is also becoming post-rights. Not long ago, the Universal Declaration of Human Rights was hailed as "the Bible of humanity" and the "last utopia," but now its rights are dismissed as Eurocentric and its foundations are said to be unfounded. (Interestingly, England's Bill of Rights in 1689 guaranteed only the rights of Englishmen because they were understood and justified within the context of English ideas and ideals. France's "Declaration of the Rights of Man and Citizen" in 1789, by contrast, was the first to claim universal human rights, though without any universal basis.) Is there a way to slow down technology and evaluate the choices it offers? No, comes the reply. Technology is unstoppable, if only because if something can be done, it will be done. And if we don't do it, someone else will.

Many people felt good about humanity when Immanuel Kant said that the secret of ethics lies in regarding each human being as an end, not a means—only for history to show how egotists and narcissists would adopt that principle. (Rabbi Heschel commented wryly, "To a person who regards himself as an absolute end a thousand lives will not be more than his own life.")[19] Many people still feel good about themselves when they resort to the ethic of utilitarianism and harp on the idea of happiness (the greatest happiness of the greatest number), but they overlook the fact that in that accounting the individual does not count at all, by definition. Others now glory in multiculturalism and trade in the currency of belonging through tribal identities, but the stress on groups defined by gender, race, age, and class has less regard for our individuality. The mighty algorithm is now king in a thousand spheres of the information society, but the algorithm has been described rightly as a "weapon of math destruction."[20]

Where then is our worth as individual human beings? Philosophically, our ideals are said to be meaningless. Scientifically, the claims for our human uniqueness are unsupportable. Ethically, if the greatest happiness of the greatest number is taken to be decisive, we are expendable as individuals. Politically, we are inconsequential as individuals in mass society. Technologically, we might as well be irrelevant as there is no stopping the runaway train. Militarily, if we get in the way, our demise is regrettable (collateral damage), and statistically we are insignificant as individuals.

THE GENESIS DECLARATION

Where then does this leave our humanity? What can be said to "the man of our time," as Rabbi Heschel wrote in the light of the death camps, "who has fallen so low that he is not even capable of being ashamed of what happened in his days"?[21] Are we no more than animals, at best superanimals who are different from other animals only in degree, not kind? Do we each gain value simply because we are part of the wider human species, or is there some justification for the feeling that each of us is somehow important on our own? Is it pure fantasy, or could it be that however small we are in the universe and however short we know our lives to be, we still somehow matter supremely? And at the grand global level, is there really a foundation for the claims that underlie universal human rights, or are they simply a passing Western way of talking and perhaps even a complete fiction? As such questions mount and the current debates intensify, it becomes evident once again that there are no solid answers about human dignity coming out of either the Eastern or the secularist families of faith. Their views of humanity and life offer little promise in terms of human dignity.

At this very point the biblical family of faiths enters the debate with bold and striking simplicity. Human beings are created in the image and likeness of God. In the ringing words of the Genesis declaration that announce the climax of the creation of the world, "Then God said, 'Let Us make man in Our image, according to Our likeness. . . . God created man in His own image, in the image of God he created him" (Gen 1:26-27). *Each human person is precious and unique. Each has dignity and worth that is inalienable and must be respected. Each must be valued, not because they are a member of the species Homo sapiens, but as an individual person in their own right.*

Thus, according to the Bible, every single human person is created in the image and likeness of God. God our Creator is himself the ground and the guarantee for the meaning and the dignity of the human person. Just as the meaning of a system must lie outside the system, as philosopher Ludwig Wittgenstein insisted, so the true meaning and the true value of humanity must come from outside humanity.[22] To insist that we can understand ourselves within a framework entirely limited to ourselves will always prove to be wrong or too small and therefore reductionist and dehumanizing in the end—humanity will be *nothing but* this or *nothing but* that (the "naked ape," the "selfish gene," and so on). What we call human dignity or worth will never be found that way. Dignity and worth can never be read off human beings looking downward, comparing humans with animals and nature. The value, dignity, and worth of each human being can only be discovered and maintained upward and in relationship to God. Humans are *made of more* than philosophy, science, or any Theory of Everything can ever know.

The Genesis declaration is brief but stunning, and it changes the status of humanity forever. It flashes across the darkness of history like the first rays of dawn and lights up humanity and the human story in its warm and brilliant light. No wonder that the Genesis declaration that humans are made in the image of God is a foundation stone of the Magna Carta of humanity

The Genesis declaration sounds out strongly from the very first chapter of the Bible, and it reverberates through the story of the exodus. The central thrust of the story is about the power of God freeing the powerless from captivity and oppression. A free God frees his people to worship him freely and to build a free society worthy of his freedom and theirs. Why? Because God himself is sovereign and free, and he has made humans in his image to be significant and free. So for his people created in his image, captivity and oppression should never have been. The world should be otherwise. Evil, injustice, and oppression are never to be taken as normal, inevitable, or final. They are always to be fought. Humans are to be free as the image-bearers of God who is free. In Rabbi Heschel's summary, "Man's greatest task is to comprehend God's respect and regard for the freedom of man, freedom, the supreme manifestation of God's regard for man."[23]

The Genesis declaration that humans are made in the image and likeness of God is the clearest, strongest, and most influential statement of the priceless value of the individual human being in human history. Whatever people may feel about themselves, however humans may treat their fellow humans, and whichever human view of humanity may be dominant in one generation or another, or one society or another, God has made his position clear. He has created human beings in his image, and each one must therefore be seen and treated as unique, precious and the bearer of dignity and worth that is inalienable. It is quite wrong to think that *special* means speciesism. Even if a person is poor, uneducated, disabled, or mentally impaired, he or she is still created in the image of God and therefore precious and unique. Each individual human is exceptional. None is ever expendable. Made in the image of God, every single human person is special, singular, and significant.

DIFFERENT FROM THE START

In a single sentence, the Genesis declaration establishes the Bible's high view of humanity and places it beyond doubt. All the rest is commentary. Humanity can learn much about itself using the rich avenues of reason, science, and nature (which was later to be called "the book of nature," as opposed to "the book of revelation"). But humans can never be understood fully if considered only *downward*. To be fully understood and to be truly fulfilled, humanity and human beings must above all be regarded *upward*, as created in the image and likeness of God (according to "the book of revelation").

The importance of humanity shines out clearly at several points in the story of creation in Genesis. First, the creation of humans is the only creation preceded by a statement of intention. Here from the very start is the (Wittgenstein-style) meaning of humanity that comes from outside humanity. With light, the earth, the oceans, the sun and the moon, and the other living creatures, Genesis simply records that God said, "Let there be . . ." and "It was so" (Gen 1:3, 6, 9, 11, 15). God executes his will through his word simply and straightforwardly. The emphasis in these phases of creation is on what God did, not on what he thought. Only with the creation of humans do we have a statement of intent. "Let Us make man in Our image, according to Our likeness" (Gen 1:26).

The powerful suggestion is that God knows men and women in a special way before he creates them, the creatures expressly made in his image. Thus the true meaning of humanity, individually and collectively, is the meaning that God designed humanity to have—and later calls each person to understand and to live. Again, that means that to understand humanity properly, *we have to understand humanity upward and not downward only*. Human beings will never be prized more highly than when they are seen as bearers of the image of God. Psychology, sociology, and anthropology are all important and invaluable disciplines and avenues of knowledge. But try to understand humans solely downward, as mere animals or as a part of nature somehow, and the resulting view of humanity will always be reductionist or unfulfilling to human beings in some way. There will always be a longing for something more because humans are made of more and made for more. Thus three foundational areas—how humanity understands itself, how humans treat each other, and how humans see the purpose of life—are each shaped decisively by the declaration that God made humans in his image and likeness.

In Genesis, which is the book of beginnings, this point is left at the general level. It is true of the first humans and therefore speaks for all humanity as humanity. Later, however, God demonstrates the same truth in addressing individuals in a more specific manner, and the truth becomes even more mysterious and wonderful. God declares to the prophet Jeremiah, for example,

> Before I formed you in the womb, I knew you.
> And before you were born I consecrated you;
> I have appointed you a prophet to the nations. (Jer 1:4-5)

Jeremiah was known by God, consecrated by God, and appointed by God, all before he was born. His call as an adult merely confirmed the design God had in mind for him even as he was conceived. If creation frees us to *be who we are*, calling frees us to *become who we can become*. Together, creation and calling mean that our entire meaning as humans and our purpose as individuals come from outside ourselves, from our Creator who knows us and has designs for us. Calling therefore escapes the inevitable reductionism and the eventual futility of the temptation to self-made meaning.

Second, the Genesis account describes the creation of a single human being rather than a species, humanity. Again, the contrast with the rest of creation is clear. The animals on the land, the fish in the sea, the birds in the air, and the vegetation on the earth are all described in general terms, as species. Only the first human is created as a single human—the word *Adam* in Hebrew being a generic name for a human rather than the first name of a particular man—Adam as opposed to Eve or Tom and Dick in distinction from Harry. In Rabbi Heschel's words, "Humanity begins in the individual man, just as history takes its rise from a singular event. It is always one man at a time whom we keep in mind when we pledge: 'With malice toward none, with charity for all.'"[24] Humanity is never an abstract mass but always specific individuals.

For the rabbis this uniqueness did not indicate species chauvinism. That is uniqueness in a perverted form. Rather, it was to teach the precious and unsubstitutable worth of each human—"the equal and absolute dignity of the human person as the image of God."[25] "Why was a single human created? To teach you that for him who destroys one man, it is regarded as if he had destroyed all men. And that for him who saves one man, it is regarded as if he had saved all men."[26] No one is indispensable, but no one can be substituted to replace someone else entirely. Every single person is as precious as the world, the rabbis said, and as such far too precious to waste on a life that defied or squandered its meaning and purpose. In Rabbi Heschel's words, "There is no ordinary man. Every man is an extraordinary man."[27] If every human is in the image of God, then every violation of any human is an offense against God, for God is "the invisible Third" person in any crime.[28]

Third, and in the same vein, the Genesis account describes the creation of humanity last. Is this simply a symptom of humanity's inflated self-importance or yet another example of history being written by the victors to justify their power? Not at all, the rabbis said again, though this time with a touch of humor. "Why was man created last? In order to say, if he is worthy, all creation was made for you, but if he is unworthy, even a gnat preceded you."[29] Overall, the emphasis on the preciousness of the individual is unmistakable. As Rabbi Heschel insisted, "We do not think a human being is valuable because he is a member of the race; it is rather the opposite: the human race is valuable because it is composed of human beings."[30]

THE IMMENSITY AND THE ENORMITY

The Genesis declaration that humans are created in the image of God is such an explosive truth that it is easy to overlook the immensity and the enormity at its heart. There is a thought-stopping mystery, perhaps even a monstrous scandal, at the center of the Bible's claim. *Created in the image of God, humans are like the utterly and absolutely unlike.* How can the likeness and the unlikeness both be true? The first chapter underscored that when God revealed himself in Exodus, Moses and the Israelites found that they were on holy ground. "He who is," God who said simply, "I am who I am" and "I will be who I will be," is Only, Other, and Over all. God is awesome in his infinite and transcendent Otherness, and all who approach the reality of his divine presence do so with a reverence bordering on terror. Yet at that very point, wonder of wonders, a seeming impossibility is thrown into the equation. God is absolutely Other, infinite, and transcendent, yet God himself states that he has created humans in his image and likeness. Somehow, humans are created to be *like* the absolutely *unlike*. In Rabbi Heschel's words, "The likeness of God means the likeness of Him, compared with whom all else is like nothing."[31]

This assertion runs headlong into one of the strongest modern objections to faith in God. According to several of the titans of modern thought, there is no God, and what is called God is purely a human projection. Feuerbach, Marx, and Freud have taken the Bible's argument and leveled it against God. They turned the Bible's critique of idolatry against itself, a critique that holds that idols are merely a projection of human or cosmic forces, and therefore "nothings."

Like all gods, they said, God is simply the self-image of humanity magnified by humanity and projected onto the sky and worshiped. If that is the case, the Genesis declaration is a self-serving fraud. There is no God, but humans use the illusion of God to promote their own special dignity—species chauvinism conjured up with the imprimatur of a nonexistent God.

To be sure, the objection is correct in arguing that the meaning of humanity depends on the character of God that humans claim to resemble. To say that humans are made in the image of God means nothing if God is made in the image of humans. If that were so, the divine would only be the human inflated to the superhuman, like a magician's conjuring trick. The argument would be circular. The difference between humans and God would only be one of degree, not kind. But that is emphatically not the God of the Bible. Creator of all, the universe, nature, and history as well as humanity, YHWH is the Lord of all, yet it is he who declares that he has created humans in his image. Nothing, no thing in the world must ever be made into an image of God, not even the world itself. But while humans must not make God in their image, God has made humans in his image.

The immensity and enormity radiate out from the very phrase *image and likeness of God* (Gen 1:26). What it says is surely unthinkable, even blasphemous. *Humans are created in the image of God who has no image, who allows no image, and who strictly forbids any image of himself.* Throughout the Bible, the two terms *image* and *likeness* are almost always negative and derogatory because they are used to describe idolatrous images. Behind this usage is the Bible's "ultimate binary," the unbridgeable difference between God and "Man," the divine and the human. God is God and "Man" is "Man," and never the twain shall be confused. "You shall have no other gods before Me," God thundered at Sinai in publishing the Ten Commandments, "You shall not make for yourself an idol, or any likeness" (Ex 20:3-4). "For I am God and not man" (Hos 11:9), as the prophet Hosea said later.

"I am God, and there is no other!" God declared through Isaiah. "I am God, and there is no one like me" (Is 46:9; 47:8, 10 NIV). "To whom then will you liken me?" (Is 40:25). Is there anyone who compares with God or anything that we can say is truly like God? No, a thousand times no, most people are surely right to say as they find they are standing on holy ground. But wait, there are beings who are like God, and God himself says so. He has created humans "in his image and likeness." Humans are not God, but what is special about them is what they have in common with God, not what they have in common with the earth. Like nature, we are created by God, but we are like God, not nature. As Rabbi Heschel notes, "The earth is our sister, not our mother."[32]

THE INESCAPABLE PARADOX

It is tempting, and many have fallen for the temptation, to stop and try to figure out what it is in humanity that is the image of God. Are there special human qualities that are God-like? Is there any particular feature that can be picked out as divine? Is it human reason, speech, freedom, love, or imagination? Should we, as some have done, call these qualities the *immortal element*, the *eternal spirit*, the *divine spark*, the *best and highest in humanity*? Wisely, the best commentators have refused to go down that road. Those who focus on any one human feature, such as reason, tend to move toward the unfortunate position that those with less of that gift are less valued as humans. (In 2016, a man in Japan stabbed nineteen disabled people in a care home because people with disabilities, he said, "had no human rights," and he "had to do it for the sake of society.")[33]

Clearly, the stronger and safer way is to regard all humans, every man, woman, and child, as the image and likeness of God. Some have one gift, others another, but all are created equally in the image of God. Far wiser not to argue about which feature *in* "Man" is the image of God, but to see that the image of God *is* "Man"—each individual human person in all the fullness of their personhood, most certainly including the handicapped and disabled too.

What is emphasized and elaborated far more in the Bible is the inescapable paradox at the heart of humanity. Humans are created "in the image of God," so the dignity and grandeur of humanity is undeniable. But humans are also made of "the dust of the ground" (Gen 2:7 NIV) and then told clearly, "For you are dust, and to dust you shall return" (Gen 3:19). So the Bible underscores the human paradox and emphasizes the dignity and the humility, the ruined glory together. Humans are formed from the dust of the earth but are living beings because "the breath of life" (Gen 2:7) has been breathed into them. Our existence "see-saws," Rabbi Heschel writes, between the animal and the divine, between what is far more and what is far less than human.[34] What a bundle of contradictions we humans are, Pascal writes, "What a chimera then is man! What a novelty, what a monster, what a chaos, what a contradiction, what a prodigy! Judge of all things, feeble earthworm, repository of truth, sewer of uncertainty and error, the glory and the scum of the universe."[35] Who on earth can unravel such a tangle?

The stress on *dust* in the Genesis account is deliberately humbling, especially in the age of modern humanism and suburban narcissism. All the other creatures on the earth in the Genesis account are formed from either earth or water, earth being the source of vegetation and life, and water being the source of life and refreshment. Humans, in contrast, are formed of dust—arid, abundant, and worthless desert dust. Created in the image of God and breathed into by the Spirit of God, humans are the highest of the high. But formed from the dust of the earth, humans are also the lowest of the low. Viewed the one way we stand higher than our fellow creatures, the animals. We are the one creature on earth able to look around us and ask why. Viewed the other way we stand even lower than the animals. In Rabbi Sacks's words, "Physically, we are almost nothing; spiritually, we are brushed by the wings of eternity."[36]

Needless to say, the stunning paradox of humanity is an inescapable feature of humanity. Stress one side of the paradox or the other and we come out either amazed or appalled. But no account of human nature is complete without both. Perhaps the most famous description of the paradox is that of William Shakespeare's Hamlet, who starts from the greatness of humanity but goes on to the other.

> What a piece of work is a man! How noble in reason! How infinite in faculty! In form and moving how express and admirable! In action how like an angel! In apprehension how like a god! The beauty of the world! The paragon of animals! And yet to me what is this quintessence of dust? Man delights not me; no, nor woman either.[37]

A century later, Blaise Pascal explored the heart of the same paradox. He used it to goad his contemporaries to think about life and their own lives, often starting from the darker side of humanity.

> What sort of freak then is man? How novel, how monstrous, how chaotic, how paradoxical, how prodigious! Judge of all things, feeble earthworm, repository of truth, sink of doubt and error, glory and refuse of the universe. Who will unravel such a tangle? . . . Man transcends man. . . . Know then, proud man, what a paradox you are to yourself.[38]

Understand the human paradox, Pascal believed, and you understand the best and worst of human behavior. "Man is neither angel nor beast, and it is unfortunately the case that anyone trying to act the angel acts the beast."[39] On the other hand, as Sacks reminds us in the words of Katherine Hepburn in *The African Queen*, "Nature, Mr. Allnut is what we were put on earth to rise above."[40]

TRUST IN EXISTENCE

The Genesis declaration is profound, and it carries rich implications for life and freedom. *First, it gives rock-solid grounds for trusting in life and existence: the final reality behind the universe is God, who is love and has a great heart for humans whom he has created in his own image.* This truth is foundational. From the perspective of the Bible there is both an ultimate origin to existence and an ultimate care and concern for existence. We may stake our very existence on God and trust in him as the guarantor of life and hope, come what may. If God is for us, then fate, chance, necessity, entropy, doom, and death do not have the last word on life. As Rabbi Sacks insists again and again, "God loves us more than we love ourselves. He believes in us more than we believe in ourselves."[41] We exist because we have been loved and are loved. The thought is marvelous beyond words: we are each God's stake in the world. God has placed a bet on history, and that bet is you and me and all around us.

This trust in existence through faith in God must never be taken for granted. To be sure, it raises questions that need to be answered, and it must always be appreciated in light of the alternatives, for the contrasts are bleak.[42] History, as historians have said, can appear to be like a grand Rorschach test. Life as we humans experience it may be a chaotic jumble of good and bad, beauty and brokenness, delights, disappointments, and disasters. And as we know well, our individual wills and desires clash repeatedly with the contrary wills and desires of others. Thus to live well and make sense of the crazy-quilt confusion of experiences, we have to discover a pattern of meaning in the jumble of dots. We do this through the ultimate beliefs that we each hold to be true, which for better or worse promise to show us the final meaning of it all.

What then is the final meaning of it all, the ultimate reality behind everything? And what will have the last word on our little lives? Is life only "a tale told by an idiot," as Shakespeare says in *Macbeth*? Is it merely a grand chain of chance and a "trash bag of random coincidences torn open in a wind," as Joseph Heller wrote?[43] Will the last word on our lives be the iron hand of fate, as happened to the hapless Oedipus? Will it be chance, necessity, karma, or power, as many people believe today? The Bible's view stands foursquare against all such bleak alternatives, and the Genesis declaration is unambiguous. Behind our little daily lives, behind the unstoppable torrents of history, and behind the universe itself is God who has created us in his image, who loves us and has a heart for us. For those who know and trust God, the universe is not ultimately deaf, indifferent, tragic, or absurd. Life may strike us at times as cruel and capricious, but fate, tragedy, chance, necessity, entropy, and doom will never have the final word. God, who created humans in his image, cares for us, and we can count on him. Whatever the appearances, whatever our circumstances, despair is never the last word, and God's silence never means he has no more to say. The last word will always be God's love, justice, and compassion. If God is for us, we can face and fight the worst that life can throw against us.

Once again, contrast is the mother of clarity, and the difference of God makes the difference in life. But sadly, even many who believe in God are missing out on this reassurance. They hesitate to speak freely of God's heart for us or even to consider that God relates to us as a person with emotions. For some the reason is an understandable reverence and the desire not to fall into the trap of anthropomorphism, speaking of God as if he were human. For others, their understanding of God owes more to Greek and Eastern ideas than to the Bible.

Hindus constantly use the two words *neti, neti* to speak of their understanding of the gods. They are "not this," "not that," and "not the other." They are always "beyond" all description and certainly untouched by emotions. The Greeks spoke similarly of the gods as impassible and beyond all feeling. Reason was always the beginning and the end for the Greeks, so thought and contemplation were appropriate in speaking of the gods, but not emotions. The Stoics held that "all passion is evil," so gods, who were "perfect in themselves," were absolutely self-sufficient and needed no one and nothing outside themselves. In Aristotle's famous description, God is the "unmoved mover" and to speak of God's passions would be unworthy as well as absurd.

Not so the Bible. According to the Hebrew and Christian Scriptures, God is infinite and transcendent—Only, Other, and Over all—and therefore awesome. But God is also personal, and he is therefore personally and passionately committed to humans created in his image. Unmoved mover? Absolutely not, Rabbi Heschel protests, God is the "most moved mover."[44] God loves, cares, grieves. God can be angry, and God can be jealous. Whereas the Stoic ideal was apathy, the Bible's ideal is empathy. Humanity is absolutely relevant to God, and humans can count on that in every situation they find themselves in.

Thus, while the Greeks favored the notions of logos and ethos in talking of God, and so does the Bible, the Bible is equally insistent on God's pathos. The characteristic "Thus says the Lord" of the prophets is an undeniable expression of logos, just as "Justice is mine" is an undeniable expression of ethos. But pathos is no less evident in the Bible. Both the major and the minor Hebrew Prophets were fired by the pathos of God's passionate engagement with his people, and once again the revelation of God's pathos was decisive at Sinai. When Moses survives the supreme test of his leadership, over the rebellion surrounding the golden calf and the mutinous desire to abort the journey to the Promised Land and return to Egypt, he was sobered. He had put the people on the line, and he had, as it were, put God on the line, and he had survived. Naturally, there would be further tests, and he prayed what is surely the most audacious prayer in the Bible, "Show me Your glory" (Ex 33:18). He wanted to know all that a fallen human being can know of God and still survive. Only the deep reality of God could see him through.

Stunningly, God's answer to Moses' prayer was rather different than he might have imagined. God answered by pronouncing in his presence what the Jews call the "Thirteen attributes of Mercy."

> The LORD, the LORD God, compassionate and gracious, slow to anger, and abounding in lovingkindness and truth; who keeps lovingkindness for thousands, who forgives iniquity, transgression and sin; yet He will by no means leave *the guilty* unpunished, visiting the iniquity of fathers on the children and on the grandchildren to the third and fourth generations. (Ex 34:6-7)

Trusting the heart of God is enough for any trial or ordeal that life may bring. God loves the world. Humanity is God's stake in history.

No one can read the Bible without seeing God's passion in action, and the consequences are profound. Life and the universe are lit up with a different light if the love, justice, and loyalty of God are behind everything and offered to us. One example is the fact that humans can have friendship with God. Abraham is described as the friend of God, but that would have been unthinkable for other religions. Friendship with God is impossible, Aristotle said, "For friendship exists only where there can be a return of affection, but friendship with God does not admit of love being returned, not at all of loving. For it would be strange if one were to say that he loved Zeus."[45]

Another example is the Jewish emphasis on joy in celebrating the Feast of Sukkot. This festival celebrates the forty years that the Jews wandered in the wilderness between Egypt and the Promised Land. Often uncertain, always exposed and vulnerable, they cannot have been happy during that time. As Rabbi

Sacks points out, happiness depends on circumstances and things going well. But they could celebrate with joy even in "a state of total insecurity" because they knew they were "under the shelter of the Divine Presence."[46] Living in tents at the time, and later celebrating the festival in the flimsiest of makeshift shelters, they were open to the elements and vulnerable before their enemies. But above them, behind them, around them, and in front of them was the ultimate reality, the presence of God who cared for them and carried them "on eagles' wings" (Ex 19:4).

I was born during the Japanese invasion of China in the Second World War, in which seventeen million were killed. My parents and I survived a terrible famine in north-central China, in which five million died in three months, including my two brothers. We then lived in the capital city, Nanking, which had suffered the horrific rape of Nanking a few years earlier and was soon to experience the first wave of communist repression under Mao Zedong. But not once in all the dangers and disasters did I ever see in my parents anything but quiet confidence in God. Trust in the final goodness of life and existence is a gift of faith from God. Whatever humans ever do to their fellow humans, God has a heart overflowing with love for the humans who are made in his image.

If ever contrast was the mother of clarity, it is here. No one who understands Babylonian astrology (the influence of "the stars"), Hindu and Buddhist *karma* (the iron law of moral causation), Greek *moira* (fate), *anankē* (necessity), and *ataraxia* (the peace of imperturbability), Stoic *apatheia* (detached indifference), or modern secularist *determinism* (chance and necessity) can fail to see the difference from the Jewish and Christian understanding of God and the universe. The chorus in Sophocles' *Antigone* counsels, "Pray not at all since there is no release for mortals from predestined calamity." Not so, declares the Bible. From first to last, and from Genesis to Revelation, there is no ambiguity: God has a heart for humanity and existence can be trusted. There are and there will be contradictions and conflicts, but all shall be well. Those who know God know peace in the storms. Neither fate nor *fait accompli* have the last word.

UNIQUE, PRECIOUS, AND IRREPLACEABLE

Second, the Genesis declaration carries the central truth that each human person is a precious individual, whether strong or weak, rich or poor, able-bodied or handicapped, intellectually brilliant or limited, beautiful or plain. Every single human person, in Rabbi Sacks's words, is "unique, non-substitutable and irreplaceable" and must be treated as such.[47] As our esteem for God, so our esteem for a human. An earlier rabbi even suggested, "A procession of angels pass before man wherever he goes, proclaiming: *Make way for the image of God*."[48] Sacks underscores this theme tirelessly. "Every child born of the genetic mix between two parents is unpredictable, *like* yet *unlike* those who have brought it into the world."[49] He quotes Hilary Putnam, a Harvard philosopher, "Every child has the right to be a complete surprise to its parents."[50] And then repeats one of his favorite *mishna*: "When a human being makes many coins in a single mint, they all come out the same. God makes every human being in the same image, His image, yet they all emerge different."[51]

Our global world is currently aggravated by racism, tribalism, and xenophobia on the right and by tribal and identity politics on the left. The Genesis declaration bluntly contradicts both. In Rabbi Sacks's words, "difference does not make a difference. Even someone not in my image—whose color, culture, caste, or class are unlike mine—is still in God's image. *This, rather than any secular philosophy, is the basis for the ideas of equality, liberty, and justice in the West*."[52] The reason is, he adds, that with all our differences we are each "an entire world," and we are each privileged (and obliged) to say, "For my sake the world was created."[53]

That is why the quantification of life is so wrong, and the almighty algorithm must be watched with an eagle eye. Human existence and human actions must never be reduced to numbers, or Stalin would be right: the death of one person is a tragedy, but the death of millions is simply a statistic. No, the rabbis protest on the basis of the Genesis declaration, "Whoever destroys a single soul should be considered the same as one who has destroyed a whole world," and whoever saves one single soul is to be considered as one who has saved a whole world." Made in the image of God, every single life matters. We must always look deeper than statistics.

That is why cloning and parenting are so different. Cloning destroys the uniqueness of both the cloned and the clone; it raises the possibility of instrumentalism in that the clone is used as a means rather than an end, and it reduces the range of diversity in the human species. Sacks's description of the glory of human parenting through "otherness" is one of the most beautiful and profound paragraphs in all his writing.

> If there is a mystery at the heart of the human condition it is *otherness*: the otherness of man and woman, parent and child. It is the space we make for otherness that makes love something other than narcissism, and parenthood greater than self-replication. It is this that gives every human

child the right to be themselves, to know they are not reproductions of someone else, constructed according to a pre-planned template. Without this, would childhood be bearable? Would a world of clones still be a human world? *We are each in God's image but no one else's.*[54]

Looked at from the outside, we are each only one in several billion humans, so we cannot expect to be viewed as other than average. But experienced from the inside, we are each unique, and we know it. The only question is whether there is anyone or anything to underwrite that uniqueness if it is not to be dismissed as an illusion. Our faces are the external clue to our uniqueness. "A face is a message, a face speaks, often unbeknown to the person," Rabbi Heschel says. "Is it not a strange marvel that among so many hundreds of millions of faces, no two faces are alike? And that no face remains quite the same for more than one instant? The most exposed part of the body, the best known, is the least describable, a synonym for an incarnation of uniqueness."[55]

No one has captured this uniqueness better and more memorably than C. S. Lewis in his wartime sermon at Oxford's University Church, St Mary's.

It is a serious thing to live in a society of possible gods and goddesses, to remember that the dullest and most uninteresting person you talk to may one day be a creature which, if you saw it now, you would be strongly tempted to worship, or else a horror and a corruption such as you now meet, if at all, only in a nightmare. . . . There are no *ordinary* people. You have never talked to a mere mortal. Nations, cultures, arts, civilizations—these are mortal, and their life to ours is as a gnat. But it is immortals whom we joke with, work with, marry, snub and exploit—immortal horrors or everlasting splendors.[56]

Philosopher Nicholas Wolterstorff summarizes this defense of the dignity of the individual human being made in the image of God with eloquent simplicity. "Wronging comes in degrees; the greater the worth of the wronged, the worse the wronging."[57] By that standard, is there any greater "wronging" than the twentieth-century view of life "unworthy of life" (*Lebensunwertes Leben*)? Nietzsche prefigured both the Nazi doctors and the American abortionists, who even now advocate the death of unwanted babies born alive, when he wrote of "the botched and the bungled," those who are "unfruitful, unproductive," and "bound to have offspring even more degenerate than they are themselves." "One should do honor," he continued, "to the fatality which says to the feeble: 'Perish!'"[58]

Revealingly, Nietzsche asserts two things in his explanation. First, if life itself is only the will to power, then "there is nothing on earth that can have any value, if it have not a modicum of power."[59] Second, the opposition to ending life that is unworthy of life was given the name God, but if God is dead, then the protest collapses. Wolterstorff is right again. The greater the standard of the worth of a human being, the greater the worth, and the greater the wronging. And if God is indeed God as he reveals himself at Sinai, the greater the judgment of all who violate his image in the poorest and most powerless bearers of that image.

EQUALITY OF DIGNITY

Third, the Genesis declaration provides the only solid foundation for the highest form of human equality—the equality of dignity. Rabbi Sacks declares forthrightly that *"Judaism was the world's first attempt to create a society of equal dignity under the sovereignty of God."*[60] Indeed, this was the inspiration for Thomas Jefferson's claim in the Declaration of Independence that "all men are created equal." Such equality, Sacks writes, is "the holy grail of revolutionary politics," but almost nothing is more elusive and controversial than the challenge of balancing equality and liberty.[61] Societies claiming to be both free and just should strive for both ideals, but knowing how to balance them is the fly in the ointment. For liberty often threatens equality, just as equality often threatens liberty, and too much inequality from too much liberty may threaten liberty just as much as too much equality without liberty does too.

For Americans and admirers of the American experiment, Jefferson's words in the Declaration of Independence shine over the discussion. They have even been described as "perhaps the best-known sentence in the English language."[62] "We hold these truths to be self-evident, that all men are created equal, that they are endowed by their Creator with certain unalienable Rights, that among these are Life, Liberty, and the pursuit of Happiness."

Sadly, Jefferson himself, and many of the American founders, failed to live up to their own declaration. But the problem is deeper than hypocrisy. As Sacks comments, "'These truths' are anything but self-evident. They would have been regarded as subversive by Plato . . . and incomprehensible to Aristotle."[63] Plato held that humanity was divided into gold, silver, and bronze people so that society was inevitably hierarchical, and Aristotle taught that some people were born to rule and others to be ruled. The plain fact is that "these truths" would have been anathema to people as diverse as Nietzsche and to the creators of the Hindu caste system. "These truths" are self-evident, Sacks concludes, "only to one steeped in the Bible."[64]

Insistence on equality runs up against numerous problems. First, there is the obvious and insurmountable fact that according to most measures—strength, speed, intelligence, talent, and wealth, for example—all humans are simply not equal and never will be. From our first brush with schooling and examinations to the heights of Olympic sports to businesses of all kinds and the story of men in war, the glory of contest and competition stands as a constant reminder of our human inequalities that no ruler, no law, and no zeal will ever eradicate.

Second, the inequalities produced by liberty today have become so severe and the contemporary foundations for the belief in human equality have become so flimsy that the traditional Jewish and Christian foundations have been dismantled, that those who affirm the ideal of equality do so over a yawning abyss. Today, the rights to liberty and equality have been made into *fiat* rights, mere paper promises and arbitrary conventions. In the words of the atheist philosopher A. C. Grayling, they are nothing more than "the result of human *decisions* to regard them as such."[65] This represents a further nail in the coffin of universal human rights and a thrust toward the post-rights age.

Third, from the French to the Russian and the Chinese revolutions, the radical and progressive left repeats monotonously that humans can only be made fully and formally equal by the most draconian measures that result in silencing dissent, flouting diversity, and flattening distinctions.

But that is only one side of the problem. Equality threatens freedom. Justice, with its eyes blindfolded, is the universal symbol that all human beings deserve equal respect under law. True justice is no respecter of persons. Its scales are balanced. But equal respect under law is one thing, and many formal notions of equality and a passion for egalitarianism are another. Three dangerous tendencies rear their head in history's recurring drives for equality and non-discrimination. Sometimes they are writ large and crude, as in the grand revolutionary drives on behalf of French *egalité*, the classless society of communism, or the progressive left's "burn it down" type of leveling. At other times they are writ small and with a more sophisticated hand, as in progressive drives for non-discrimination now. But for those who would defend the liberal society, the damaging tendencies need watching.

First, when the pursuit of equality is elevated to being the ultimate good, rather than one ideal among others, it is likely to be driven by resentment until it grows into a passion for formal equality or equality as uniformity. If this happens, it will grow in turn into a zero-sum game in which competitors brook no rivals, scorn any negotiation of rights, and obliterate all claims to rights that stand in their way. Today, this lethal brand of egalitarianism, crusading under the banner of nondiscrimination, is often fueled by a passion for moral purity that allows no other moral criteria apart from equality and therefore becomes as zealous for its ruthless consistency as Torquemada was for his orthodoxy.

Second, the pursuit of equality and nondiscrimination has a broad flattening effect because it confuses equality of personhood with equality of behavior and therefore opens the door to amorality. On the one hand, it irons out diversity by reducing individuals to members of groups labeled according to sex, race, class, and age. On the other hand, it rules out all moral and social criteria and considerations other than equality and therefore encourages the equal rights of all behaviors regardless of moral criteria or social consequences. Thus in a liberal society prizing radical equality, behaviors that were once considered wrong now become one more practice in the mosaic of diverse practices that can each demand equal rights with all others.

If equality is the sole standard, for example, on what grounds should anyone withhold equal rights from the advocates of polyamory, polygamy, child marriage, female genital circumcision, pedophilia, incest, and sex with animals? By the standards of the progressive left those who advocate such behavior are minorities and therefore members of oppressed groups and candidates for liberation. And if equality alone is the criterion, how can anyone who votes against such practices be able to escape the accusation of prejudice, bigotry, and hatred? The truth is that equality alone is a dangerous criterion. It must always be balanced by the dignity of the individual and the morality and social consequences of the behavior.

Third, the pursuit of equality and nondiscrimination requires a strong authority to adjudicate the claims of the "disadvantaged" and the "victims," and then impose the socially engineered solutions in their favor. This becomes more urgent all the time because an equality-based society produces ever more claimants to be aggrieved and victimized because they are not treated equally. Thus engineered equality increases lack of trust between groups and reinforces rivalry, insecurities, jealousy, and paranoia. The result carries an almost mathematical certainty: The drive to achieve a more formally equal society ends with more and more legal interventions, a steady erosion of individual liberty and personal responsibility and the relentless strengthening of the central deciding authority. Society may be made more equal, but individuals will become less free, and the umpiring state (or university) will become stronger and more intrusive.

The answer, Rabbi Sacks argues, is to appreciate the difference between equality over "physical goods" and equality over "spiritual (or social and public) goods." The former, such as money and power, always represent "zero-sum games" in which some win and some lose, whereas the latter have a different logic. They are "non-zero-sum games. The more love or influence or trust I give away, the more I have. That is because they are goods the existence of which depends on being shared. They give rise to structures of co-operation, not competition."[66] Thus Exodus puts forth a vision of a "republic of faith" and a "society of equals." But the covenant people were equals in a special way—they enjoyed equality before the law (which is the easiest equality), equality in schooling for all (which is rarer but crucial, as we shall see in chapter six), and equality in dignity and worth (which is the rarest of all in history and possible only for those who see humans as God sees them, made in his image and therefore possessing dignity and worth that is inalienable).

Equality in access to schooling, civic education, and knowledge is critical to the biblical view. As Rabbi Sacks reminds us, "Almost every culture has placed a premium on forms of knowledge available only to an elite."[67] He cites the decipherers of Egyptian hieroglyphics, the Delphic oracle, the medieval restriction of the Bible to the priests, and the modern snobbery of arcane academic theory and language. True to its antihierarchical ideals, Judaism is different. "In Judaism, if something can be said, it can be said simply. God says about Moses: 'With him I speak face-to-face, clearly and not in riddles' (Num. 12:8)." Knowledge must be accessible if it is to be the common property of the people. "Democracy in Judaism is less a matter of one person, one vote; it is more a matter of education and culture. Everyone must be articulate in the literature of citizenship. . . . Everyone must understand the way of life they are to lead."[68] "That education is the key to human dignity and should be equally available to all is one of the most profound ideas in all human history."[69] The splendors of Solomon's temple and the treasures of the Vatican far outshine the humble synagogue, the plain Reformation meeting house, and the average school classroom, but the latter and not the former are the expression of the equality of dignity.

RIGHT OVER MIGHT AND JUSTICE OVER ALL

Fourth, the Genesis declaration carries a further and equally momentous implication. *Created in the image of God, each human being is God's stake in both humanity and history, and God insists that every single one be treated with justice.* Survey the gods of China, India, Mesopotamia, Egypt, Assyria, Persia, Greece, Rome, and the ancient European tribes, and you will find no one and nothing like the God of Sinai. Some, like the gods of India, are utterly beyond any consideration of justice (*neti, neti*). For others, like certain of the gods of Greece and Rome, justice is merely the defense of their own preserves against trespass or the insistence that humans do not escape the fate determined for them (*Oedipus Rex*). There are none for whom justice is central to their character and central to their commands to humans when dealing with their fellow humans.

The God of Sinai is a God of justice. His character is just, and his commands are just in themselves and all about justice for humanity. God cares passionately about justice in all human relationships because justice is the matter of how humans made in his image treat other humans equally made in his image. If justice is to prevail, *right* must always prevail over *might*. God's justice therefore constantly opposes all forms of prejudice and abuse of power—and above all, the abuse of power through which some humans oppress other humans. This point is central in the Prophets. Because their passion for justice comes from God's own passion for justice, their concern is not primarily for an ideal or a theoretical definition of justice but the desecration of justice in practice in the lives of the weak and defenseless.

Rabbi Heschel underscores that God's stake in humanity also means God's stake in history. Just as God created the universe as his masterpiece, so God creates humanity to be his partner in creating history as their masterwork together. God's work in creating the universe is finished, and his celebrated verdict on the outcome was that it was "very good." But his partnership with humanity in shaping history is ongoing, and any verdict on the outcome so far must be mixed—mainly because of the ways humans treat their fellow humans so inhumanly. This means that those who know and love God have a high calling to play their part in working to restore the earth. Justice and love are the standard, and oppression and the abuse of power are the evils to be fought. At the heart of this restoration is the truth that oppressing any person made in the image of God is an affront to God himself and a desecration of the image of God in the person. As the Hebrew proverb states, "He who oppresses the poor taunts his Maker, he who is kind to the needy honors him" (Prov 14:31).

There is no earlier, stronger, or more timely critique of the abuse of power than this striking feature of the Hebrew Scriptures. God's justice means that injustice to God's children is a flaming affront to God himself. All admirers and supporters of reform should take note. The greatest reformers in history, whether Bartolomé de Las Casas in sixteenth-century Spain, William Wilberforce in eighteenth-century Britain, William Carey in nineteenth-century India, or Martin Luther King Jr. in twentieth-century America, all shared one conviction that was a driving concern in their action: humans are made in the image of God, and the oppression of any single human or an entire group of humans is a violation of their creation and an outrage to God himself. Las Casas thundered to his fellow Spaniards, "You cannot be saved while still holding Indians!" Or as he wrote, Indians are "free human beings, and ought to be treated as human beings and free."[70]

If each human being is made in the image of God and therefore unique, precious, and unsubstitutable, then the abuse of any human being by any other is an outrage against creation. Lord Acton's dictum is justly famous, "All power tends to corrupt and absolute power corrupts absolutely." He was writing as a Christian and writing about the inevitable corruptions of the hierarchical power of the medieval church, but it is important to appreciate that both the problems of abuse and the remedy to abuse are central to the Bible's understanding of humanity and freedom. Thousands of years before Acton, Exodus shows that right prevails over might. Under God there are moral limits to power, and unlimited power carries unlimited dangers. All human sovereignty is under God's sovereignty.

It would be almost impossible to exaggerate the significance of this point. As Rabbi Sacks notes, the Abrahamic family were "latecomers" in history.[71] The Bible never pretends that they were archetypally human in any way. God's call to Abraham comes after the story of the Tower of Babel that is the symbol of ancient civilization. No, the truth is different and far deeper. "*Judaism does not represent the birth of civilization; it represents a critique of civilization.*"[72] The people of God are to be an anti-Egypt, an anti-Babylon, and counterculture to all the cultures from the Greeks to the Romans to the Spanish, the French, the British, the Americans, the Russians, and the Chinese. Called to be countercultural, it is a travesty when the people of God become the holy oil sprinkled on the status quo, the religious rationale for bolstering cultures under stress and a vile travesty if ever they become flowers on the chains that oppress. The people of God are to be an eternal critique of all that is wrong and a signal of transcendence pointing to a better and brighter way. They are called to be revolutionary, not reactionary, and a revolution that repairs and restores the world, turning its upside down to be the right way up.

That is why Rabbi Sacks insists again and again that Exodus is not only the master story of freedom but the strongest and most sustained critique of the abuse of power—and, importantly, that unchecked power has a dark consequence that is often overlooked. *Power not only oppresses the weak, power corrupts the powerful.* "Power destroys the powerless and the powerful alike, oppressing the one, while corrupting the other."[73] For any human to exercise power over another human, without their consent and against their will, is an abuse of power and potentially a form of violence.

The Exodus story, Sacks says, is "the eternal critique of power used by humans to coerce and diminish their fellow-humans."[74] That is why the monotheism of the Bible was

> a revolution thousands of years in advance of the culture of the West. . . .
> If the image of God was to be found not only in kings but in the human person as such, then all power that dehumanizes is *ipso facto* an abuse of power. Slavery, seen by all ancient thinkers as part of the natural order, becomes morally wrong, an offense not only against man but against God.[75]

Created in the image and likeness of God, humans have an inalienable dignity and worth. Each is free, responsible, and consequential, and—unless there is freely chosen consent—none should be under the dominion of anyone but God. "Power is a zero-sum game," Rabbi Sacks continues,

> I use it to buy my freedom at the expense of yours. It is a way of getting you to do my will despite your will. It turns you into a means for my end. Dominance, the use of force, brutality, whether raw as in primitive societies, or hierarchical, class- or caste-based social orders, is an act of defiance against the principle of the first chapter of Genesis, that we are all created equally in the image and likeness of God.[76]

In Genesis, God gave humans dominion over their fellow creatures, the animals, to be stewards over the earth. But he did not give them dominion over each other. Yet because of sin, the abuse of power, the domination of humans by humans, and the prevalence of hierarchical societies that become abusive are central facts of history, and they go back almost to the beginning. Sacks points out how John Milton agrees with the Jewish sages in tracing the abuse back to Nimrod, the first great ruler of Assyria and by implication to the builders of the Tower of Babel.

In *Paradise Lost* when Adam is told that Nimrod would usurp "dominion undeserved" over his fellow men, he bursts out in horror, "O execrable son to aspire Above his Brethren, to himself assuming Authority usurped, from God not given: He gave us only over beasts, fish, fowl Dominion absolute; that right we hold by his donation; but man over man He made not Lord; such title to himself Reserving, human left from human free."[77] "A major root of freedom," Rabbi Heschel writes, "lies in the belief that man, every man, is too good to be the slave of another man."[78] God tells Pharaoh, the most powerful ruler of the ancient world, Sacks notes, that "though these people may be your slaves, they are My children."[79]

Rabbi Sacks underscores how radical Milton was, and before him how radical the Torah's critique was.

> To question this—the right of humans to rule over other humans, without their consent, depriving them of their freedom—was at that time and for most of history, utterly unthinkable. All advanced societies were like this. How could they be otherwise? Was this not the very structure of the universe? Did the sun not rule the day? Did the moon not rule the night? Was there not in heaven itself a hierarchy of the gods?

Unthinkable in the pagan world, Sacks agrees, but belief in the God of Sinai is not only theology but "a political philosophy with revolutionary implications. If there is only one God, then there is no hierarchy in heaven. And if He set His image on human beings as such, then there is no justified hierarchy-without-consent on earth either."[80] Any oppression of humans by other humans, such as racism, is a supreme abuse of power and a violation of their status created in the image and likeness of God himself. Such evil and such injustice cry out to heaven itself. And as philosopher David Berlinski reminds us, violence is even deeper and wider than lists of atrocities can demonstrate, terrible though such records are. Violence also includes terror and its express goal of reducing a society to quivering fear. "Violence is not simply a matter of what is done but *what might be done*."[81]

The Bible's critique of the abuse of power is unsparing, and this fact is all the more striking in view of the current strength of critical theory, which uses the concept of power to critique all relationships. Charges and accusations are going wider and wider and higher and higher. As I write, long-cherished institutions, such as the Boy Scouts, and highly revered spiritual leaders, such as Jean Vanier of L'Arche communities, have been exposed. The fallibility of humans and the corruptibility of power is no surprise to anyone with a biblical viewpoint. The vital difference between the Bible and critical theory (as we shall see in chap. 7) is over how the abuses are addressed and the wrongs resolved.

Rabbi Heschel raised a searching question. "Why were so few voices raised in the ancient world in protest against the ruthlessness of man? Why are human beings so obsequious, ready to kill and ready to die at the call of kings and chieftains?"[82] Perhaps, he ventures, it is because humans worship might and those who command it. The root lies in the human impulse to idolatry. As Dostoevsky remarked in *Demons*, "The whole law of human existence consists in nothing other than a man's always being able to bow before the immeasurably great. If people are deprived of the immeasurably great, they will not live and will die in despair."[83] The result, long before the current philosophy of postmodernism, is the destroyers of nations—guilty men, "whose strength is their god," as the prophet Habakkuk cries out in horror (Hab 1:11). Mao's infamous dictum that "Power grows out of the barrel of a gun" was therefore only the modern world's restatement of Tacitus's "The gods are on the side of the stronger," and both are merely a commentary on the bloody course of history. The Bible stands across the path of all such attitudes and actions. "The prophets," Heschel wrote, "were the first men in history to regard a nation's reliance upon force as evil. . . . The prophets proclaimed that the heart of God is on the side of the weaker."[84]

This relentless critique of the abuse of power lies behind a small but striking feature of the Hebrew Scriptures: the prohibition of census-taking. In an age mesmerized by statistics, the repudiation offers a triple reminder. First, what counts is the meaning of the statistics, not just the surface facts in the numbers. Second, the attempt to measure strength through numbers alone will often give a false assessment. And third, as Rabbi Sacks points out, the best way to assess a people is through their contributions to society, not their numbers. "If you want to know the strength of the Jewish people, ask them to give, and then count the contributions."[85]

Milton Himmelfarb, for instance, wrote that all the Jews in the world were "smaller than a small statistical error in the Chinese census. Yet we remain bigger than our numbers. Big things seem to happen around us and to us."[86] The Jewish contributions to the worlds of philosophy, science, medicine, finance, and entertainment have been out of all proportion to their tiny numbers. The outcome is a staggering rebuke to Christians whose numbers dwarf the Jews by far. It is also a stirring lesson in the assessment of power itself, especially for a free people. As Rabbi Sacks writes, to win "the battle of the spirit, the victory of heart and mind and soul, you do not need numbers. You need dedication, commitment, study, prayer, vision, courage, ideals, hope. You need people who are instinctively inclined to contribute. Give, then count the contributions: the finest way ever devised to measure the strength of a people."[87]

FOLLOWING ORDERS IS NO DEFENSE

Beyond this small but significant point the Bible's critique of the abuse of power includes two notions that are hugely important for resisting oppression and therefore for protecting freedom. One is the long-held notion of civil disobedience, which goes back to the Hebrew midwives in Exodus (They "feared God and did not do what the Egyptian king had commanded" [Ex 1:17]). The other is the more recently asserted principle of "crimes against humanity," which was established by the Nuremberg Charter in August 1945 and applied the next year at the Nuremberg trial of the Nazis. Whatever the laws and leadership of any country may be, there are certain crimes whose enormity rules out the defense, "I was only following orders." Such radical evil has been described as the *fleur du mal* ("the flower of evil" or the ripened decadence of malignant evil). In such situations moral and civil disobedience is fully legitimate and not only possible but required. It is notable, Sacks points out, that the story of the heroic midwives in Exodus who refuse to obey the "slow genocide" of the Pharaoh is the first mention of civil disobedience in history.

Decades later there is a significant chorus of those who dispute the reasoning behind the Universal Declaration of Human Rights and the Nuremberg notion of "crimes against humanity." Such crimes, it is said, are only "winner's justice" (Stalin: "Victors are not put on trial"),[88] and "Eurocentric" rather than universal (though in fact the basis for the notion is the Bible, so the notion is European only to the extent that Europe adheres to the Bible). But beyond all arguments about the basis for the Nuremberg Charter and the Universal Declaration of

Human Rights, the twentieth century established two truths with unquestionable clarity, one negative and one positive.

The negative truth is the fact that the horror of "crimes against humanity" was even worse than slavery and racism. Slave masters and racists see humans as inferior and therefore fit for servitude; Stalin and Hitler saw humans as less than human and therefore fit for extermination (the Jews, the gypsies, the handicapped, and the unborn were treated as "life not worth living"). The worst evils combined both levels of dehumanization (Himmler: "Whether ten thousand Russian females fall down from exhaustion while digging an anti-tank ditch interests me only in so far as the anti-tank ditch for Germany is finished").[89] The positive truth concerns the principle on which the fight for humanity and freedom must rest. The clearer and higher the view of humanity, the stronger and more outrageous is the violation of any speech and actions that denies the dignity of the human person—and the Bible's view is the highest of all.

This whole point about power and the abuse of power deserves deeper reflection as we survey our world today. The bookends of history, as mentioned in the introduction, are authoritarianism and anarchy, order without freedom and freedom without order. Within the opening two books of the Bible, authoritarianism is demonstrated by the builders of Babel in Genesis and the pharaohs of Egypt in Exodus. (A Jewish midrash says that when the Tower of Babel was being built, no one noticed when a human being fell to their death, but when a brick fell, people lamented.)[90] Less obviously, anarchy is demonstrated by the sexual lawlessness that recurs constantly at the edges of the story, especially in Genesis—with its stories of seduction, abduction, incest, heterosexual rape, homosexual rape, and accusation of rape.

Both bookends, and not just the first, represent the gross abuse of power. Authoritarianism abuses humans through tyrants and political power, whereas moral and sexual anarchy abuses humans (particularly women and children) through predators and the unchecked license of sexual desire and power. Hugh Heffner's *Playboy* magazine provided a fantasyland for alpha males, but long before the permissiveness of the 1960s gave a green light to sexual predators, the Bible was realistic about the dangers of sexual *anomie*. All-out sexual freedom with no norms at all converge on the place where sexual desire and sexual dominance meet. The pagan world once pursued outlandish sex in its pursuit of fertility; the modern world now promotes it in the name of freedom. But the predations of power are no different. As Rabbi Sacks argues, *eros* allied to power is a threat to justice, the rule of law and human dignity. The combination of sexual desire and lawless power results in people being used as means to ends, with no respect for persons.

The Bible emphatically condemns the link between sexual desire and violence. This link should be pondered as it becomes clear how the sexual license of the 1960s has led directly to the evils protested by the #MeToo movement. Sacks's comment is worth quoting at length.

> Such behavior privileges some people against others. It turns women into instruments of male desire. It places power, not love, at the heart of human relationships. It treats women as objects rather than as subjects with equal dignity and integrity. It divorces sex from compassion and concern. *It dishonors the most intimate human bond, the one in which we are most like God Himself: the love that brings new life into the world.* Above all, though, it leads to violence, and the Torah regards violence—the cause of the Flood—as the single greatest threat to humanity.[91]

Too few people realize the links between the French Revolution and what Wilhelm Reich later called "the Sexual Revolution." Of those who do, many think only of the radical perversions of the Marquis de Sade and dismiss him at once as if his diseased fantasies were a complete aberration. But if the Palais Royale in Paris was ground zero for the political revolution, sexual liberation was also at the heart of its complex of cafes, galleries, and exhibition halls. The reform-minded Duc d'Orléans opened it to the public as a pleasure center where "all desires can be gratified as soon as conceived," and the duke's mistress was described as "a princess among the prostitutes."[92] The author of *Les Liaisons dangereuses* (*Dangerous Liaisons*), a pioneer of "liberating," set up shop at the Palais, and it was said that every form of sexual gratification that he described in the book was available in the precincts.[93] Andre Malraux, France's Minister of Culture under General de Gaulle, argued later that the novel's hero is the first character in Western literature to be driven by an ideology.

We must make no mistake. Sadism is a vile and horrendous extreme, but the Marquis de Sade was a philosopher as well as a pervert, and many who turn their back on his life are closer than they realize to his logic. It is fashionable to celebrate Hugh Hefner as an apostle of sexual freedom and to denigrate Harvey Weinstein as a monster and sexual predator, but the logic of the former and the logic of the latter are linked, and they were both prefigured in the French

Revolution. The just critique of the abuse of power by humans over other humans and by men over women applies to the permissive lifestyles of Western societies as much as to the brutal oppression of totalitarian dictators. The Genesis declaration stands defiantly across the path of both. The declaration that humans are made in the image and likeness of God is no empty truth. To talk of "the stupidity of dignity," as leading atheists have, is foolish and dangerous. The Genesis declaration is a statement of the highest human worth, and the strongest barrier against the desecration of the image. Being human is the noblest expression of the human being. And any human who violates a fellow human desecrates the One in whose image, in the beautiful words of the Hebrew poet, we are each "fearfully and wonderfully made" (Ps 139:14).

America cannot endure permanently half 1776 and half 1789. The compromises, contradictions, hypocrisies, inequities, and evils have built up unaddressed. The grapes of wrath have ripened again, and the choice before America is plain. Either America goes forward best by going back first, or America is about to reap a future in which the worst will once again be the corruption of the best.

3

EAST OF EDEN

THE GREAT ALIENATION

PRINCIPLE 3: FREEDOM MUST BE REALISTIC

The great divide in the world is between those who see a great divide in the world and those who don't. That old comment has been pressed into service in many different debates, often ending in fruitless arguments between optimists who see the glass half full and pessimists who see it half empty or between those who think this is "the best of times" and those who see it as "the worst of times." But there is one question where its relevance is inescapable: Is there something wrong with the world or not?

The divide between those who say there is something wrong and those who say there isn't has always been deep and consequential, but it widened fatefully in the twentieth century. In hindsight it became clear that there has been a link between utopianism and revolution and between utopianism and the most horrendous evils. In the seventeenth century the Diggers' aim was not only to remove "the Norman yoke" and restore Saxon laws but to restore "the pure law of righteousness before the Fall."[1] In the eighteenth century Adam Weishaupt's short-lived Illuminati society, which played a key role in the history of revolution, was originally called "The Club of the Perfectible." Tom Paine wrote with all the confidence of the eighteenth-century Enlightenment that the revolutionaries were making the world anew. "What were formerly called revolutions were little more than a change of persons or an alteration of local circumstances . . . what we now see in the world . . . is a renovation of the natural order of things, a system of principles as universal as truth."[2]

In the twentieth century Mao Zedong pictured himself as a revolutionary artist painting on a blank canvas. And in the twenty-first century the role of the utopian improver will be played by the transhumanist revolutionary as well as the political revolutionary, all in pursuit of nothing less than the human being who is both perfect and immortal. Francis Crick, codiscoverer of the DNA in 1953, offers the watchword: "I do not see how contemporary man is so perfect that we should not seek to improve him."[3] George Orwell confessed that he had spent time in the "Never-Neverlands of Grand Theory" until he came to see that the philosopher Michael Oakeshott was right: the utopian was like King Midas, "always in the unfortunate position of not being able to touch anything without transforming it into an abstraction."[4]

Almost as dangerous as the utopians are the dualistic thinkers—those who see the world in terms of we-they, good-bad, and children of light-children of darkness. The divisions themselves are real enough and evident for anyone to observe. What is dangerous is the presumption that while there is real evil in the world, the evil is all on the side of "our" enemies, whoever "we" are, whereas "we" and "our" friends are good.

Alexander Solzhenitsyn punctured the pretensions of all such thinking in his stunning verdict from *The Gulag Archipelago*: "It was only when I lay there on the rotting prison straw that I sensed within myself the first stirrings of good. Gradually it was disclosed to me that the line separating good and evil passes not through states, nor between classes, nor between political parties either, but right through every human heart, and through all human hearts."[5] Or again, "If only there were evil people somewhere, insidiously committing evil deeds, and it were necessary only to separate them from the rest of us and destroy them. But the line dividing good and evil cuts through the heart of every human being. And who is willing to destroy a piece of his own heart?"[6]

Realism and responsibility, rather than either utopianism or dualism, are essential requirements for facing up to evil and injustice and putting wrong right—and they both begin with an understanding of what is wrong with the world. Perhaps the most famous response to that question was the answer of the author and journalist G. K. Chesterton. When asked by the *Times* (London), along with other eminent intellectuals, what was wrong with the world, his answer was short enough to send on a postcard: "I am."

As befits a philosopher, Rabbi Sacks's answer is slightly longer but no less honest and simple. There is a haunting human question we all face, he writes, "How is it possible to live the ethical life without an overwhelming sense of guilt, inadequacy and failure?" His answer is candid, and one that almost everyone can identify with.

The distance between who we are and who we ought to be is, for most of us, vast. We fail. We fall. We give in to temptation. We drift into bad habits. We say or do things in anger that we later regret. We disappoint those who had faith in us. We betray those who trusted us. We lose friends. Sometimes our deepest relationships can fall apart. We experience frustration, shame, humiliation, remorse. We let others down. We let ourselves down. These things are not rare. They happen to all of us, even the greatest. One of the most powerful features of biblical narrative is that its portraits are not idealized. Its heroes are human. They too have their moments of self-doubt. They too sin.[7]

Rabbi Heschel, a champion of the civil rights movement alongside Dr. Martin Luther King, agreed.

There is nothing we forget as eagerly, as quickly, as the wickedness of man. The earth holds such a terrifying secret. Ruins are removed, the dead are buried, and crimes forgotten. Bland complacency, splendid mansions, fortresses of cruel oblivion top the graves. The dead have no voice, but God will disclose the secret of the earth.[8]

Yes, if we are honest, almost all of us can second Chesterton and admit, the problem of the world is me. It is in my heart too. None of us is truly always and only among the innocents. In the language made popular by the spread of the coronavirus in 2020, humanity has "an underlying condition." In Rabbi Heschel's admission, "We all suffer from an ego-centric predicament."[9] Or in Rabbi Sacks's words, "the problem of chaos is not out there, but 'in here,' in the human heart."[10] But, many people would object, does there have to be any mention of *sin*? For everyone who would chuckle at the two-word treatise of G. K. Chesterton or warm to the candor of Rabbi Sacks, there are others who would bridle at the word *sin*. That term is surely old-fashioned and over the top, a dreaded word that once sent shivers down people's spines and now elicits responses ranging from disdain to amusement and unease—as if *sin* was a preacher's word reserved for the flagrant and the unrepentant—and not for you and me or our neighbors.

So what does sin have to do with the world? Or at least, what does it have to do with the modern world and with the ideals of freedom and revolution? The Bible's answer is everything, and there are two major reasons why realism about human nature is essential. First, no one can hope to put anything right unless they know what has gone wrong. That is as true of revolution as it is of a cell phone or a light switch. A revolution with a faulty analysis of what is wrong in society will never be more than reactionary. It can never be truly revolutionary. Realism about wrong is essential to putting things right, and realism in revolution is indispensable to the task of working for genuine transformation. Oddly, today's radicals proclaim loudly and in unison that evils such as racism and sexism are systemic, yet they adamantly resist any thought that there is anything wrong with humanity other than the problems that they attack through their causes.

Second, realism is essential because freedom and especially the moment of liberation can be intoxicating. Too many people, unaccustomed to its heady delights, have become so drunk that they have lost their wits and are swept away in their enthusiasm. The twenty-three-year-old poet William Wordsworth is often cited as the arch example of such folly—which he later came to regret. Not long after graduating from Cambridge, he traveled to Paris in 1791 and fell in love with both the revolution and a young French woman. "Bliss it was in that dawn to be alive, but to be young was very heaven."[11] Dostoevsky noted the same euphoria sweeping Russia at the first rumors of the emancipation of the serfs (as it did more recently over the so-called Arab Spring in the early 2010s)—"the whole of Russia suddenly became exultant and all ready to be reborn."[12] His own years in the Omsk prison gave him an insatiable thirst for freedom ("Those four years I consider a time in which I was buried alive and closed up as in a coffin").[13] Liberation to him was therefore almost a resurrection. As the narrator says in *Notes from the Dead House*, "Freedom, a new life, resurrection from the dead. . . . What a glorious moment!"[14]

Overall such naivety a simple warning should be posted. The glory of liberation is heady, intoxicatingly so, but to enjoy lasting freedom requires realism, including an understanding of how freedom easily goes wrong.

CULTURAL DYNAMICS OF SIN

According to the Bible, when God created humans "in his image and likeness," he gave them freedom and responsibility. He was sovereign and they were significant. But in doing so, God, as it were, took a risk. In Rabbi Sacks's words, "He had made the one life form capable of defying him and destroying the entire order of creation itself."[15] Or again, humans "are the first and to this day the only life form endowed with the capacity to undo the work of creation."[16] Defying him is, of course, what happened. The result led to our "underlying condition." It caused the disruption of the harmony between humanity and God, humans and other humans, and humans and the earth (destroying the earth is a point on which even the nuclear pacifists and climate change alarmists now appear to agree).

But the book of Genesis not only records the fact that it happened, it describes how and why it happened, and it also shows how those who come to know God are called to the task of healing the wound and repairing the damage. But for the purposes of understanding what has gone wrong with the world, Genesis also shows how the dynamics of that original sin have had such enduring power down through the centuries and across the continents—for both individuals and whole societies. In sum, Genesis shines light on the cultural as well as the personal dynamics of human sin and how an understanding of these dynamics can unlock many of the destructive trends at work in our day. Sin is anything but inactive, and the notion of sin is anything but archaic. Yet there is a massive irony in the relationship of the modern world to the Bible. As modern people we believe that we are very superior to the Bible and its view of sin and are quick to dismiss it as old-fashioned. So we completely ignore what the Bible says about us when the Bible's descriptions of sin and us have proved far more accurate and enduring than our modern dismissals of the Bible, many of which are outdated already.

If we pay attention to the account of the temptation and the outcome of the first human sin, it is clear that its potency grew out of three distinct elements in the appeal and in the consequences that followed. Together, these components empowered the seduction and devastation of the first sin, and their dynamics have been in play in the world ever since. These dynamics have combined and recombined in various forms over time, depending on the social conditions of each generation. Under the extreme conditions of the advanced modern world, these same dynamics of sin can be traced clearly in our day.

FREEDOM WITHOUT FETTERS

The first component in the cultural dynamics of sin is *the temptation to suspicion of God and by implication a temptation to a deeper, wider suspicion of others and everything outside us as a threat to our freedom.* "Indeed," the tempter asked, "Has God really said, 'You shall not eat from any tree of the garden'?" (Gen 3:1). The question raised is disarmingly factual and innocent sounding. Trust is the foundation of all human life, all good relationships, and all good societies. But the tempter's question carries a subtle query that must have detonated like a time bomb. Could the truth be that, in setting a boundary to their freedom and restricting their choice, God was out to keep them on a short leash and reduce their freedom? But if they were really created free, then surely they would have to be completely and absolutely free? Doesn't that mean that any limit on freedom is a denial of true freedom and therefore that they are not as free as they thought, let alone truly free? God was in the way of their freedom. In trusting God, they had been suckered.

The logic of that suspicion is rife today, and it moves in three main directions: against boundaries, against others, and against the past. First, the suspicion is directed against boundaries. It fuels the drive to transgress, as any boundary around freedom is seen as a block on freedom. Dostoevsky captured this thought in *Notes from the Dead House.* Imagine building a palace, he wrote, and furnishing it with gold, marble, paintings, hanging gardens, and delights of every sort. You would never wish to leave it—unless, that is, you suddenly discovered that

> your palace is enclosed by a fence and you're told, 'All this is yours! Delight in it. Only you must not take a single step outside the fence!' Believe me, at that same moment you'll want to be free of your paradise and step over the fence. And what's more, all this magnificence, all this luxury will provoke even more suffering. The luxury itself will cause you pain.[17]

Second, the suspicion is directed against others. It will always throw a cloud over the presence of others and their motives. Free societies have come to value freedom to the point where the idea of freedom has become the idol of absolute freedom. And to those mesmerized by the lure of absolute freedom, all external considerations and constraints are made suspect. God, religion, tradition, duty, truth, families, children, and even others have become enemies of freedom for some people. *I* will always be hampered by *We.* Better not to be married, and better not to have children. But the problem now goes even deeper. All limits to individual freedom are now suspect. If freedom is our ability to choose what we wish, then anything that hampers our choice limits our freedom. An old Chinese saying asked, "Why do you hate me? I didn't give you anything." But that mistrust now runs deeper and threatens to touch all commitments, ties, and obligations. *To be free, depend on no one, receive nothing from anyone, and you will not owe anything to anyone.*

Third, the suspicion will be directed against the past. "Did God say?" has now been followed by "Did I say?" Suspicion will challenge all ties from the past that constrain the present. All words are commitments in some sense, but promises, promise keeping, and loyalty all depend on a word of honor given in the past that binds together the past, the present, and the future. A husband and wife are faithful to the vows made on their wedding day. The loyalty of citizens and patriots is expressed in a pledge of allegiance, a salute to the flag, or the singing of an anthem. In each case the past is binding on the present and the future. But as skeptics such as Machiavelli and David Hume have long pointed out, that is easily challenged. Why should anyone be bound for the whole of life by words uttered at a particular moment earlier in life? The past, they say, is dead and gone, and so too are its promises, vows, and oaths. All that was yesterday, and today is another day. What matters is that we must be free and unfettered in the present moment, so forget the past and let the future take care of itself when the time comes.

The net effect of all such suspicions and rejections is disastrous. Did humanity once believe that humans were created? It is time to reject all givens and treat everyone and everything as socially constructed, not created. (Simone de Beauvoir: "One is not born a woman. One becomes so.")[18] Were we told that history and the past shape who we are today. Forget them, and focus only on the present and the future. Do we each stand in a particular tradition? Break it off and think only of yourself and your generation. ("It's a generational thing. They wouldn't understand.") Does biology determine who we are? Then choose to be whoever you feel you are, for "your truth" and "my truth" are what matters, and how you feel today is decisive. (Rousseau: "What I feel to be good is good, and what I feel to be bad is bad.")[19]

Do our families, our ancestry, and our biology constrain us? Then break out of their narrow confines and offer life choices to children from the kindergarten on. Do social conventions box you in and hamper your expression of who you are? Flout them, and do your own thing. Do other people crowd into your space? Shut them out. ("There's no need for red hot pokers. Hell is other people.")[20] Do your own previous decisions and ways of life tie you down like a ball and chain? Then break them off, be mindful only of the present, and do what you want right now. ("You only live once.") Do commitments hamper your freedom as "ties that bind"? Then cut them off or make them all conditional and for the moment only.

The overall trend is clear: if freedom is absolute and the goal is autonomy, then *others* and *otherness* of any kind are suspect—God, history, biology, customs, parents, family, peers, society, duty, commitments—they must all be overthrown if they get in the way. The assault on family is the most poignant but deadliest of all for a simple reason: the family is still the one place where, despite all the breakdowns and hurt, love, self-giving, service, sacrifice, and protection are still most natural and instinctive. Yet in all these cases the dynamics of sin and the conditions of modernity advance together to arouse suspicion, incite mistrust, and promote separation, isolation, and breakdown. In the name of freedom, break with anything and everything that ties you down and constrains your freedom. Advanced modern conditions conspire to reinforce all forms of atomistic individualism, and current philosophies that reflect such conditions and reinforce such thinking are not hard to find.

IDEAS AS ALIBIS FOR INTERESTS

This suspicion-fueled resentment and autonomy blazed out early in the French Revolution. Louis Antoine de Saint-Just, the so-called youthful revolutionary, composed a huge pornographic poem comparing traditional values to madness and striking out in his own way—"original, original . . . I want to live henceforth in my own way."[21] The same attitude can be seen in the calendar proposed at the French Revolution, starting life anew in the "Year Zero." The revolutionaries abolished the seven-day week—it was based on the Bible's account of the seven days of creation. Then they abolished Sundays, Saints' Days, and Christian festivals such as Christmas and Easter. They replaced them with feasts consecrating trees, fruits, and animals rather than historical events. Rousseau proclaimed "the universal religion of Nature," and the revolutionaries rejoiced that "cultivation" had replaced "cult."[22]

Ayn Rand's *objectivism* is an obvious example of a similar philosophy in our day. Sometimes called "Nietzscheanism in a pinstripe suit," its central tenet is that selfishness and self-assertion are the highest good, so dependency of any kind—whether economic or relational—is wrong. In Rand's novel *Atlas Shrugged*, the motto carved over the door of John Galt's home has become the motto of countless readers: "I swear by my life and my love of it that I will never live for the life of another man, nor ask another man to live for mine." Or as Galt expands on his philosophy of life, "Do you ask what moral obligation I owe to my fellow men? None, except the obligation I owe to myself, to material objects and to all of existence: rationality."[23]

Postmodernism provides another popular alibi for bowing to the idol of freedom. God is dead, and truth is dead, it claims, so the ultimate determinant in society is power. But if all relations are negotiated solely by power, the best protection against the unwanted power of others is to approach everyone with suspicion (the infamous "hermeneutics of suspicion"). The outcome is an aging society fueled by pervasive suspicion, mistrust, rumor, conspiracy theories, and cynicism. Nothing is what it appears to be and no one can be trusted, so suspicion is the best insurance against the mounting menace of manipulation by the power of others. What the suspicious and cynical forget is that freedom is an ideal, naivety about an ideal may be a mark of immaturity, but suspicion and cynicism about an ideal are the sure symptoms of an aging and declining society.

PORN AND POWERLESSNESS

As the mention of Saint-Just shows, yet another natural example of specious freedom through rejection of others is pornography. Pornography is fantasy freedom, and all at the expense of the other. Love and the sexuality of love are the highest and most intimate tribute to the worth of another human being, whereas pornography stands at the opposite extreme. Short of rape and murder, pornography is one of the lowest forms of respect for another. The other is brought into the relationship as I-It rather than I-Thou. She, and sadly *she* is mostly the right term, is merely an instrument. She may have volunteered, and she may be doing it to be paid, but she is there only as an object to gratify his desire. (Andrea Dworkin's title says it all: *Pornography: Men Possessing Women.*) That is why pornography is naturally critiqued in terms of power. One person uses another person purely for his pleasure.

But in fact the focus on power is often an alibi and only half the story. As Yale Law School professor Paul Kahn argues in his defense of love in politics, pornography is as much about powerlessness as power: "pornography is not so much a form of power over others as a reaction to the ultimate lack of power that individuals experience."[24] In real life most people do not feel greatly empowered. We are each tied down by a web of commitments, responsibilities, and obligations—to our families, our work, and our governments. For most of us except the rich and powerful, our freedom to move is limited. Thus, Kahn writes, the "pornographic is both the simplest and the most compelling form of fleeing from the burdens of history."[25]

In the fantasyland of the porn world, all wider commitments and responsibilities are absent or deliberately excluded. There are no entangling loves, no children, no neighbors, no colleagues, no need for words (only deeds), no sense of past or future, and no real others at all. There is only the pseudopower and pseudofreedom of the individual's body getting its way, operating solely as a body with its desires and cordoned off even from the individual's heart and mind. All actions are certainly insulated from any consideration of love and respect for the other person. They are also separated from any thought of children generated as the fruit of sexual love (as opposed to children objectified and brutalized in pedophilia). Pornography, in short, can be both a bid for power and a salve for the lack of power, though an obsession with pornography underscores the aspect of weakness by leading to addiction. But either way, the fashionable status of modern pornography represents another form of attempted freedom through repudiation of the other.

The general trend in all these ideas is plain. Whenever freedom is reduced to being only power, any restriction of power is viewed at once as a restriction of freedom. That erases the importance of the traditional distinction between liberty and license, and absolute freedom becomes permission to do what we like rather than the power to do what we ought. Which of course turns society into a power game with no rules, a game that favors the strong against the weak and justifies the abuse of power. But the term "*abuse*" should be in quotation marks because it is a moral consideration and therefore unwarranted under postmodernism. To be sure, a moment is bound to come when abuse truly becomes egregious and cries out for a moral judgment in which right can prevail against might (when, for example, the logic of the power-based permissiveness of the sexual revolution becomes so abusive that it raises the outrage of the #MeToo movement.) But until that moment, there is no "abuse" as such. There is only the natural course of events and the outworking of power. Under the philosophy of postmodernism, might always makes right. If power is the sole umpire in the game, how can "abuse" be flagged as abuse when the powerful are simply being powerful and the weak are simply being weak? (Will the #MeToo movement prove radical enough to go beyond protesting the symptoms to protesting the root of the problem?)

ROCKS AND ISLANDS

Evidence of the madness and destructiveness of unbounded freedom can be found in many places throughout the West. "No man is an island," John Donne wrote famously. But today many advanced modern city dwellers might well sing with Paul Simon and Art Garfunkel, "I am a rock / I am an island."[26] Living radically isolated lives their relational deprivation has cut them off from the richness of traditional community and the continental solidarity of humanity. ("Bowling alone," as per Robert Putnam or "Alone together," as described by

Sherry Turkle.)[27] Even the reduced time they are with others gives them only a smattering of the fellow feeling they crave. Their loneliness is deep and silent.

Responses to such atomistic individualism and the loss or rejection of the other are varied. For some people the separation leads to the new Prometheanism and lifestyles of thrusting egotism and narcissism, as careless of others as their individualism allows them to be. Freedom is the ever-expanding assertion of the individual will ("I and who but I?").

For many others the separation leads to loneliness, the sad epidemic of the urban world of modernity. In Dostoevsky's brief summary, relationships of all sorts would be attractive were it not for a single barrier. "The law of individuality on earth is binding. The *I* stands in the way."[28]

For still others the separation leads them from being lonely to becoming *loners*, those whose resentment and revenge is taken out on their neighbors and colleagues in conflicts and massacres. (In America's domestic massacres, loners, and not simply guns, are the constant, a problem that will never be solved by gun laws alone.)

For yet others the separation of autonomous, commitment-averse people leads from suspicion to fear and deep insecurity about criticism of any kind and eventually to a Hobbesian-style "hatred of all against all."

Saddest of all, the separation leads to a rise in the incidence of suicides. Suicide is the most tragic modern epidemic, as cosmically separated individuals defiantly assert their freedom against the walls of shame, failure, hostility, or despair that they feel closing in on them.

America's rising tide of suicides ought to be read as writing on the wall. The combination of extreme individualism, extreme isolation, the shift from a guilt culture to a shame culture, the coercive power of the internet, and a general lack of meaning and purpose have become toxic. Classical writers such as Seneca and Pliny the Elder, philosophers such as David Hume and Arthur Schopenhauer, and novelists such as Fyodor Dostoevsky have long commented on the idea of "logical suicide"—the idea that suicide can be the ultimate expression of individual freedom over against society and the unwanted pressure of others. Dostoevsky is well known for the way he presses ideas to their extreme. In *Demons* the argument for suicide is put forward by Kirillov, an atheist in the revolutionary cell who argues that suicide is the perfect expression of his freedom and his atheism.

If someone disbelieves in God, Kirillov argues, they should become God themselves in a supreme assertion of their self-will. ("If there is God, then the will is all his, and I cannot get out of his will. If not, the will is all mine, and it is my duty to proclaim self-will.")[29] But the supreme demonstration of self-will is suicide—the godlike freedom to do exactly what you will and so flout the hold of all physical laws. Everything we do in life, from making coffee to making love, has some practical purpose and to that extent is hemmed in by the causality of all the physical forces that make up life on earth. But freely to will one's own destruction, to give up the unassailable title to one's own life, and to relinquish the world altogether is an act of ultimate freedom against life and all consider-ations and constraints of any kind. (Kirillov: "The fullest point of my self-will is—for me—to kill myself.")[30]

Needless to say, the icy logic is chilling, but the commentary it sheds on the suicide's view of life and the weight it leaves on the hearts of those left behind create an unfathomable sadness.

Lord James Bryce, Queen Victoria's ambassador to Washington, DC, warned of such a social unraveling a long time ago. America did not have Europe's constraining sense of tradition or the social cohesion that came from living in small towns and villages. Instead, America was so large, so free, and so mobile that its freedom might always end in chaos were it not for the one factor that held the country together—the spiritual, moral, and social bonding of religion. If religion were ever to lose its power in America, Bryce mused (and he was writing at the start of the twentieth century when that prospect seemed un-thinkable), he could foresee what Americans are beginning to experience today—a social unraveling that would be difficult to stop. After all, America is "the country in which the loss of faith in the invisible might produce *the completest revolution*, because it is the country where men have been least wont to revere anything in the visible world."[31]

HOMO DEUS

The second component in the cultural dynamics of sin is *the temptation to strive to be as God* ("You will be like God, knowing good and evil" [Gen 3:5]). A small infringement of the rules, perhaps, and the first humans could be like their creator. What a rich prize for so small a risk. What could be more appealing? This impulse to idolatry was introduced in chapter one, though it is notable that the original temptation was not to idolatry in general but to self-idolatry and self-adulation in particular. The reason for the difference is that to think we are truly God is quite beyond most of us. We are rather obviously small, imperfect people, so to pretend to be God would look absurd or comic. So general idolatry is the easier human move. Reject God and put ourselves at the center of life in his place while looking to someone or something bigger than us to replace our need for God and serve our interests at the same time.

The greatest souls of history need no such dodge. They feel well capable of posturing as God. From Nimrod to Napoleon, the great captains of history have thrust themselves forward time and again as Promethean men gods in their generation. Heinrich Heine described Karl Marx as "the godless self-god."[32] Nietzsche highlighted the dynamic in the nineteenth century for himself ("If there were Gods, how could I stand not to be a God?"),[33] but he was following the logic he had read in Dostoevsky. In *Demons* the great Russian novelist portrays the dynamic of idolatry in Kirillov, the engineer and revolutionary. ("To recognize that there is no God, and not to recognize that at the same time you have become God, is an absurdity. . . . I have found it: the attribute of my divinity is—Self-will.")[34] Yuval Harari expresses the same point unambiguously in the strutting bravado of his bestselling *Homo Deus*. (We are the "Gods of planet earth," the "new godlings," and "Scientists today can do much better than the Old Testament God.")[35]

The overall movement is clear. Whenever there is a man or woman with colossal pride, or whenever some breakthrough in science and technology appears to warrant a new stage of human self-reliance, self-idolatry takes off again. For most humans, in contrast, rejecting God means having to replace God, and the deepest temptation is to play God in our own lives, even though we need the help of idols that are less than God but greater than us.

For the builders of the Tower of Babel the technological breakthrough came through the invention of brick kilns. For Yuval Harari, humans can hail their new status as "godlings" thanks to the fruits of artificial intelligence and biogenetic engineering. But if the claims to be God are the same across the centuries, so also will be the outcome. In Rabbi Sacks's words, "when humans try to be more than human they end up less than human."[36]

NOT ME, SIR! HIM!

The third personal and cultural dynamic in the original sin was *a shifting of responsibility*. If suspicion destroys the trust that underlies all relationships, evasion of responsibility is equally fundamental as a denial of freedom. Freedom and responsibility are indivisible. Freedom entails responsibility, and responsibility expresses freedom. Choices have consequences, and responsibility means shouldering the consequences of the free choices we have made. Yet that is exactly what the personal and cultural dynamics of sin attempt to deny.

As the rabbis understand Genesis, evasion of responsibility was at the heart of the personal and cultural dynamics of sin. When God confronted Adam, Adam refused to take personal responsibility. He blamed Eve for leading him astray. "The woman whom You gave *to be* with me, she gave me from the tree, and I ate" (Gen 3:12). Similarly, when God confronted Cain after the murder of his brother Abel, Cain refused to take moral responsibility. "Am I my brother's keeper?" he said famously (Gen 4:9). Later still, the builders of the Tower of Babel thrust their ziggurat upward into the heavens and refused to accept any existential responsibility for their lives on earth before God. "Let us make for ourselves a name" (Gen 11:4).

Complete autonomy? No human beings who have ever lived created themselves or brought themselves into being. Choosing and choice are critical to freedom, but as Rabbi Sacks says, "It is a peculiar post-Enlightenment delusion to think that the only significant things about us are those that we choose. The truth is that some of the most important facts about us we did not choose. We did not choose to be born. We did not choose our parents. We did not choose the time and place of our birth."[37] Whether we are aware of it or not, and grateful or not, we were all once children and therefore heirs, recipients, and debtors from the start of our lives.

We are never completely autonomous. We are all always dependent and indebted in some way, and life itself is essentially our response to all we have received—to God, to life, to our fathers and mothers, to our families, to our education, to our countries, and to the wider civilization we were born in. Even orphans once had parents, and it is ludicrous to think that the only way to be free is to cut ourselves off from all commitments and debts and in effect make ourselves cultural orphans. Simply to describe such folly is surely to see it.

It should be equally obvious that no human being is absolute. No one, not even the richest and most powerful masters of the universe, can possibly live according to their own will alone, and no one is ever completely autonomous. Such possibilities are a mirage. We are relational to the core of our being, and try as we will, we cannot ever be anything else. Responding to others, from our parents on, we are responsible before we have rights, and we have rights only to the degree that we and others prove responsible. Dependency is therefore inevitable at some point, and in itself dependency is not an insult to our dignity or a cramp on our freedom. The only question is whether it is a good dependency or a bad dependency, for dependency in the bonds of trust and love is freedom and not servitude. In sum, there is no such thing as a completely "self-made man" (or woman) or an absolutely free and autonomous person, and those who fancy that they are one or the other are either blind or foolish and a danger to those around them.

For both Jews and Christians, freedom starts as a gift rather than an achievement. We are creative because we were created. From Abraham on, the heart of our responsibility in life is to respond to God's call and to live all life as a calling to God and to his way of living. Others too have glimpsed the centrality of responsibility in human life. Václav Havel, for instance, the playwright and dissident turned president of the Czech Republic, explored this truth in his *Letters to Olga* (his wife). Why should someone pay the fare if they are traveling alone in the second car of a streetcar with no conductor and no one to see what they do? The answer, he says, is more than a matter of conscience and upbringing. It is a matter of responsibility, which means vouching for ourselves and standing behind everything we do. "Who stands fast?" Dietrich Bonhoeffer wrote, as a man who faced up to Hitler and stood fast to the point of death. "Responsibility means that the totality of our life is pledged, and that our action becomes a matter of life and death."[38]

Where are such responsible people? Bonhoeffer asked. He might well raise that question today when the frequency of women aborting their babies and men abandoning their families is only the beginning of how modern life is turning nonresponsibility into a philosophy and irresponsibility into a way of life. We are living in the golden age of exoneration, which represents a massive acceleration in the art of making excuses and ducking responsibility. From birth we are taught to blame others, resent others, and sue others, while always excusing ourselves. The culture of victimhood has developed an armory of slogans to justify itself—"born this way," "hard-wired like this," and "My parents made me do it."

In all the problems created by victim playing, three are common today and clearly evident in American politics. The danger for individuals is that those who portray themselves as victims eventually perceive themselves as victims and then paralyze themselves as victims. When it comes to groups, those who wish to identify themselves as victims end by becoming instruments for the political purposes of others, thereby compounding their dependency and victim-hood. The danger for society is that when young people are allowed to learn only the negative lessons from history, to justify the victim narrative, they end in reinforcing the evils from their past rather than remedying them. They have been trained to use the injuries of the past to serve the interests of their future and thus to ignore the real responsibilities of the present.

REAPING THE WHIRLWIND

No one who explores the Bible's description of the cultural dynamics of sin can seriously say that the notion of sin is obsolete. It carves open the logic of many of today's trends with unsparing precision. So too does the Bible's description of the outcome of such dynamics. Some of these descriptions are well known—for example, the description of sin as "transgression" (the wrong of crossing boundaries) and as "missing the mark" (the equal wrong and the tragedy of falling short of what should be and what might have been). Or again, the notion of the "hardening of the heart" as repeating a sin means reducing the seri-ousness of sin so that "never again" becomes "again and again." But other de-scriptions of the outcomes are less well known and highly illuminating—for example, the description of how sin results in "exile" and the "loss of home."

As the Bible tells the story, to know and love God is to be at home in the universe, and to reject God is to become alienated from him and to find ourselves as "strangers in a strange land"—"exiled," "wandering," "lost" and "east of Eden." After they had sinned, Adam and Eve were exiled from the Garden of Eden (Gen 3), and after he had murdered his brother, Cain was sentenced to perpetual exile (Gen 4). Centuries later when Israel abandoned God, the result was exile under Babylon. And needless to say, alienation and homelessness of one sort or another have repeatedly been diagnosed as the chronic ailment of the modern world. But have we not brought the problem down on ourselves? As the prophet Hosea commented, "They sow the wind, and they reap the whirlwind" (Hos 8:7).

In each case the dynamics of the alienation are the same. Freedom means responsibility, and choices have consequences. In response to human sin and false choices, God either leaves us or drives us toward the logic of our own settled choices, and the outcome is a form of judgment as "measure for measure." Thus, as Rabbi Sacks writes, "A sin, *het*, is an act in the wrong place. The result, *galut*, is that the agent finds himself in the wrong place."[39] In short, for the Bible, "sin leads to exile."[40]

As we shall see in chapter seven, exile and homelessness are a serious predicament, but they are not hopeless because the Bible holds out the offer of a homecoming. There is a way back from exile. A turnaround is possible because *repentance*" in the Bible means both "return" and "homecoming." As Rabbi Sacks underscores, the Hebrew word *teshuva* means both a spiritual act and a physical act. It requires a double turning—first, a spiritual turning that is a change of mind and heart and, second, a physical turning that is a return home— "homecoming," with all the relief, warmth, and joy that homecoming means to a wanderer or an exile.

Yet we never escape the realism of the need for humility. In his study of the reign of terror in the French Revolution, David Andress gives a salutary twist to the well-known saying that "the price of liberty is eternal vigilance." The phrase, he points out, is usually restricted to external dangers and enemies, but we must never forget ourselves, which is where the greatest vigilance is required. The French revolutionaries forgot to watch themselves.

> Of far more significance, and the true and tragic lesson of the epic descent to the terror, is the summons to vigilance against ourselves—that we should not assume that we are righteous, and our enemies are evil; that we can see clearly, and others are blinded by malice and folly; that we can abrogate the fragile rights of others in the name of our own certainty and all will be well regardless.[41]

We too are the problem. The human problem is never simply *out there* but always *in here too.*

IT SHOULD HAVE BEEN OTHERWISE

The Bible's realism yet hope in the face of the great alienation of humanity is unique, and many implications flow from this view. One is that *the Bible does full justice to the intuitive outrage of the human heart in the face of evil and injustice.* This outrage is the natural and the right response to evil and injustice. It is also a crucial ingredient in the human calling to reform and revolution, and thus to help repair and restore the world. In the Bible's view, evil is monstrously evil and injustice is horribly wrong, *but it should have been otherwise. It was never supposed to be this way.* To conclude that evil is normal, inevitable, or final is itself a license for more evil. From the beginning of the Bible to the end, there is no shred of ambiguity about evil and injustice. Evil and injustice are totally, radically, and flagrantly counter to the character and purpose of God. They are disruptive and destructive by definition. They are both a perversion and a privation—the absence of good in something that by its very nature should be expected to have this good. Contrary to Leibniz, Alexander Pope, and all who believe that this is the best of all possible worlds, *whatever is, is emphatically not right.*[42]

A tree, a cow, or a rock without love is no less a tree, a cow, or a rock. But a human being is made in the image and likeness of God, so a human being whose heart is filled with the intent to harm rather than to seek another's good is disordered and decisively less of a human being. Evil is therefore in essence what was not supposed to be, a rupture in the cosmic order of things, a cancer whose malignancy has spread to every part of life, a form of red-handed mutiny against life as it was supposed to be. Thus evil and injustice are not the results of ignorance but of the will. They have nothing to do with the essence of creation, but with a shattering intrusion after creation. Evil and injustice are alien. They are parasites on a healthy body, gatecrashers in the grand celebration of life and existence. To accept evil as fated or final is worse than excusing evil, it encourages evil. To recognize evil as alien is always to be ready to resist evil.

In his memoir *Errata*, George Steiner, the eminent literary critic, captures the outrage we feel in the face of evil and injustice.

> At the maddening center of despair is the insistent instinct—again I can put it no other way—of a broken contract. Of an appalling and specific cataclysm. In the futile scream of a child, in the mute agony of a tortured animal, sounds the "background noise" of a horror after creation, after being torn loose from the logic and repose of nothingness. Something— how helpless language can be—has gone hideously wrong. Reality should, could have been, otherwise.[43]

Evil and injustice raise a host of deep questions, above all the challenge of the ancient trilemma (How can evil be evil, and God be all-loving and all-powerful at the same time?).[44] A full discussion of the issues is beyond us here, but what matters for our exploration is straightforward. The world is not as it should be. Something is terribly wrong. The conviction born of that outrage must lead to whatever can be done. Condemnation is right, but never enough. What is needed is rescue and deliverance. However great or small our efforts are, whether they are successful or a failure, the outrage triggered by the wrong must mean a determination to make things right. But those attitudes and those responses are made both right and natural by the realism born of understanding the great alienation.

YOU BAD, ME GOOD

A second implication of realism is humility and candor. *If the problem of the world is me or us, then whatever the evil and injustice we fight, the problem is within us too and we must be aware of the dangers for ourselves.* This realism stands in direct contrast to two perspectives that repeatedly make the problem worse by forgetting that evil is in their own hearts too—and thereby end in compounding evil.

One error is dualism, the view that divides the world into two camps: discerning evil in others and denying it in ourselves—*us* and *them, good* and *bad, black* and *white, children of darkness* and *children of light. We* are obviously on one side, the "good" side, and *they*, whoever we disagree with, are on the other side, the "bad" side. Taking sides in disagreements is inevitable and often right, and there truly is evil and injustice in the world. That is the whole point of the realism. Not all cats are gray, and the search for moral equivalence can be disastrous. But it is dangerous to generalize about opponents, and it is wrong to stereotype. There truly are monsters and monstrous evils to be fought, but there are exceptions in every group and good sides to all but the worst of people. Above all, dualism is deadly because it blinds us to our own flaws, and it may even lead to our projecting onto others the evils we do not admit in ourselves—which of course is rank hypocrisy. Jesus gave a stinging rebuke to such hypocrisy. The hypocrites were concerned about the splinter in their neighbor's eye but ignored the plank in their own. Or, as Nietzsche warned in *Beyond Good and Evil,* "Whoever fights monsters should see to it that in the process he does not become a monster."[45]

The other error is utopianism, the belief in human perfectibility and progress that denies evil in human nature and views history as the path to ever-upward improvement. Few beliefs are more natural to the revolutionary mind, for who at some stage in life has not thrilled to the appeal of Tom Paine's famous claim, "we have it in our power to begin the world over again"?[46] But as the last century demonstrates, the most murderous tyrannies in history were the fruit of un-grounded confidence in politics, science, education, and psychology and in what they could do to improve human nature and society. Stalin, Mao, Pol Pot, and even Hitler, all talked in their turn of making humankind "anew." Mao exulted that he was the artist to paint a new vision for China: "A blank sheet of paper has no blotches, so the newest and most beautiful words can be written on it, the newest and most beautiful pictures can be painted on it."[47]

Each of these utopians presided over a monumental catastrophe that grew directly from their utopianism. The chief problem was that they could only bridge the gap between the ideal and the real in one way—through coercion, terror, and violence at the cost of the lives of millions of their own people. Solzhenitsyn notes that in the correspondence between Marx and Engels, they frequently stated that terror would be indispensable after achieving power. ("It will be necessary to repeat the year 1793. After achieving power, we'll be considered monsters, but we couldn't care less.")[48] Robespierre even justified "virtuous terrorism." In a speech to the Convention in 1794, he made it chillingly clear: "If the mainspring of popular government in peacetime is virtue, amid revolution it is at the same time both virtue and terror: virtue without which terror is fatal; terror without which virtue is impotent. Terror is nothing but prompt, severe, inflexible justice; it is therefore an emanation of virtue."[49]

It is true that justice and freedom may be fought for and won in the name of utopian visions. But without realism and humility, such political movements and revolutions can never achieve their ends. They are certain to degenerate into chaos or tyranny. The Russian Revolution was a Bolshevist *coup d'état* that Lenin called "the Revolution," and his critics saw from the start that such a tiny handful of radicals could only succeed in shaping the majority through violence and terror. "Their dictatorship is not one of the laboring people, but the dictatorship of a clique. And precisely for this reason they will have to resort more and more to terroristic methods"—which they did.[50] (A close feature is what Walzer calls "the radicalism of the writing desk."[51] The further intellectuals are from military action, the more likely they are to advocate brutal war.)

James Billington concluded his magnificent study on a hopeful note, based on the demise of utopianism. He believed that "the end may be approaching of the political religion which saw in revolution the sunrise of a perfect society."[52] I am more inclined to believe that such passionate utopian faith springs eternal and will not die out so easily. Yet regardless, we must never lose the courage to speak out against evil and injustice and to stand against them. But as we speak and as we stand, we must never forget who we are. The problem of the world is me or us. Rabbi Sacks's warning is once again apt: "When humans try to be more than human, they end up less than human. Only when God is God, can we be us."[53]

THE GREATEST ENEMY OF FREEDOM IS FREEDOM

A third implication of the realism is that nothing in a world gone awry ever turns out as it was intended. Life is strewn with ironies, unintended consequences, and unforeseen aftermaths. This means that the wise must always stay humble and remain on the alert, not least in dealing with freedom. Freedom is so elemental to human life that it is not surprising that the irony of freedom is itself elemental. *The great paradox of freedom is that the greatest enemy of freedom is freedom.* No one and nothing enslaves free people as much as they enslave themselves.[54]

The repeated failure of free societies is a fact of history that can easily be demonstrated. Freedom commonly fails when it runs to excess and breeds permissiveness and license. Or again, freedom fails when people who love freedom so long to be safe and secure that their love of security undermines their freedom. Or yet again, freedom fails when free societies become so caught up in the glory of freedom that they justify anything and everything done in its name, including things that quite clearly contradict freedom—such as the abuse of others.

But what is behind these failures and the paradox itself? One reason is political. As Exodus demonstrates and the French philosopher Montesquieu later elaborated, freedom requires both the *structures* of freedom, such as the covenant/constitution and laws, and the *spirit* of freedom. But the tendency, alas, is to rely on the former and to forget the latter and so to lose both. Freedom cannot keep itself alive. It is not self-sustaining.

Another reason for the paradox is ethical. Freedom requires order and therefore restraint, yet the restraint that is most appropriate to freedom is self-restraint—Burke's "chains on the appetites" and Lord Moulton's "obedience to the unenforceable"—but this self-restraint is the very thing that freedom undermines when it flourishes.[55]

Yet another reason for the paradox is spiritual and psychological. Freedom means and requires responsibility, but the responsibility of freedom can be a burden and even cause suffering. At some point, down in the dark labyrinths where we humans rationalize our evasions of responsibility, things become twisted. People who desire to evade responsibility get to the point where there appears to be tyranny in freedom, because of its responsibility, and freedom in tyranny, because there is no responsibility required, only dependency. *The result grows into a fear of freedom that ends in a desire for freedom from freedom.*

Erich Fromm's *Escape from Freedom* is a classic modern discussion of the paradox of freedom, but the realism in the Hebrew and Christian Scriptures long predates the modern analysis. There are three major examples in the Bible. First and most remarkably is the fate of the Pharaoh himself. Such was the hierarchical power structure of Egypt that Pharaoh was the freest man in all the land, if not in the entire world of his time. Such too was the inequality between the status of Pharaoh and the status of Moses that there was no question which of the two contestants had greater power and freedom. Yet Exodus is the story of how the freest man in the whole world came to rule over everybody but himself and so became a slave.

As Rabbi Sacks points out, "evil has two faces." The first is turned to the outside world, in terms of what it does to the victim. "The second—turned within—is what it does to its perpetrator. Evil traps the evildoer in its mesh. Slowly but surely he or she loses freedom and becomes not evil's master but its slave."[56] Thus as Pharaoh stubbornly refused the request for freedom, hardening his heart each time, the stubbornness hardened into an obsession that became irrational and self-destructive. Eventually, even his advisers counseled him to let Israel go ("Do you not realize that Egypt is destroyed?" [Ex 10:7]), but he adamantly refused. He was no longer free and thinking clearly. His stubbornness had become an obsession and his obsession slavery. "It was not the Hebrews but he who was the real slave: to his obstinate insistence that he, not God, ruled history."[57]

"Pharaoh is every man writ large," Sacks concludes.[58] Freedom is not a matter of either-or but of more or less. There are degrees of freedom and degrees in losing freedom too. Free people can truly become free, exert their freedom over others, and trumpet their own freedom, yet in failing to rule over themselves they can still become slaves to their own chosen ideas (obsessions) and their own chosen behavior (addictions).

The second example of the paradox was the chronic grumbling and ingratitude of the Israelites as soon as they were liberated. Once the waters of the Red Sea had closed over the Egyptian horses and chariots, the Israelites were genuinely free. God had rescued them, and they were out from under Pharaoh's control. But were they fully free? Clearly, they were and they weren't—as they betrayed in their infamous three Gs: their *grumblings* (and the ten incidents of complaints that mirror the ten plagues), their *going back* (or the repeated threats to do so), and the other *gods* they lapsed into worshiping (and in particular the golden calf of the Egyptian bull-god Apis).

Walzer calls this effect the "attraction-revulsion" principle of freedom and slavery. After a lifetime in the most advanced and prosperous nation of their day, the Israelites were more attracted to the world and lifestyle of Egypt than they admitted to themselves. It was one thing to be set free and another to live free. Liberation is the beginning of liberty, but liberty is deeper and more demanding than liberation. Personal and social transformation takes longer than revolution. As the Jewish sages noted wryly, it took God one day to take the Israelites out of Egypt, but forty years and counting to take Egypt out of the Israelites.

The third and most troubling example of the paradox of freedom comes much later in the Hebrew Scriptures. It concerned the building of the temple by King Solomon. Nearly five hundred years after the exodus, Israel had entered the Promised Land, had grown rapidly in power and prosperity, so that the building of the temple represented both a completion and a closure. Yet the wording of the account is strewn with red flags. The construction of the tabernacle was voluntary, whereas the construction of the temple was compulsory. Words used in Exodus to describe the harsh work and the cruel overseers in Egypt were now used to describe the building of the new temple. The fault line that was soon to split the nation apart was beginning to show. "Why?" Rabbi Sacks asks. "Because Solomon in effect turned the Israelites into a conscripted labor force: the very thing they had left Egypt to avoid."[59] Solomon had become a second Pharaoh and Israel a second Egypt.

The warning in the paradox sounds out again. Rabbi Sacks minces no words.

The Temple was intended to stand at the heart, geographical and spiritual, of a nation that had been taken by God from slavery to freedom. The faith of Israel therefore had to be an expression of liberty. Its Temple should have been built out of voluntary contributions, just as was the Tabernacle. This was no minor detail. It lay at the very heart of the project itself. Faith, coerced, is not faith. Worship, forced, is not true worship. A Temple built by conscripted labor conflicts with the very nature of God to whom it is dedicated. For a moment, Solomon acted as if he were an Egyptian Pharaoh, not a king of Israel, and the pent-up frustration and anger of the people eventually exploded after his death, splitting the nation into two.[60]

A PARADOX WITHIN THE PARADOX

Dare I point out that there is a paradox within the paradox? Those who respond to the paradox falsely only prove the paradox all the more forcefully. The lesson of the paradox is that freedom is a rare achievement and thus essentially—and properly—human freedom is always insecure. No individual and no nation can ever be entirely secure and danger proof. Freedom, like life, is vulnerable. It depends on the fire of freedom being passed on from heart to heart and generation to generation and with eternal vigilance. Thus to counter the paradox by attempting to guarantee freedom's permanence and security by the wrong means is a false response that only proves the paradox. What Rabbi Sacks calls "immortality projects" that are a bid for permanence, such as armies, walls, and monuments, never work.[61] Whether Pharaoh's pyramids, China's Great Wall, Solomon's temple, Rome's triumphal arches, or Napoleon's Grand Armée, such titanic bids for invulnerability and immortality deliver neither. Confusing freedom with power, they end as monuments to the paradox and demonstrations of the fate of Shelley's "Ozymandias." Free people must thrive on the risk and daring of sustaining freedom as freedom requires.

Is it too late for the United States and the Western world to stop and think? For all who claim to love freedom, there is nothing more urgent for free people at the height of their power and prosperity than to ponder the paradox of freedom. American self-congratulation is almost boundless today, and the farewell address by American presidents has become an occasion for the last self-hurrah by the departing leader. They are bidding for their place on the Mount Rushmore of history. Nothing could be further from the burden of Moses' farewell address. The real test of freedom and greatness is power plus prosperity plus time. In Rabbi Sacks's summary, "The real trial, he said, was not in the past but in the future, not in the desert but in the Promised Land. The greatest challenge to faith would not be poverty but affluence, not slavery but freedom, not exile but home. People who believe they have arrived become complacent, self-satisfied, self-congratulatory, and that is the beginning of the end of national greatness."[62]

Freedom is still the greatest enemy of freedom. Failure to take seriously the paradox of freedom has always been a sure road to becoming its eventual victim, but the advanced modern world has added a sting in the tail to the paradox. Until the eighteenth century the West was shaped by ideas that came from either the classical ideals of Greece and Rome or from the Hebrew and Christian Scriptures. People who loved freedom in the West therefore faced a straightforward choice over freedom—either to control themselves and so to live as they knew they ought, according to truth, character, and the way of life that freedom requires or to live as they pleased and let their desires and passions control them.

As this choice was presented for two thousand years, desires and passions were the chief menaces to freedom, and both the classical and the Jewish and Christian accounts advised people unashamedly how to deal with the desires and passions in order to sustain freedom.

The combined influence of the Enlightenment and modernity has changed this situation and tipped the scale toward the paradox in two ways. According to the sexual revolution and other secular philosophies of freedom, desires and passions are no longer the problem but the goal. Freedom, as they see it, is the freedom to pursue desires and passions wherever they lead. But this cultural revolution has come with a steep but hidden price. In the post-Christian age the bonds once provided by faith and ethics must now come from elsewhere, and the search is on for social control by whatever means.

Through the influence of Weishaupt's Illuminism on revolution in the eighteenth century ("Know everything in order to control everyone"), and the rise of the internet, Google, and Facebook in our own time, the new freedoms come at the price of new controls. Companies in the West (and governments in other parts of the world) collect more and more of the comprehensive data (total data) of our desires, our passions, our habits, and our buying habits, which allows them to influence and control our desires, passions, and habits. Those who control the commercial stimuli control the consuming stimulated. Once again, freedom without bounds is pulling us toward control without bounds, and the paradox of freedom is harder to sidestep than ever.

America cannot endure permanently half 1776 and half 1789. The compromises, contradictions, hypocrisies, inequities, and evils have built up unaddressed. The grapes of wrath have ripened again, and the choice before America is plain. Either America goes forward best by going back first, or America is about to reap a future in which the worst will once again be the corruption of the best.

4

LET MY PEOPLE GO

THE GREAT LIBERATION

PRINCIPLE 4: FREEDOM MUST BE WON

None of us are as free, as good, or as profoundly transformed as we think we are. When the American Declaration of Independence was published in 1776 as a fanfare for freedom, the English essayist Samuel Johnson famously mocked its pretensions in words that haunt America today. He was an arch-Tory, but he could recognize hypocrisy an ocean away. "How is it that we hear the loudest yelps for liberty among the drivers of Negroes?"[1] A century later, Henry David Thoreau was equally unsparing, though writing as an American. "Do we call this the land of the free?" he wrote in his *Journal*, "What is it to be free from King George the Fourth and continue slaves to prejudice? What is it to be born free and equal and not live? What is the value of any political freedom, but as a means to moral freedom?"[2] After all, as he wrote in *Walden* later, "It is hard to have a southern overseer; it is worse to have a northern one; but worst of all when you are the slave-driver of yourself."[3]

What is true of individual freedom and change is true too of revolution. Few revolutions are as revolutionary as their revolutionaries think. There are simply too many flaws and faults in the theory and practice of revolution. Originally, the term *revolution* was scientific. It described the motion of something circling until it came back to the place it started from. For those who followed Ptolemy, revolution was the motion of the sun going around the earth, whereas for Copernicus and most people today, it is the motion of the earth going around the sun. Thus today's more common political use of the term represents a double shift. First, revolution generally moved in common use from science to politics. Second, it moved from a sense of "eternal recurrence," through which things always came back to where they started, to the goal of decisive transformation, through which revolution means a breakthrough to a completely new and improved situation.

But in truth, the words *revolution* and *revolutionary* are widely abused and overused. Change in human nature and human societies is far more challenging and takes far longer than most people realize. Which means that social and political revolutions are rarely as complete a turning of the wheel as their partisans believe. For a start, rhetoric and protest are one thing; revolution is another. There are far more political *springs* than *summers* and far more so-called revolutions than successful revolutions. Revolutions that truly overturn governments with lasting improvements are rare. The sluggish inertia of human nature, the seeming immovability of a status quo, or the power of an authoritarian government can each prove more of a dead weight than most political movements can move. Then too, a coup d'état is not a revolution; it changes the government only and not the society.

Even "successful" revolutions are rarely as successful as their revolutionaries hope. For one thing, many revolutions are built on faulty assessments of human nature, often with flawed, utopian notions of human potential and perfectibility. For another thing, new governments often carry forward more of the old regimes than they like to admit. Napoleon Bonaparte was twice as dictatorial as Louis XVI, Comrade Lenin and Comrade Stalin were far more brutal than most Russian czars, and Chairman Mao was more autocratic and murderous to his own people than the worst of emperors from any Chinese dynasty. The recurring revolutionary longing for "total revolution" or "complete revolution" is a telltale symptom of all the unfulfilled and stillborn hopes left over from earlier dreams of revolution.

Those who are naive about human nature will find themselves disappointed again and again. Change, revolution, and transformation are much harder than many people realize. Rabbi Sacks summarizes the need for realism: "Revolutions, protests, and civil wars still take place, encouraging people to think that removing a tyrant or having a democratic election will end corruption, create freedom, and lead to justice and the rule of law—and still people are surprised and disappointed when it does not happen. All that happens is a change of faces in the corridors of power."[4]

PEERLESS BUT NOT PERFECT

The Exodus revolution stands alone in history as the superlative revolution, not perfect but peerless, including the fact that it does not romanticize its leaders. The festival of Passover, which celebrates the exodus, is the favorite festival for Jews, but it carries immense significance for every last man, woman, and child on the earth. Not only is its vision of freedom deeper and more comprehensive than any other, but its portrayal of the errors and shortcomings of the leading players is realistic and never airbrushed. The book of Exodus is therefore a classic that beggars the power of language to describe it. It is one of the most powerful stories of all time. It is one of the greatest turning points in human history. It is an archetypal saga of a journey that far transcends Homer's *Odyssey* and Virgil's *Iliad* and differs completely from more individual journeys such as Miguel Cervantes's *Don Quixote,* John Bunyan's *Pilgrim's Progress*, and Herman Hesse's *Siddhartha*.

Exodus is history's supreme precedent and pattern for revolutionary change and therefore for hope and the very notion of possibility. After the exodus, as Rabbi Sacks notes, the world has never been the same. The contagion of freedom has been released. Everything can now always be other than it is, what happened once in the exodus can happen again, and nothing need ever stay as it is. History has been put on notice. Chance, necessity, and fate have all been given their comeuppance. Nothing is inevitable. Nothing is beyond challenge. Everything can be overturned. A great civilization that measured its permanence in millennia and symbolized its achievements in monuments that are the wonders of the world had been overcome. The untroubled sleep of Pharaoh and all the tyrants of history has been disturbed forever.

In Rabbi Sacks's summary,

> No story has been more influential in shaping the inner landscape of liberty, teaching successive generations that oppression is not inevitable, that it is not woven into the fabric of history. There can be another place, another kind of society, a different way of living. What happened once can happen again for those who have faith in the God who had faith in humankind. The God of freedom calls on us to be free.[5]

If the French Revolution trumpets its claim to be "the great revolution," the exodus stands forever as the great liberation, the greatest large-scale liberation of all time. Under God, the impossible is now always possible. Freedom and justice can prevail over oppression. In short, "No story has had greater influence in inspiring revolution or evolution toward a just and humane society. It is the West's great meta-narrative of liberty."[6]

As a matter of plain historical fact, certain people in slavery were freed from a certain ruler in a certain society on a certain date in time.[7] But as a matter of precedent, principle, and possibility, the power of exodus is even more revolutionary, and it has resounded down through history ever after. The absolutely powerless found a champion who liberated them from the supreme power of their day and from one of the longest-lasting powers in all history—and liberated them not just for their own sake but for the sake of humanity itself. Freedom is once again abroad on the earth.

The old truth may continue: power destroys the powerless and the powerful alike, oppressing the one and corrupting the other. But Exodus not only models freedom, it has also launched a successful and sustained critique of the abuse of power that continues to this day. Contrary to the dictators of history and the apostles of postmodernism, power is no longer self-evident and self-justifying. Might no longer means right. Exodus has called into question both oppression and the abuse of power. The world need no longer carry on as before.

No account of any revolution is less romanticized, yet the Exodus Revolution still stands as the most revolutionary revolution in history, as well as the most positive and influential. The liberation at the heart of Exodus is the ultimate revolution, just as its vision remains the deepest and most comprehensive pattern for freedom. The exodus rescue of the Hebrew people from bondage and brutal oppression is a great liberation that teaches more about personal and political freedom than any other event or text in history. To dismiss the exodus as a mere "slave revolt in morals," as Nietzsche did in his *Genealogy of Morals*, or diminish it to being simply the forerunner of anyone's personal salvation, as many religious believers do, is a folly that humanity cannot afford.[8] The exodus, as its influence has played out in history, is truly the master story of human freedom and the Magna Carta of humanity.

GOD VERSUS THE GODS

The main contours of the book of Exodus are well known. The Hebrews, who centuries later were to call themselves Jews, went down to Egypt numbering only seventy people and returned 600,000 men strong, not counting their wives and children. They moved from being an insignificant family of tribes to being a nation that would grow into world-historic significance, from being a tiny minority in a surrounding sea of paganism to being the bearers of the world's most powerful religious truth, and above all, from being a people oppressed in abject slavery to being the exemplars of the mightiest vision of freedom ever outlined. And their story goes from a saga of family relations to a chronicle of the politics of a nation and the emergence of a new type of national leader. Exodus is a gigantic milestone for the Jewish people, for the entire Abrahamic family of faiths, and for humanity.

But what are the major themes of Exodus? Beyond all doubt, the first, last, and central theme is the sovereign freedom of God, the one who frees his people from slavery under one of the most powerful civilizations of all time. *A free God frees his people to worship him freely and to live before him freely with each other.* At one level the protagonists in the conflict are obvious—Moses and Pharaoh. For all who have watched the epic films of Cecil B. DeMille, Charlton Heston as Moses and Yul Brynner as Pharaoh will always stride across the screen and the imagination. But for all their salience in the films, Moses and Pharaoh are only small players in the story of Exodus. The central protagonists are not Moses and Pharaoh but God and the gods of Egypt.

To describe the conflict as a contest between *monotheism* and *polytheism* does not capture its significance, for those words are only abstractions. In reality, the Lord, who revealed himself to Moses as the great "I am who I am," the One who "will be who he will be," was in a titanic showdown with the gods of Egypt, whether Ra, the sun god or any other god, including the god of the River Nile. Exodus stands as the ultimate story of freedom because it turns on the ultimate conflict over power—the contest between the power of God and the power of the gods of Egypt.

Needless to say, supernatural power is at the heart of the contest. As countless sermons, lessons, and bedtime stories will attest, no account of the exodus can afford to ignore the dramatic miracles that punctuated the conflict—the mounting pressure of the ten plagues, the last-minute rescue through the parting of the Red Sea, the timely uncorking of water from a desert rock, and the daily provision of bread-like manna in the wilderness. But as the Jews have always argued, extraordinary though they are, the miracles are secondary. What is primary is God and the character of God as revealed through his power in liberating action.

In the pagan world, polytheism, territoriality, finiteness, and limitation went hand in hand. There were many gods, and each had their place and importance. In essence they were human projections of this or that finite force in the universe—the sun, the moon, the stars, the river, the thunderstorm, the harvest, and so on. As projections of the forces of nature and therefore of the finite world, they were necessarily limited by definition. The Nile was not the sun, and the god of the Nile was not the god of the sun. In the same way, it was held that the gods of the nations were unique to those nations and therefore limited. The gods of Egypt were not the same as the gods of Assyria, Babylon, or Persia. Pharaoh expresses this conventional view perfectly when Moses cried, "Let my people go," and Pharaoh replied, "Who is the LORD that I should obey His voice to let Israel go? I do not know the LORD, and besides, I will not let Israel go" (Ex 5:2). The gods of Egypt were the gods *in* Egypt and the sole gods in Egypt. The Pharaoh neither knew nor acknowledged any other gods but Egyptian gods within the borders of Egypt.

But Pharaoh, quite simply, did not know the Lord God, so he did not know who he was up against. YHWH, the God who spoke at Sinai, is quite different from all other gods. He is God, and not one more god among the gods. He who says, "I am who I am," is not one force of nature among many. He is not even the supreme sum of all the forces of nature, as Nature, Being, or Existence. He is transcendent, the creator of it all, the earth, humanity, and the very cosmos itself. As such, YHWH, the living God, is both singular and sovereign. Sovereignty means freedom, and freedom means sovereignty. He therefore rules over all. He is not limited by territory. He is God of everyone and anyone, and the Lord of "anywhere and everywhere."[9] When God stretches out his hand over Egypt and frees his people from Egypt, "The Egyptians shall know that I am the LORD" (Ex 7:5). That disclosure of who God is, and that demonstration of what God can do, is at the heart of Exodus. Later, for all who sign on to be the people of God, it is unthinkable to hold any conviction except "There is no god but God." As Exodus recounts the story, that truth was signed and sealed for Moses at Sinai and then for the entire people of God at Sinai.

Familiarity can once again breed inattention, and I for one never read the story of Exodus without reminding myself of the awesome power, wealth, and seeming permanence of imperial Egypt. All who marvel at the golden splendor and extravagance of King Tutankhamun and his treasures should remember that he was a young, short-lived, and minor Pharaoh as the rulers of Egypt go. The greatness and glory of Ramses II, for example, boggles the imagination. His self-celebrations and immortality projects outstrip the greatest egotists and narcissists in history. Few human beings can have been so full of themselves and with such solid grounds for believing so. As for the Great Pyramid at Giza, it is the last and greatest of the seven wonders of the ancient world. It had already stood for a thousand years before Moses stood before it. For nearly four thousand years it was the tallest manmade structure on the earth—until surpassed by Lincoln Cathedral and then the Eiffel Tower. Constructed with more than two million stones, each weighing at least one or two tons, some weighing sixty tons, and all built in twenty years and before the invention of the wheel, the Pyramid of Khufu expresses the power and permanence of a civilization that none would dare defy from within.

Yet God defied and defeated the might of Egypt, rescuing his powerless people from the hand of the greatest power of that day and perhaps any day. That, of course, was the significance of the contest over the ten plagues. Each one was commanded by God and used to address a particular point in the pantheon of Egyptian beliefs, thereby demonstrating the superior power of God. That contrast between God and the gods is crystal clear by the third plague, the infestation of lice. With the first two plagues, Pharaoh's magicians were able to match what Moses did—though not quite. As Rabbi Sacks observes, they were so intent on copying Moses that they failed to notice the irony in what they were doing. Moses produced blood in the Nile and then frogs on the land, and they too were able to produce blood in the Nile and frogs on the land. But in adding to the blood and the frogs, they were doing Moses' work for him and making the problem worse, not better.

The satire and the humor grew clearer with the third plague. As Sacks notes, Egypt was the epitome of the massive, the vast, the monumental, the splendid, the solidly grand, and the apparently permanent. Yet what defeats them is the smallest and most miserable of creatures, a louse, a gnat, or perhaps a mosquito. For all the brilliance of the Egyptian magic arts, for all their vaunted expertise in controlling the forces of nature, Pharaoh's elite magicians and supersorcerers could not produce a wretched louse, a humble gnat, or a pesky mosquito. They were beaten, and they admit to Pharaoh, "This is the finger of God" (Ex 8:19). The magic arts in the ancient world were what science and technology are in the modern world, but the best of their Egyptian science and technology had come up short. The experts of Egypt had met their comeuppance in a louse. The master magicians of Memphis had been defeated by a mosquito.

Sacks points out two things during the third plague that are different sides of the same coin and evident at this early turning point in the contest between God and the gods. First, the magicians' failure highlights the Bible's use of humor to mock the pretensions of humans who think they can play God and rival God through their creations—then and now. "One thing makes God laugh—the sight of humanity attempting to defy heaven."[10] The Egyptians can build pyramids that last thousands of years and create objects of such magnificent beauty that centuries later people will queue for hours to marvel at them in exhibitions, but they cannot create a louse or a gnat.

Second, the magicians' excuse to Pharaoh demonstrates the wrong way to respond to human ignorance or impotence. Their argument is the first-known example of the "god of the gaps." "It is the finger of God," they say, when they admit they are stuck. They attribute something to God simply because they cannot explain it or do it themselves. But as Sacks notes, that puts science and religion at loggerheads and risks diminishing faith as science is able to explain more and more of the world. "The more we can explain scientifically or control technologically, the less need we have for faith. As the scope of science expands, the place of God progressively diminishes to vanishing point."[11] What the Torah is saying, Sacks continues, is that this is a pagan way of thinking. The God of the Bible, as Francis Bacon and others have put it, reveals himself through two books and not just one: the book of nature and the book of revelation. He is the God of the natural as well as the supernatural. A *miracle* is not a stopgap explanation of the so-far inexplicable. God is in the ordinary and the extraordinary, the everyday as well as the absolutely singular.

Exodus is unquestionably a gigantic and calculated affront to Pharaoh and all the strutting captains of war and masters of the universe and thus to human hubris. Sacks concludes,

> Technological prowess has led human beings, time and again, to believe they are like gods. They could scale the heavens, bend nature to their purposes, and construct vast edifices to their glory. Yet in their wake they left a trail of devastation, and the civilizations they built declined and died, to be remembered only in relics and ruins. Humility is the only antidote to hubris. However great we are, we are small in the scheme of things. That is what God showed the Egyptians in the plague of lice.[12]

PARTNERS IN THE ULTIMATE PROJECT

The sovereign freedom of God is the first and last lesson of the exodus, so it is natural to focus on the signs and wonders as the demonstration of God's power over against the gods of Egypt. But while Exodus is all about God, the supernatural, and miracles, it is also a story of human responsibility. Here is the balance to the stress on God's sovereignty. To let God be God does not excuse humans from their responsibility as they are invited to become partners with God in the great venture of freedom.

To be sure, the supernatural power (and grace, mercy, and compassion) of God is prominent and indispensable in Exodus. The English word *exodus* comes from the Latin that translated the Greek word *exodos*, which meant "going out" or "departure." Such migrations were not uncommon at the time, but they depended entirely on the goodwill of the nation from which people wished to vote with their feet and leave. To leave imperial Egypt against the will of the Pharaoh was unthinkable. To escape from the Nile Delta and the might of the Egyptian army at the height of its power was beyond a mere human challenge. No ordinary protest would have made a dent on the status quo of any dynasty, let alone prove strong enough to secure the release of a million slaves from forced labor on the vast royal building sites. Egypt at the zenith of its power could not be overcome from within. The complete failure of Moses' early attempt to take justice into his own hands shows the fate of all would-be liberators. Even when the Israelites followed God's commands, the situation had initially grown worse.

Only the sovereign freedom and power of God were able to liberate Israel successfully from the power of Egypt, and such decisive supernatural power is needed today when people require genuine liberation from oppressions and addictions. But that said, the Exodus account carries a subtheme too. It contains what Rabbi Sacks calls "double narratives"—two battles (before and after the Red Sea), two sets of stone tablets (one written on by God and one by Moses), two announcements of the covenant (first by God and then by Moses), two accounts of the construction of the tabernacle (before and after the incident of the golden calf), and so on.[13] "*In each case,*" Sacks notes, "*the first is the work of God alone, while the second involves a human contribution.*"[14]

The significance of this point will be clearer in chapter five, but it enters here as an advance lesson in the Bible's insistence on both God's sovereignty and human significance, on human responsibility as well as divine initiative. The exodus pays the supreme tribute to the sovereignty and power of God. As Moses reminds the people a generation later, "Has a god tried to go to take for himself a nation from within another nation by trials, by signs and wonders . . . as the LORD your God did for you in Egypt before your eyes?" (Deut 4:34). The answer, of course, is no, yet at the same time numerous individuals play a vital role in the exodus. In Sacks's words,

> That is the ultimate significance of the politics of covenant, born at Mount Sinai. More than any other type of politics, covenant makes demands of its citizens. A covenantal society is one in which everyone has responsibilities as well as rights, in which everyone is expected to study the law as well as keep it, in which parents are duty bound to tell the story of freedom to their children; in which we are collectively as well as individually responsible for the common good.[15]

NO REVOLUTION WITHOUT A PRICE

To be sure, God is supreme, sovereign, and all-decisive in the story of Exodus. Without the intervention of God, there would have been no exodus, no deliverance, and no revolution, and it is God's victory that lifts the exodus to be the paean to freedom that it is—as Moses and Miriam were quick to acknowledge after the miracle at the Red Sea ("Sing to the LORD, for He is highly exalted; / The horse and his rider he has hurled into the sea" [Ex 15:21]). Almost cheekily, the Israelites hailed how God had rescued his people with an outstretched arm or a strong hand (Ex 3:19-20, 6:1) knowing full well that the Pharaohs routinely titled themselves "Lords of the strong arm."

New Kingdom pharaohs celebrated their victories in stone, in massive monuments to themselves, whereas the Israelites celebrated in song, not stone, and they sang to God their deliverer. But to focus only on God's part in the story leaves the account lopsided in another way too. Triumphalism is misguided. Along with the responsibility of human actors, a further key factor is the cost of the deliverance. The truth is that every revolution—the English, the American, the French, the Russian, and the Chinese too—has a price in blood that has been paid and must be counted, and that is true too of Exodus.

The cost of the exodus has to be measured against at least four things: the power of imperial Egypt that had to be confronted, the depth of the Israelite degradation in slavery that had to be remedied, the strength of the stubbornness with which the Pharaoh opposed their demands for freedom, and the severity of the judgment Pharaoh called down on his own head in resisting God's calls for freedom and justice. The Egyptians paid a heavy price for enslaving Israel and for the irrational stubbornness of their Pharaoh.

We have observed the first two factors already. Imperial Egypt was one of the mightiest powers in human history, and the pitiful cry of the Hebrew slaves was the trigger for God's moving into action to deliver his people. But the third and fourth factors grew more prominent as the contest continued and the plagues accumulated, and up until the last plague it was the people and not Pharaoh who paid for his policies. After each of the first five plagues, we read that Pharaoh stubbornly refused Moses' demands, and there are variations on the comment that followed, "Pharaoh hardened his heart" (Ex 8:32). Which means too that in Pharaoh's pride, he thought only of himself and left the Egyptian people to face the consequences of his decisions. But from the sixth plague on, as Pharaoh grew even more recalcitrant, to the point of rejecting the urgent counsel of his advisers, the text says, "The LORD hardened Pharaoh's heart" (Ex 10:27).

Was God's intervention unfair? Was God usurping Pharaoh's freedom? Earlier, God had simply respected Pharaoh's freedom. Each of Pharaoh's choices had consequences, and God had left him to the logic of his own choices—even though his choices were bringing down consequences, in the form of plagues and judgments, onto his people, and thus to some extent on his own head as their ruler. But as Pharaoh chose to be even more willfully stubborn, there was a change. God did not simply *leave* Pharaoh to the logic of his choices, he *drove* Pharaoh to the logic of his settled choices—as a stronger and stronger form of judgment as the consequence of his choices.

Finally, Pharaoh in his stubbornness was standing alone. He had resisted God, he had resisted Moses, and he had resisted the urgent appeal of his advisers. "Let the men go. . . . Do you not realize that Egypt is destroyed?" (Ex 10:7). At that point God's judgment became a full-blown "measure for measure" with a supreme and sobering cost to Pharaoh and his subjects. God's repeated requests to "Let my people go" were summed up most forthrightly yet poignantly in the words "Israel is My son, My firstborn. So I said to you, 'Let My son go that he may serve Me;' but you have refused to let him go" (Ex 4:22-23). Pharaoh refused to surrender God's firstborn, and God replied in kind. "Behold I will kill your son, your firstborn" (v. 23).

After the three plagues that touched on the waters and the creatures around them, three that touched people directly, and three that were airborne, the tenth and last plague was the most terrible of all. The killing of the firstborn, from the royal family down, brought Pharaoh and all Egypt to their knees and opened the door for the Israelites to leave. But even then deliverance was carried out only through the solemn and enduring action of the Passover. The angel of death struck down the firstborn across Egypt, from the richest palace to the humblest hut, but passed over the homes of all whose doors were marked by the blood of sacrificed lambs. From Moses through Marx to Mao Zedong, there must be no romanticizing of revolution. There is always a cost, a steep, steep cost. Great injustices require great redress, and only heaven's scales of justice can weigh the price of the redress. The innocent suffer along with the guilty, ordinary people along with their leaders, and they suffer because of the decisions of their guilty leaders. Only God, and to some extent later history, can gauge the suffering and the justice and estimate the worthwhileness of the price that was paid.

A PRECEDENT AND A PATTERN

The implications of the great liberation of Exodus are boundless. Exodus was the birth of the Jewish people as a nation, and it has been the fountainhead of personal and political freedom for more individuals, more movements, and more revolutions than any other precedent in history. The debts owed to the inspiration of Exodus are countless and unpayable. Among the most famous and influential are the Swiss, Dutch, Scottish, and English reformations. Oliver Cromwell declared that Exodus was the direct parallel to what he was trying to do in the English Civil War. It is behind Governor Bradford's Mayflower Compact as well as John Winthrop's "Modell of Christian charity" on the Arbella. It was a key theme in the dynamism of Puritan New England, and both Benjamin Franklin and Thomas Jefferson proposed to use it for the Great Seal of the United. African American spirituals, such as "Go down Moses," have resonated with its themes, as did the stirring speeches and sermons of the civil rights movement. Moses' great demand to Pharaoh, "Let my people go," has been echoed in a thousand protests. And the Jubilee cry, "Proclaim liberty throughout the land to all the inhabitants" (Lev 25:10 NIV) has been stamped on bells, stamps, rifles, and whatever symbols were cherished and brandished in countless fights for freedom down the years.

In short, Exodus has been, still is, and will remain the leading wellspring of English-speaking freedom, of much of Western freedom itself, and increasingly in the future of freedom around the entire world.

FREEDOM OVER TIME

The central implication of Exodus, then, is it stands as a towering precedent—as a beacon for freedom, liberation, change, transformation, and hope. But two further implications should be underscored here. *The first is the understanding in Exodus that human freedom begins with freedom over time.* Intriguingly, as Rabbi Sacks points out many times, the Torah uses the same word *avoda* to describe both slavery to Pharaoh and service (and worship) to God. That surely is a hostage to fortune. God's service, the skeptic will say, is no less slavery than bondage in Egypt. All that has changed is a shift from one master to another master. It is not real freedom.

Not so, the Bible answers. Service to God is service that (in the words of Archbishop Cranmer's Book of Common Prayer) is "perfect freedom." For there is one all-important difference between the two forms of service. Rabbi Sacks quotes earlier rabbinic teaching that the difference between a slave and a free human being does not lie in how hard or long each works. "Free people often work long hours doing arduous tasks. The difference lies in who controls time. A slave works until he or she is allowed to stop. A free person decides when to begin and end. Control over time is the essential difference between slavery and freedom."[16] Needless to say, Israel had long had *Shabbat* as a day of rest and recreation in its week. Now, significantly, God's first command to Israel, and one that was given while they were still in Egypt, was the command to establish their calendar and celebrate the Passover. "They were given authority over time. The first command to the Israelites was thus an essential prelude to freedom."[17] In a manner that is both a rebuke and a recommendation to our advanced modern world with its never-resting drivenness, the Israelites experienced genuine liberation when they were liberated from being time slaves.

CHANGE TAKES TIME, NOT FORCE

A second implication of Exodus also involves an understanding of time. *Liberation may take no more than a moment, but freedom is a way of life that takes longer and requires patience and persistence.* However fast or slow liberation is, change in human nature must respect the nature of freedom, which means that it requires time—and failure to understand this principle leads to violence. This can be seen in the famous diversion through which God led his people to the Promised Land by an indirect route.

> Now when Pharaoh let the people go, God did not lead them by the way of the land of the Philistines, although it was near, for God said, "The people may have a change of heart when they see war, and return to Egypt." Hence God led the people around by the way of the wilderness to the Red Sea. (Ex 13:17-18)

Behind this diversion lies God's knowledge of the condition of his people after their liberation and his refusal to accelerate change through force or violence. There were things they needed to do for themselves, and God would not do for them. Rabbi Sacks states the point behind the diversion incident with daring. "In creating humanity, God, as it were, placed Himself under a statute of self limitation."[18] This principle is the counterbalance to the emphasis on the sovereignty and power of God in Exodus. Without God's sovereignty, there would have been no exodus. In the great era of the Pharaohs, no power on earth was greater than the power of the Pharaohs, Ramses II supremely. The contest had to be what it was: God against the gods. And of course, God's power won. Yet astonishingly, the Exodus account gives a fuller picture than that. It balances its stress on the sovereignty of God with a principle that is vital for a biblical understanding of human nature and change and therefore of politics and revolution. This principle is critically different from the views of change and revolution in today's secular accounts.

Once again, according to the Bible, God respects the freedom of humans made in his image, and this time in the arena of human change. Following Maimonides, Sacks notes that change in nature is always slow. There is "no such thing as sudden, drastic, revolutionary change in the world we inhabit. Trees take time to grow. The seasons change imperceptibly into one another. Day fades into night. Processes take time, and there are no shortcuts."[19] He then goes on to assert that what is true of nature is all the more true of human nature. Humans develop slowly and change slowly. Total change and fast change too often lead to violent change. But this raises a deep and obvious question, When God wants humans to change, does God circumvent human nature?

Maimonides's and Sacks's answer is radical, in that it goes to the root of freedom. "God sometimes intervenes to change nature. We call these interventions miracles. But God never intervenes to change human nature. To do so would be to compromise human free will. That is something God, on principle, never does."[20] God respects the human heart and never invades human freedom.

> Wisdom is not wisdom if it is coerced. Virtue is not virtue if we are compelled by inner or outer forces over which we have no control. . . . He could not force the pace of the moral development of mankind without destroying the very thing He had created. . . . He gave humanity the freedom to grow. But that inevitably meant that change in the affairs of mankind would be slow.[21]

True freedom is Lord Moulton's "obedience to the unenforceable" and Tocqueville's "habits of the heart."

Does that point sound purely theoretical? It is anything but. As Sacks notes, it demonstrates the foundational difference between change and revolution according to the Hebrew Bible (and therefore the revolutions of 1642 and 1776) and change and revolution according to secular philosophy, whether Rousseau's or Marx's (and the revolutions of 1789, 1917, and 1949). The former respected the importance of time and human responsibility in political change and therefore tolerated slow transformation, whereas the latter did not, and there relied on violence and social engineering to enforce change. "Political change can be rapid. Changing human nature is very slow indeed. It takes generations, even centuries and millennia."[22] The revolutionary violence of the twentieth century was morally disastrous, and the source of the disaster lies in a flawed view of human freedom and change.

America cannot endure permanently half 1776 and half 1789. The compromises, contradictions, hypocrisies, inequities, and evils have built up unaddressed. The grapes of wrath have ripened again, and the choice before America is plain. Either America goes forward best by going back first, or America is about to reap a future in which the worst will once again be the corruption of the best.

5

SET FREE
TO LIVE FREE
TOGETHER

PRINCIPLE 5: FREEDOM MUST BE
ORDERED AND CULTIVATED

As the dark menace of Hitler lowered over Germany in the 1930s, Martin Buber, the eminent Jewish philosopher, became concerned for his nine- and eleven-year-old granddaughters who were living with him and his wife. He was not concerned for himself, though his own freedom to speak and publish was steadily curtailed, but the young girls were experiencing the threat differently. At their school they were no longer addressed by name, but simply as "You there," and the harshness of the changes was unsettling their world.

In response Buber wrote an article titled "Die Kinder" (The Children).

Children experience what happens and keep silent, but in the night they groan in their dreams, awaken, and stare into the darkness: The world has become unreliable. A child had a friend: the friend was taken for granted as the sunlight. Now the friend suddenly looks at him strangely, the corners of his mouth mock him: Surely you didn't imagine that I really cared about you?

A child had a teacher, a certain one among all others. He knew that this person existed, so everything was alright. Now the teacher no longer has a voice when he speaks to him. . . . What has happened? A child knows many things, but he still doesn't know how it all fits together.[1]

The urgent need, Buber argued, was for the Jews to rebuild trust for their children as a matter of spiritual resistance.

> For its spirit to grow, a child needs what is constant, what is dependable. There must be something that does not fail. The home is not enough; the world must be part of it. What has happened to this world? The familiar smile had turned into a scowl. I know nothing else but this: to make something unshakable visible in the child's world. . . . It is up to us to make the world reliable again for the children. It depends on us where we can say to them and ourselves, "Don't worry, Mother is here."[2]

HIGH TRUST, WIDE FREEDOM

Life for the Jews in Europe in the 1930s is an extreme case, but it takes an extreme case to shine a light on a truth so simple that it might otherwise be dismissed as a cliché. Character, ethics, trust, trustworthiness, faithfulness, honesty, loyalty, reliability, dependability, and predictability are all essential to both life, freedom, and free societies. By definition they have to be taken on trust to a large extent. Anyone who insists on checking out everything that they would like to trust and count on in a single day would soon find themselves paralyzed and unable to act at all. From our trust in inanimate objects (such as the chairs we sit on and the meals we eat) to institutions of all kinds (such as the post office and the police) to our relatives, friends, and colleagues, we would quickly find that trust is an inescapable requirement for daily living. Life requires trust. For anyone who wants a life, life could never be checked out constantly and continually.

Talk of trust is so basic and pious sounding that it leaves many Americans unconcerned. Too obvious to need mentioning, it is treated as irrelevant. But the fact is that due to the crisis of trust, America is unraveling and American freedom is decaying—due to a silent trio of poisons that are all deadly to trust. Philosophical cynicism destroys truth and objectivity, moral corruption undermines integrity and justice, and social collapse works its way through institutions such as the family because of the dissolving of ties and bonds. Truth and trust are dying in postmodern America, and freedom too will inevitably die.

Yet the stress on trust is only half the story. Without a certain amount of trust, we would be paralyzed, but without a certain amount of mistrust, we would be gullible and taken for a ride. In the world after the great alienation, there are lies, deceptions, and betrayals, and people we should never trust. Freedom and responsibility thrive on trust, and the wider the circle of trust, the wider the freedom that can thrive. Freedom flourishes in a high-trust society and degenerates in a low-trust society. Trusting the trustworthy is beneficial but so too is mistrusting the untrustworthy. *The integrity that is loyalty to our word is quite simply the foundation of all human relationships and the indispensable necessity for freedom and a good society.*

That of course means that we must be able to know whom we can trust, whom we should mistrust, and how to get the balance right. It means assessing people's claims, promises, commitments, and intentions, their character and their competence in being able to keep promises and keep their word. Too much mistrust and fear, suspicion, cynicism, and aversion to risk are deeply destructive, not only to trust and good relations but to freedom. Today's common insistence on transparency is understandable but naive and dangerous when taken to excess and yet another way of undermining trust and freedom. The transparency of life before the all-seeing eye of closed-circuit television is the Big Brother version of freedom that is not free. In such a world we can be trusted only when we are transparent to the camera.

Notice the influence of the fashionable philosophy of postmodernism that moves in the same direction. It is essentially uncongenial to freedom because its sole principle is power, which means that might prevails over right. But beyond that, its basic operating method is suspicion, because suspicion is the best way to protect against the power moves of others. (Hence the much-touted hermeneutics of suspicion: "nothing is ever as it appears.") The result is that postmodernism can never create anything other than a low-trust society. But the spiral then descends sharply. A culture of suspicion raises ever more demands for excessive accountability, which undermines trust all the more. Being trusted is an important key to trustworthiness. Those who cannot be trusted must be watched, constantly, so the freedom engendered by trust and trustworthiness is destroyed by the drift toward its complete opposite—the world of the excessively monitored workplace, the police state, and the growing surveillance of our hi-tech world. Studies show that employers who monitor their workers' work rate too closely have the effect of reducing their employees' work rate.[3]

The so-called Trump Derangement Syndrome of the die-hard Never Trumpers had the same effect on America. By their account, every word President Trump uttered was wrong or a lie, and every action he took was ill-conceived, bad, or had an ulterior motive. There was little benefit of the doubt or any attempt at fairness. There was only instant and automatic wholesale rejection. Even if the President had cured both cancer and Alzheimer's in a single week, his supporters said, he would still have been blamed. The result was the default position of suspicion and precaution through which calls for his impeachment even preceded his inauguration, and the suspicious were driven to the perversions of the secret FISA court and the violations of the civil liberties of American citizens.

Such attitudes are disastrous because the ability to trust our leaders and our fellow citizens, our bosses and our colleagues, is essential for a free society. This means that with a maximum of trust there can be a minimum of surveillance, so when trust breaks down, freedom shrinks. The opposite is true for authoritarian societies from the start. With the minimum of trust there has to be the maximum of surveillance. The ability to "trust" (aka control) their people is essential for totalitarian leaders and governments, which means there must be a maximum of surveillance—as with China's two billion watching cameras and its social credit system. One official document from China expressed the goal with poetic candor: to "allow the trustworthy to roam everywhere under heaven while making it hard for the discredited to take a single step."[4]

That raises a basic question for anyone concerned with living a good life and building a free society. *What sort of arrangement can create a high-trust/high trustworthy society, building and fostering trustworthiness and trust so as to expand freedom and safeguard against the corrosive effects of suspicion, mistrust, cynicism, and control?* The answer offered in Exodus, and pointed to in American history at its best, is a covenantal and constitutional commonwealth. "Order turns individuals into community," Sacks writes, "and communities into a people."[5] And covenantal order does so while all the time respecting individuality, building trust and trustworthiness, and protecting freedom.

THE SHRINKING OF THE CONSTITUTION

The truth is that the covenantal vision of Exodus holds the promise of the greatest trust, freedom, and relational richness found in any social and political system in history—but it carries requirements. If loyalty underlies all relationships at every level—loyalty to our families, our friends, our neighbors, our colleagues, and our fellow citizens—then covenant loyalty gives seriousness to loyalty and stability and endurance to relationships. For those for whom faith in God is the supreme covenant commitment and loyalty, faith in God becomes what Rabbi Heschel can call "the loyalty of all my loyalties."[6]

This deep, rich meaning of covenant, promise keeping, trustworthiness, and trust, has been lost in America today, in faith itself as well as in marriage and public life. Ironically, many nations have recently followed the precedent and prestige of the US Constitution and especially its Bill of Rights. But in an individualistic age the covenantal solidarity has been lost. And in a secular age the interpersonal and moral layers of constitutionalism have shrunk even as the shell has been copied. Constitutionalism has therefore been severed from its roots in the Hebrew covenant and cut off from such personal and moral notions as promises, promise keeping, and loyalty. Constitutionalism today is only a pale shadow of covenantalism, and what remains is little more than a legal construction that is the privileged preserve (and battleground) of lawyers and judges.

Even in America, where the Hebrew and Puritan covenant was foundational, little of the original richness of covenant remains, and the idea of *constitutional* and *unconstitutional* has been thinned to the breaking point. Then, with notions such as the "living constitution" and the postmodern idea that words are whatever anyone says they are, *constitutional* is weakened even further. Whoever has the power to say what the US Constitution means becomes a law to themselves and the rule of law as restraint is weakened. As the Trump impeachment hearings showed, *constitutional* has become a word with which any group can preen themselves when occasion serves, and *unconstitutional* has become a verbal weapon of choice to be hurled by those whose politics pays scant attention to the original constitutional system of government. Yet when neither *covenant* nor *constitution* bears much resemblance to what they were and should be, trust and freedom are the losers unless the situation is remedied.

COLLECTIVE RESPONSIBILITY, NOT GOVERNMENT

Jews live by covenants, and so does freedom. The nation of Israel is unique in that it was founded twice, as Michael Walzer points out. Israel was founded once as a family and once as a nation, but founded both times through a covenant.[7] The second founding, the national founding at Sinai, was truly revolutionary, and its originality in its time, as well as its profound influence on later history, both deserve recognition. As Sacks says, "For nowhere else do we find anything like the politics of Mount Sinai, with its radical vision of a society held together not by power but by the free consent of its citizens to be bound, individually and collectively, by a moral code and a covenant with God."[8] Standard thinking, he submits, traces freedom back to Athens, even though seventeenth-century explorations in freedom engaged not with the Greeks but with the Bible. "Hobbes quotes it 657 times in *The Leviathan* alone. Long before the Greek philosophers, and far more profoundly, at Mount Sinai the concept of a free society was born."[9] "At Sinai the politics of freedom was born."[10]

For a start, covenantalism is different from the classical understanding of politics put forward by the Greeks and the Romans. According to Plato, Aristotle, Polybius, and Cicero, politics should be classified and understood according to different types of rulers and governments. There are three major types of government—monarchy (the rule of one), aristocracy (the rule of the excellent few), and democracy (the rule of the people). Each in its turn has an ideal and a corrupt form—monarchy degenerates into tyranny, aristocracy degenerates into oligarchy, and democracy degenerates into anarchy or mob rule.

In the last generation a Jewish scholar, Daniel J. Elazar, expanded the limitations of this government-centered perspective on politics. He proposed different categories and an alternative way of understanding politics and society. He shifted the focus to look at societies rather than at governments alone and on how the societies were founded rather than simply how they were ruled. Seen this way Elazar set out three major types of societies and how they are founded.

The first type is *organic*, societies that are organically linked through blood and kinship, such as an African tribe or a Scottish clan. While natural in the past, such organic societies have been made rarer and more difficult by the conditions of modernity.

The second and main type is *hierarchical*, societies that are founded through force and conquest, such as kingdoms and empires. Again, while always natural and all too common today in the form of authoritarianism, this type of society, based on power, is always prone to become corrupt and oppressive. ("All power tends to corrupt" and so on.)

And the third type is *covenantal*, societies that are founded by a common binding agreement between the people in order to found what is essentially a republic or commonwealth—supremely the Jews, the Swiss, and the Americans.

Elazar's shift in focus sounds purely academic, but it was far more. It was significant because it highlights a vital point that was stressed later by the Jews and is still vital for America and the West today. *The form of government matters less than two other things: the collective responsibility of the people and the moral limits to the power of any authority.* As Rabbi Sacks explains, if God is sovereign and all of life is viewed and lived under God, then two things follow. First, "all human power is delegated, limited, subject to moral constraints."[11] Second, "this has nothing to do with political structures (monarchy, oligarchy, democracy—Jews have tried them all) and everything to do with collective moral responsibility. . . . God has given us freedom; it is for us to use it to create a just, generous, gracious society. God does not do it for us but He teaches us how it is done. As Moses said: The choice is ours."[12]

The idea of covenant uniquely reinforces these two points, but the form was neither new nor unique to Exodus. As historians point out, the notion of covenant formed the Hittite treaties in the ancient Near East as well as the Celtic oath societies and Alexander the Great's Hellenic League. Rabbi Sacks describes covenant as "a standard device in the politics of the ancient Near East. Essentially it was a non-aggression pact between two powers, tribes, clans or city states."[13] Such covenants were either between equal powers (parity treaties) or between a stronger power and a weaker power (suzerainty treaties). The two most famous biblical covenants prior to Exodus were God's covenant with humanity after the flood, made with Noah (Gen 6), and God's covenant with Abraham and his family (Gen 15).

THE UNIQUENESS OF SINAI

The covenant at Sinai, however, is unique. It represents the central founding event for the Jewish people, just as the life, death, and resurrection of Jesus do for Christians. Three things, Elazar argued, set the Sinai covenant apart from all other covenants of that time.

First, *God himself was a partner to the covenant.* All surrounding covenants were sworn to by their respective parties "under God" (or under their respective gods). But though the gods of the ancient world were limited and not absolute, they were absolute in their own spheres, so it was unprecedented, even unthinkable, to view any god as a covenantal partner on a level with human partners in a covenant—least of all YHWH, the God of Sinai. But at Sinai, God, the creator of the universe and the sovereign king, bound himself as a partner to the subordinate king, the people of Israel. Significantly, as we saw in discussing the *great revelation*, the notion of divine self-limitation entered at that point, and from then on it becomes a critical component in the covenantal view of freedom.

Second, the covenant was with the entire nation or people of Israel, and it was the covenant that made them a people. Other covenants covered nations in the sense that the nation as a whole came under the umbrella of the terms of the covenant, but the covenants themselves were signed only by the rulers, whether kings or tribal leaders. Moses was the leader of the Israelites, in fact their first and still their greatest leader, but he did not make the covenant with God. He only reported and relayed the terms. The account insists twice that the Exodus covenant was not made by Moses or the tribal elders but by "all the people" (Ex 19:8; 24:3). It prefigures the celebrated formulation of the American Constitution, "We the people." The covenant was not a social contract forged out of multiple expressions of self-interest. The covenant created and constituted the Jewish people, and the Jewish people were and are the Jewish people only in covenant.

The covenant at Sinai included men, women, children, and both the born and the yet to be born. In Michael Walzer's words, "The agreement is wholesale; all the people accept all the laws," and the result is "an almost democracy."[14] Strikingly, this point stands in strong contrast to most other suzerainty treaties, in stark contrast to the hierarchical and top-down governments of the rulers of Babylon and Egypt, and also in contrast to the Athenian government, whether by aristocrats or democrats. Through the emphasis on the whole people, it obviously stands in contrast to today's individualism. And through the startling emphasis on the born and the yet to be born, it also stands in contrast to the modern world's exaggerated "generationalism."

Instead of marking off each generation as absolutely unique and radically different from the previous generation (boomers, millennials, Gen Z, and so on), it builds the Jewish people into an intergenerational community across the reaches of time. It binds together the past, the present, and the future to form a living tradition that links all generations. Thus each generation is a pulse beat in the life of humanity, and no individual Jewish life is ever a purely private concern. Rabbi Heschel writes, each life "is a movement in the symphony of the ages."[15]

Third, the covenant was comprehensive and lasting. Covenants in that day were limited in that they typically covered only external relations between the parties. As with modern contracts, the aim was to make the binding agreement over a clearly limited point. But the Sinai covenant was different. Freedom was not just a moment of liberation but a way of life for a whole people and for generations to come. In Isaiah Berlin's terms, freedom was not only *negative* (freedom from) but *positive* (freedom to be or freedom for).[16] The covenant included how they worked and rested, how they farmed, what they wore, how they ran their businesses, how they treated the poor and the stranger, and how they understood time and history. It was comprehensive and lasting, and it set out an entire way of life. Indeed, the covenant was so comprehensive, lasting, and deep that it came to be viewed as the bonding of the ultimate relationship between God and his people.

AT THE HEART OF HUMANNESS

It is almost impossible to exaggerate the depth, richness, and centrality of covenant in the Hebrew and Christian Scriptures. How do we best relate to God and to each other? How do we best negotiate our deepest differences with each other so that diversity becomes a source of strength and not weakness? There is no deeper human answer than covenanting: a way of life lived through the giving and receiving of promises. *Covenanting is foundational for a triangle of relationships that are themselves foundational for a good life and a good society—first, faith in God; second, marriage between a man and a woman as the core of family life and the generator of new life and future generations; and third, membership in a community or citizenship in a nation.* What covenanting does in each case is make promises that foster trust and trustworthiness and thus freedom and responsibility. As such, covenanting is an expression of freedom rather than coercion or fate, and it empowers more freedom in return. As Rabbi Sacks notes, covenant is "the decision to make love—not power, wealth, or *force majeure*—the generative principle of life."[17] Thus, in principle, covenant can replace self-interest, power, and dominance with liberty, love, and loyalty, though only if the covenanters remain true to the promises made.

SINAI'S ENDURING CONTRIBUTION

This central point about covenanting is powerful and suggestive in itself. But growing out of it, three further points have proved momentous in shaping the social and political life of Israel and other covenantal societies down the ages. (I have explored this theme in the first chapter of an earlier book *Last Call for Liberty*, which overlaps with the next few pages.)[18]

First, *the covenant was a matter of freely chosen consent.* Three separate times the Jewish people were asked for their response, and they answered, "All that the LORD has spoken we will do," and they answered "with one voice" (Ex 19:8; 24:3, 7). In other words, the people ratified the covenant voluntarily. There are three simple words, "Here I am," which recur repeatedly in the Bible (by Abraham, Jacob, Moses, and Samuel, for example). They express the humility, willingness, and readiness of individuals who know God to follow God. But the freely chosen consent to the Sinai covenant is collective and momentous, and Rabbi Sacks underscores the profundity of what was happening. "A far-reaching principle is here articulated for the first time: *there is no legitimate government without the consent of the governed, even if the governor is creator of heaven and earth.* . . . God is not a transcendental equivalent of a Pharaoh. The commonwealth he invites the Israelites to join him in creating is not one where power rules, even the power of heaven itself."[19] From then on, as Sacks notes, the Jewish sages believed that "an agreement must be free to be binding."[20]

Jewish commentators also point out that, though the Torah contains 613 specific commands, there is no Hebrew word for *obey*. The nearest is *shema*, the word for *listen*, best translated in the old English terms *hearken*, *heed*, or *pay attention*. The meaning of *shema* emphasizes active listening. It requires the freedom and responsibility to listen, to deliberate, to decide for oneself, and then to act accordingly. There is no sense of blind obedience in the Muslim sense of Islam as "submission." The Jews were indeed bound by the law, but as Walzer underscores, they were "freely bound."[21] Their assent to the covenant was not simply a matter of power and obedience, as the Hittite vassal treaties were. Their assent and adherence was a threefold blend of obedience, gratitude for their liberation, and admiration for the laws they were accepting. ("What great nation is there that has statutes and judgments as righteous as this whole law which I am setting before you today?" [Deut 4:8].)

Importantly, Rabbi Sacks points out, the result is a *nomocracy*, the freely chosen rule of law, rather than a *theocracy*, the direct rule of God. Josephus fatefully chose the latter term when trying to explain the Jewish system to the Romans, but *theocracy* was an unfortunate choice. It came to mean the oppressive rule of clerics rather than the free consent of the entire people, which is what Exodus describes. Thus, importantly, the account in Exodus is the earliest and weightiest example of the notion that is vital to all free societies—"the consent of the governed." For the Jewish people from then on, that was the source of their strength: "that unforgettable moment at an otherwise unmemorable mountain, when God gave the people His word, and they gave Him theirs. 'All that the Lord has spoken, we shall perform.'"[22]

Second, the covenant was a matter of a mutually binding moral pledge. A promise is an obligation that someone picks up or puts themself under. Such a promise assumes and requires integrity—the person trusted must have both the character to keep the promise and the competence to be able to do so. In that sense, "Covenant is essentially an exchange of promises. Two or more parties agree to be bound by certain undertakings, pledging themselves to each other in an open-ended relationship of mutual care."[23]

A covenant is therefore promise keeping and trust writ large and made lasting. It is the trust that underlies all healthy families and all good relationships now expanded to become the foundation of an entire society and even a nation. A covenant is a commitment that makes life worth living and enables life to be lived well. It is a word of honor given at a point in time that binds together past, present, and future, making possible lasting love, enduring freedom, flourishing lives, and a healthy community.

For freedom-loving people like Americans, these foundational ideas must never become clichés. They must be read slowly and pondered deeply, and kept alive in acts such as the Pledge of Allegiance. Ours is a day when lip service to ideals is common, hypocrisy and double standards are rampant, and worst of all, suspicion and cynicism are cultivated by postmodernism as necessities to safeguard us against manipulation. In short, promise keeping, character, and trust are in short supply today. Yet without integrity, and without character and competence, trust is meaningless and freedom is endangered.

Trust starts from integrity, trust continues only with integrity, and trust lasts only as long as there is integrity. That link between trust and integrity is indissoluble, so much so that Rabbi Heschel can write stunningly, "The person in whom I trust is present in my trust."[24] Covenant is therefore nothing less than the enlargement of that promise keeping and that trust to a community and national level. So long as covenantal promise keeping is maintained, from the top of society to the bottom, the integrity of individuals others can rely on can become the integrity and solidarity of a community on which all can rely. Conversely, the crisis of trust in American institutions, including the White House, Congress, and the mainstream media, spells trouble for freedom in America.

The opening words of the *Shema* (Deut 6:4) are the first words taught to a Jewish child, and they led to the solemn commitment that is the Hebrew equivalent of the American Pledge of Allegiance. ("We pledge allegiance to the One God, Sovereign of the Universe, to whose authority all earthly powers are answerable.")[25] God can be trusted, and in the act of declaring trust in God, God himself is trusted and comes close. The result of pledging together was the mutuality of the covenant. As Moses pronounced later, "You have declared this day that the LORD is your God. . . . The LORD has today declared you to be His people, a treasured possession, as He promised you" (Deut 26:17-18).

It is notable that words are *performative* here, and not merely descriptive. They bring into reality something that was not there before and bind the future as well as the present. The full reality of all that the covenant means is created through words, the words of honor that form the promise and commit the future. You have vouched for your word, Moses says, and God has vouched for his word, and a new reality is born. For as in the covenantal oath of a marriage covenant (I do), the words bring into existence a new reality. As Sacks says, such words are "not *stating* a fact but *creating* a fact." They are "speaking a relationship into being."[26]

The moral dimension in the pledge is what makes a covenant different from a legal contract, what makes a political covenant stronger than a social contract, and a covenant of marriage before God deeper and more lasting than a civil marriage. (The Old English term *wedlock* was far from what it sounds like—a relationship that is a form of locked-up captivity and the butt of countless wedding jokes. *Wedlock* is a compound of the word *wed*, or pledge, and the word *lac*, or gift, so that marriage was the freely given pledge of love.)

A covenant is based on the foundational moral act of one person making a solemn promise to another person or to many others—and the others making the promise to them in return. The mutuality is essential and inescapable. This promise is both an expression of freedom and an assumption of responsibility that entails obligation by all for all. The freedom that is at the heart of the consent to the covenant carries within it the responsibility that is the heart of the obligation to the covenant. The people who covenant, whether in faith, in marriage, or in community and nation building, make a morally informed and morally binding mutual pledge to each other that creates trust, loyalty, and reliability. The trust created by this mutual pledge is all-important because it replaces the need for regulations and control in the community. It acts as the glue that binds as well as the oil that smooths. It helps to form the essential ecosystem that freedom needs to thrive.

The symbolism surrounding covenant-making underscored the seriousness of the commitment and stands in stark contrast to America's current "kneeling crisis" that started in the National Football League. All protest against injustice is right, and many of the injustices protested during the singing of the anthem were real, but still the protest was misdirected. In disrespecting the anthem (or the Pledge of Allegiance and the flag), the protest disrespected the Declaration of Independence that they each symbolized. Thus the protest cut itself off from the source and standard of the freedom and justice appealed to—the promise at the heart of the Declaration (which Martin Luther King Jr. called the "promissory note"). All that was left was a power-based protest that is an expression of postmodern progressive radicalism.

The Hebrew word for *making* a covenant was to *cut* a covenant (as in "cutting a deal"). In an ancient covenant ceremony (Gen 15:9-18), an animal or birds were sacrificed and cut in half, and the parties to the covenant either walked or sat between the two halves. The meaning was clear and profound. As Sacks describes it, "The division of things normally united or whole stood as a symbol of the unification of entities (persons, tribes, nations) previously divided."[27]

LOVE, LOYALTY, AND LIBERTY

These simple truths must always be kept alive in *words that are more than words*. A covenant (and a constitution) is a law and far more than law. It provides an external framework in which freedom can flourish, but it is never just a framework. It depends on an initial promise and a solemn once-for-all commitment, but it also requires a continuing obligation—ongoing promise keeping. A covenant (or constitution) is certainly a foundational law, it provides a framework for freedom, and it truly begins with a pledge given at a certain moment in time. But the structure is dead without the spirit within it, the framework is empty without the promise keeping that sustains the trust that nourishes the freedom, and the inaugural dedication has to issue in a way of life that continues strongly in the same manner, or it will die.

In other words, freedom and trust are living truths. The Pledge of Allegiance dies if it is ever allowed to become rite words in rote order. Freedom and trust are part of a social and political ecosystem of freedom that must be cultivated with care. Like a garden or a rain forest, they depend on an ecology that must never be taken for granted. (In America today, carelessness about the Constitution and the Pledge, and conflict and incivility in public debate, have all reached levels that are ruinous to American freedom.) At best, we now say that when trust and trustworthiness, dependability, and loyalty are strong, they create "social capital." That is an understandable picture in a society dominated by money and economics, but it is unfortunate because the image is inorganic and lets the citizenry and their promise making off the hook.

Abraham Lincoln captured the human dimension better when he spoke in his first inaugural address of "the mystic chords of memory, stretching from every battle-field, and patriot grave, to every living heart and hearthstone, all over this broad land."[28] But the Sinai covenant goes deeper still. The keepers of the covenant were to "love the LORD your God," to "love your neighbor as yourself," and to "love the stranger, because you were strangers" (Deut 6:5; Lev 19:18; Deut 10:19). Covenantal politics at its heart is far, far more than a matter of social capital. From first to last it is about relationships, promises, commitments, trust—and love.

Covenant is therefore a form of binding and bonding rooted in love that is common to both a family and a nation. As mentioned in the introduction, Rabbi Sacks sets out two foundational questions underlying human life. First, how do we *relate* to each other and to God? (And the answer we saw lies in the Bible's rich understanding of words.) And second, how do we *negotiate* life with each other when we all desire freedom and we are all very different? In short, how do we create *freedom with order* and in a form that defies the pull of the two great extremes, the authoritarianism of order without freedom and the anarchy of freedom without order?

If the answer to *how we relate to each other* is words, the best answer to *how we negotiate life with each other* is covenant. The covenantal commitment of freedom creates the moral responsibility of mutual obligation that in turn creates ordered freedom in which all can flourish. A major difference between a family, a community, and a nation is of course size. Rabbi Sacks describes covenantal-constitutional politics as "a tightly interconnected fabric of love, loyalty, and liberty," and even as the "politics of love."[29] Truth breeds integrity, integrity breeds trustworthiness, trustworthiness breeds trust, trust breeds reliability and loyalty, and loyalty is the faithfulness that is the expression of love. Such covenanting is challenging for a family and still more challenging for a nation, but if America insists on thinking and education that are rife with cynicism and mistrust, covenantal (or constitutional) freedom will soon be impossible.

"Judaism," Sacks notes, "was the first moral system to place interpersonal love at the center of the moral life. . . . All moral systems have at their heart a principle of justice, or reciprocal altruism: do as you would be done by. But love is something different and more demanding." "This was later adopted by Christianity and remains a distinctive element of the Judeo-Christian ethic."[30] That emphasis is behind the important difference between patriotism and nationalism. Even politics should be understood as the proper ordering of love. T. S. Eliot warned of the folly of dreaming of a society so perfect that no one would need to be good. In the same way, it is dangerous for an elite of experts to dream of a society so well-governed that there is no need for love or good relationships. It is the realist, not the sentimental dreamer or the bureaucratic manager, who understands the relationship of love, loyalty, liberty, and life, and it is the realist who knows why stable families built on love are essential to lasting freedom.

THE COVENANTAL-CONSTITUTIONAL WAY

This means that every citizen in a covenantal (or constitutional) society must live out certain simple principles if the culture of trust and freedom is to flourish. *Know your way of life.* Freedom is not the permission to do what we like, but the power to do what we ought, so free people should be committed to living what they believe is the best way to live according to their understanding of freedom—what that way is and why they believe it is best for them. In other words, there can only be freedom and human flourishing if a certain kind of people live a certain kind of way—the way of freedom.

The American founders understood this well and expressed it in what I have called "the golden triangle of freedom": "Freedom requires virtue; virtue requires faith; and faith requires freedom."[31] But for centuries the Jewish people have rightly taken great pride in the fact that, in strong contrast to the surrounding cultures, their laws were explained and not simply imposed. (Their laws were *apologetic* and given a reason why, and not simply *apodictic* and imposed as a command without explanation—"Because I say so.")

Exercise your freedom. Freedom is a gift and an inheritance, but it is also an art that requires practice, discipline, and perseverance—whether voting, debating, or assuming the demands of neighborhood and citizenship. As with the 10,000 hours principle in the arts, freedom is not just a gift but a lifetime work in progress that is the fruit of Alexis de Tocqueville's "apprenticeship of liberty," and Nietzsche's "long obedience in the same direction." Nelson Mandela rightly called it the "long walk to freedom."[32] It is a journey on which, as Sacks says, there is "no short cut to liberty."[33] Freedom is "immensely demanding" and "hard work."[34] Robust democratic civility is taught better in town halls than on Twitter. "For the journey is not just physical, a walk across the desert. It is psychological, moral, and spiritual. It takes as long as the time needed for human beings to change."[35]

Keep your promises. It is only as free people do what they say and follow through on all that they promise that they become predictable and trustworthy to others—which in turn strengthens the bonds of the wider web of social trust that strengthens the collective freedom of everyone. Conversely, leaders who lie and do not keep their word are a disaster. A chronic failing of our time is to think of both identity and freedom in purely individual terms. We therefore break our commitments easily, whether in marriage or as citizens and leaders, if we feel our commitments are not in our best interests or not fulfilling us.

But the blunt truth is that we are moral and social beings. We can and must be alone at times, but we cannot even be ourselves all by ourselves. And our word is our integrity and character. Political freedom is therefore never only individual. Political freedom is shared freedom and shared responsibility. As the title of this chapter insists, free people are those who have been "set free to live free *together*," and the deepest challenge in that sentence lies in the final word. Citizenship in a free society is not for Robinson Crusoes, egotists, or narcissists, but for team players.

Respect your neighbor. Communal freedom is always shared freedom, and shared freedom always requires self-limitation. A right for one is a right for another and a responsibility for both. Rabbi Sacks even goes so far as to say that Martin Buber was wrong when he called his famous work *I and Thou*. "In Judaism the primary relationship is *We and Thou*. Despite its insistence on individual responsibility ("If I am not for myself, who will be for me?"), Judaism is equally insistent on collective responsibility ("And if I am only for myself, what am I?").[36] As we saw with the great revelation, even God limits his freedom with respect to human freedom. ("Is God everywhere?" "No," the rabbis answered, "God is omnipresent, but he does not enter and invade the human heart"—a truth pictured in Holman Hunt's much-loved painting *Light of the World* that hangs in Keble College, Oxford.)[37] All others have their own integrity and their own rights, and we are all sometimes an other to others. Freedom's challenge, then, is to know when each individual can and must assert their own freedom, and when it is time to respect one's own limit in light of the equal freedom of others.

What would happen, Rabbi Sacks remarks, if we each insisted on speaking a language of our own—entirely of our own choice and devising? Freedom in that sense would lead to a babble of incomprehension and chaos. Language by its very nature is a shared exercise, and to ignore this fact would lead to less freedom, not more. In the same way, he notes, freedom is shared freedom and requires a common moral understanding of how we respect each other and deal with each other. "Morality is like a language, and just as we cannot invent our own language and hope thereby to communicate with others, so we cannot invent our own morality and hope to live graciously with others in a community of shared ideals."[38]

In sum, it is demanding to be a citizen in a covenantal (and constitutional) republic. That is not always the case with subjects under a monarchy or a dictatorship. They can often be passive because the king or the dictator is responsible for the nation. But that is not the case with citizens in a covenantal (or constitutional) society. "We the people" are always responsible. They have a collective authority and responsibility. They must therefore always be active—or they are likely to get the government their passivity deserves.

ALL FOR ONE AND ONE FOR ALL

Third, the covenant was a matter of the reciprocal responsibility of all for all. Long before the celebrated motto of the Three Musketeers, "All for one and one for all," the Jewish covenant embedded the pledge of responsibility to God and all other Jews. It included the profound new ethic, "You shall love your neighbor as yourself," and it reached out in care for the widow, the orphan, and even the stranger: "Love the stranger, for you were strangers in the land of Egypt" (Deut 10:19 NKJV). Indeed, as the rabbis pointed out, the celebrated command to love one's neighbor comes only once in the Torah, whereas the far more unlikely command to love the stranger and so to resist tribalism, ethnocentrism, and xenophobia comes no fewer than thirty-six times.

In Walzer's words, "We are responsible for our fellows—all of us for all of us."[39] In the words of Rabbi Shimon bar Yohai, "Israel is like a single body with one soul. When one is injured, all feel the pain."[40] The implication is simple and stunning. "*It meant that the basis of social order in Judaism is not power but collective responsibility.* Power belongs to God. Responsibility belongs to us."[41] Each person is both an individual and a member of the community. As an individual, each person has rights—but only to the extent that, as a member of the community, each also has responsibilities.

Behind this principle is the Bible's understanding of commonality and diversity. This is hugely significant today as the advanced modern world swings between the extremes of anarchic individualism and authoritarian collectivism (tribalism, multiculturalism, and socialism in the West, and communism elsewhere). Rabbi Sacks summarizes the balance succinctly:

> Humanity is formed of our commonalities and differences. Our differences shape our identity. Our commonalities form our humanity. We are neither completely different, nor all the same. If we were completely different, we

could not communicate. If we were all alike, we would have nothing to say. Our differences matter. But so too does the truth that despite our religious differences, we share a common humanity.[42]

Thus, across the differences of our genuine diversity, which might otherwise divide us, the reciprocal responsibility of all for all binds us together yet while still safeguarding against the collectivism that would diminish or deny our individual identity.

Remarkably, the reciprocal responsibility of the covenant included even the rights of the future, for its terms covered not only the born but the unborn and the yet to be born. ("The LORD did not make this covenant with our fathers, but with us, *with* all those of us alive here today." [Deut 5:3].) There was an equality of dignity for each individual before the covenant, and there was also equality of responsibility of all for all others who were within the covenant. By definition, the "stranger," the "foreigner," the "outsider," and the "other" are not "people like us," to use Aristotle's term. But while none of them are in our image and "people like us," they are all in God's image, and as such they must be treated with dignity and compassion. "By creating all humans in His image," Rabbi Sacks comments, "God sets us the challenge of seeing His image in one who is not in my image: whose color, culture, class and creed are not mine. The ultimate spiritual challenge is to see the trace of God in the face of a stranger."[43]

The ethic of responsibility later became the Jewish principle that "all Israelites are responsible for one another." It meant, one rabbi said, that there was not one covenant at Sinai but 600,000 covenants, as all the Israelite men signed on to the covenant's pledge. No, another rabbi said, there were really 600,000 times 600,000 covenants as everyone made a covenant not only with God but with all their fellow Israelites. When the celebrated Rabbi Hillel was asked if he could explain the essence of Judaism while standing on one leg, he replied that nothing could be simpler: "Do unto others as you will have others do unto you. The rest is commentary."

In our day Rabbi Sacks underscores the simple but profound result. "A covenant is a pledge between two or more partners, each of whom respects the freedom and integrity of the other, to be loyal to one another and to do together what neither can do alone."[44] Excessive dependency is a problem in any society, and so also is excessive autonomy. But such is the covenantal responsibility of each person and the responsibility of each for each other, and all for all, that a covenantal community becomes a community with a partnership and a project at its core.

What is sad is that even to state these principles is to underscore how far a covenantal-constitutional country such as America has strayed from them.

POLITICS IN THE COVENANTAL COMMUNITY

The salient features of politics in the covenantal community should be no surprise by now, beginning with its soaring audacity. The central Jewish project, Sacks says, is "constructing a society radically unlike any that had existed before and most that have come into existence since. It poses a fundamental question: can we make, on earth, a social order based not on transactions of power but on respect for the human person—each person—as the image of God?"[45]

Certain simple truths comprise this vision: the fact that covenantalism is essentially political, though more; the centrality of relationships based on the worth of human dignity and responsibility; and the insistence on a sustained critique of the abuse of human power—in stark contrast to the oppressive fusion of power and politics in all the other regimes of the ancient world and many regimes today. Together these features helped to create a horizontal rather than a vertical society and a devolved rather than a centralized society. As Sacks emphasizes, *"The forms of government are not eternal truths, nor are they exclusive to Israel."*[46] What was distinctive and more important was the purpose— the "moral limits of power" and the "delegation, distribution, and democratization of leadership."[47]

Several other points are prominent. First, reciprocal responsibility means what Sacks calls *"the primacy of the personal over the political."*[48] Exodus is unashamedly clear about a principle that runs through the whole Bible. People matter more than politics. Politics, of course, is all about the government of people and people governing people. Politics and international relations are therefore prominent in the Bible, with its unfolding story of empires, dynasties, emperors, kings, queens, battles, and coups. But for the Bible, politics is never an end in itself, for power is the currency of politics and power as an end rather than means becomes an idol, corruptible, and oppressive. Thus, in contrast to Babylon, Egypt, Persia, Greece, Rome—and Paris, Moscow, and Beijing—the personal has the primacy over the political and the ethical over the political. As Rabbi Sacks underscores, the Bible knows well the force of Lord Acton's dictum that all power tends to corrupt, and the wisdom of Oliver Goldsmith's insight,

"How small of all that human hearts endure, / That part which laws and kings can cause or cure."[49] "In Judaism people do not exist to serve the state. The state exists to serve the people, and the people exist to serve God."[50]

Second, reciprocal responsibility means that everyone was required to play their part. As Rabbi Sacks puts it, "Each is responsible for playing his or her part in the maintenance of a just and gracious order—by helping the poor, acting justly, honestly, and compassionately, educating children, not neglecting marginal members of society, and so on."[51] Through this responsibility of all for all, the character of a covenant society is determined by its relationships at every level—the people in relation to other people, the leaders in relation to the people, and the people in relation to the marginalized and the outsiders.

Thus, relationships in the covenantal community were not simply private. Personal relations were a public good, and it can even be said that relationships matter more than regimes. Indeed, the condition of society shapes the character of the state. It is noteworthy that Israel lived within the covenant centuries before there was a king, and one influential tradition held that the monarchy was not an ideal but a concession only because the covenant people failed to keep the covenant. Covenant communities require covenant-keeping people, which means that the deepest political challenges are pre-political. They are spiritual, personal, ethical, and communal before they are political. Politics is always downstream from covenant keeping. As Rabbi Sacks concludes, *Political change cannot be brought about by politics alone. It needs human transformation.*"[52]

Third, the role of the Hebrew leaders was strikingly different from that of leaders in other nations. For a start, there was no single or absolute human authority in Israel. Rather, there was an early version of the separation of powers or checks and balances—the so-called three crowns of authority: the king, the priest, and the prophet. For another thing, the Jewish kings were never considered sacred. They were not divine, they did not embody the gods on earth, and they were never to usurp the role of the priest. Remarkably too, they could lead the nation in war, but they had no role in legislation. God had given the law, and the task of the king was not to add to it but to see that it was carried out. But if the kings or the priests strayed from the terms of the covenant, they were open to the challenge of the prophet, the social critic whose calling was to be the guardian of the covenant and to challenge the king under the authority of the Word of the Lord. As Rabbi Heschel put it, "Elsewhere the king was a god, in Israel it was God who was king."[53]

It is notable too, as Rabbi Sacks points out, that the role of the king, which appeared to be a concession, is described negatively rather than positively. It is not spelled out in terms of its tasks and mission but in terms of its restrictions. "He must not accumulate horses, wives or wealth (Deut. 17:17). . . . These are all negatives, not statements of positive purpose."[54] And of course, when the monarchy was established, "it was haunted by failure."[55] If all these political notions were to be expressed in contemporary terms, it would be said that the power of leaders in the covenant community was both *secularized* and *relativized*. Jewish leaders were servant leaders, not leaders to be served. The great pyramids of Egypt still stand as monuments to the immortality of the Pharaohs, but as the Torah records, it was the Lord himself who buried Moses, "but no man knows his burial place to this day" (Deut 34:6). Sinai leadership has nothing to do with the contemporary cult of celebrity and power.

Fourth, power at every level—political, military, economic, and even the demographic power of numbers was critiqued. At the very peak of the power and prosperity of the Jewish monarchy, King Solomon flouted all the warnings given to him. He accumulated horses, wives, and wealth, and paid for it when they went to his head and turned his heart. As Rabbi Sacks comments, "Solomon, the wisest of men, thought himself wiser than the Torah. Hubris led to nemesis."[56] Or as he noted in more general terms, "The emphasis was always on the few against the many, the weak against the strong, intelligence against brute force, and the unexpected outcome through unconventional means."[57] It was as if the saying of the prophet Zechariah was the Jewish national motto: "'Not by might nor by power, but by My Spirit,' says the LORD of hosts" (Zech 4:6).

To be sure, politics in the Hebrew Scriptures is set in an agrarian society that is a far cry from the world of the White House, the Kremlin, Downing Street, and the Élysée Palace. But the principles of politics in the Bible are illuminating and suggestive for our day. Overall, there is no question that freedom was safeguarded because covenantal politics was both morally and constitutionally limited. It was built to guard against the abuse of power. The old maxim fits covenantal politics well and stands in stark contrast to power-based postmodern politics: "The first thing to say about politics is that politics is not the first thing."

FULL RICH FREEDOM

Once again, the implications of the Exodus way of freedom are profound and need to be explored in many areas. But one implication is unequivocally clear and beyond debate. *Covenantal freedom is a vision of full, rich freedom, and it comes down squarely on one side in the historic debates over freedom.* Is freedom the permission to do what we like or the power to do what we ought? Is freedom simply negative freedom (freedom *from* whatever coerces or controls us), or is it also positive freedom (freedom *for* whatever it takes to be ourselves)? Does revolutionary freedom simply mean the overthrow of an old regime, or does it also mean a commitment to an ongoing transformation and a new society? In each case, covenantal freedom emphatically disagrees with the first of the alternatives. But it does not merely agree with the second, it represents history's highest expression of this full, rich, and complete view of freedom.

Hebrew has two words for freedom, and the exodus demonstrates them both. One word *ḥofesh* covers the meaning of "freedom from" (Isaiah Berlin's "negative freedom"). It describes what makes the exodus "the great liberation." God rescued Israel from Pharaoh and slavery, decisively and effectively—Israel's great "freedom from." The other word *ḥerut* covers the meaning of "freedom for" (Isaiah Berlin's "positive freedom"). It describes what makes Exodus "the great constitution." God gave Israel the covenant, including the Ten Commandments, setting out how they should live in freedom together—Israel's great "freedom to be."

Over against lopsided libertarianism, this comprehensive view of freedom must be emphasized tirelessly. Negative freedom, liberation, emancipation are all good and essential. They must never be diminished for a second. But they are only half the story. There must be no choice between the two sides of freedom, for neither is complete without the other. Through the *great liberation*, God set Israel free, and through the *great constitution* he set out the covenant as a way of life in which they can live free together. "Set free to live free together." The unashamed insistence on all three components in that sentence is the watershed truth for freedom. Negative freedom is good, but it is only the beginning. It is fulfilled only in positive freedom. But positive freedom in an individual sense is not enough. It is shared freedom that requires equal freedom for others—all of which lead to three basic principles.

- *First, freedom is not permission to do what you want but the power to do what you ought.*

- *Second, each person's freedom is free only to the extent that each one respects the equal freedom of all others too.*

- *Third, communal freedom means freedom for each person and freedom for all in the service of the good of all.*

The blend of richness and realism in this view of freedom stands in contrast to many contemporary views, such as libertarianism. Negative freedom or *freedom from* is always foundational and essential. No one subject to the will of another or under the power of any external force can be said to be free, whether the external force is a colonial power, an abusive husband, a schoolyard bully, or addiction to drugs and alcohol.

Understood in that sense, the Israelites were not free until they were the other side of the Red Sea. Only then were they beyond Pharaoh's kingdom and truly free of his rule and the threat of his formidable cavalry. Yet Moses' insistence on that negative freedom can be seen even earlier in the contest. As Pharaoh's bargaining began to weaken, he offered to let Israel go with the proviso that they leave their herds and flocks behind (and would therefore be sure to return). No, Moses countered, "Not a hoof shall be left behind" (Ex 10:26). "Let my people go" meant freedom and an exodus that was complete, total, lasting, and final.

Yet the completeness of Israel's victory at the Red Sea did not mean complete freedom. As the rabbis underscored, freedom meant much more and it would take much longer. For Israel's "freedom to be" faced a major obstacle: the Israelites had been so chronically conditioned by slavery for so long that they could *go free* but they were unable to *live free*. As the Jews express the point themselves, "It took one day to take the Israelites out of Egypt. It took forty years to take Egypt out of the Israelites."[58] If freedom is the power to live as we ought, then freedom requires truth, character, and a way of life to make freedom possible, and views of freedom that are based on negative freedom only are inadequate.

Put differently, freedom, along with love, is the most powerful form of human energy. But as Sacks reminds us, all sources of energy, from a fire in a cottage hearth to nuclear energy, require some form of containment. Without that, they would be dangerous. The covenant "has always acted as a container for the spiritual and intellectual energy of the Jewish people. That energy 'has not merely exploded or been dispersed; it has been harnessed as a continuous power.'"[59] Again, what Exodus offers is the road to full, rich freedom.

BELIEFS NOT BLOOD

Covenantalism, as Daniel Elazar stressed, was the alternative to organic societies on one side and hierarchical societies on the other. In contrast to organic societies, the Hebrew covenant was not about blood and kinship but beliefs, words, promises, and binding obligations. The first reference to Israel in the book of

Exodus is when the Pharaoh refers to "the nation of the children of Israel" (Ex 1:9). Importantly, as Dennis Prager underscores, there are two words for *nation* in Hebrew, and Pharaoh does not use the one that refers to a nation defined as a political unit (the Hebrew word *goy*) but the one that refers to a nation defined by blood (the word *am*). "Pharaoh is saying, in effect, the purity of the Egyptian people is being threatened by an alien presence, the children of Israel, who are of a different bloodline."[60]

Identity and solidarity through blood ties have been a major source of cruelty and evil in history, such as slavery in Egypt and ethnic cleansing today. Judaism, in contrast, was a matter of covenant and not kinship. It depended on beliefs and not blood ties. Abraham, as Prager notes, was not born a Jew, Jacob's brother Esau was not considered a Jew, and Ruth the ancestor of Israel's greatest king, David, though a foreigner, was able to become a Jew. What constituted Judaism and what made the Jew a Jew was the covenant and all that the covenant meant.[61]

The same was once true of the American republic, but no longer. America is a project and an experiment. America was founded as a nation *by intention and by ideas*, and *not by kinship*. Yet Paris in the form of tribal politics and identity politics is changing all that. Whereas Martin Luther King Jr. spoke of the "content of character" rather than the "color of skin," the progressive left has reversed that. Tribes of sex, class, race, and age now matter more than ideas. The left hails the death of the White majority and the coming of the minority majority. But that is muddled thinking, and nothing shows more clearly the death of Sinai and the triumph of Paris. It should not matter whether the majority of Americans are English, Scottish, German, Irish, Italian, African, Mexican, Asian, or whatever. If Sinai and 1776 are to endure and the great experiment in freedom is to last, all that matters is that the majority in any generation understand and adhere to the founding principles of American freedom and keep alive the strong *unum* that America needs to balance the expanding American *pluribus*.

THE ARGUMENT WITH HEAVEN FOR THE SAKE OF HEAVEN

Another major implication of the covenant leads in an entirely different direction. God's character and covenant give all who know him the grounds for arguing with him on behalf of justice for his world. This "argument with heaven for the sake of heaven" is not only possible but right, good, and a matter of faith.[62] Far from blasphemy, it is one of the great Jewish traditions. God and his people are bound together as partners by the Sinai covenant, so humans can claim justice in appealing to God over apparent injustice, just as God in his justice can challenge his people over their injustice. What matters is that such an argument with heaven is not opposed to faith, it is part of the life of faith. As Rabbi Sacks observes, "it is notable that it is not heretics, skeptics, or atheists who raise these questions, but heroes of the faith."[63]

What is surely the most stunning example of all occurred when some of the Jews in Auschwitz challenged three rabbis to put God on trial for murder. They convened a court, held a full trial, and returned a verdict: God was guilty. The enormity of what had happened hushed the entire hut into a dark silence, which was only broken when one of the rabbis announced, "And now it is time for the evening prayer."[64] The story of the trial was dismissed as fiction after the war until Elie Wiesel stated publicly that he had been present at such a trial. The malevolence of the evil of the death camps called faith in God into question, though most admitted that faith in humanity was called into question even more deeply. What does it say of us as humans that the people who did these things are the same species we are?

The Bible rarely explains why God called Abraham and his family—but one comes when God says that he chose Abraham that he and his household would "keep the way of the LORD by doing righteousness and justice" (Gen 18:17-19). Abraham was therefore doing precisely that when he queried the justice of God's judgment of Sodom. "Shall not the judge of all the earth deal justly?" (Gen 18:25). There is even a suggestion that the Lord was inviting Abraham to enter the debate and challenge his verdict and so become part of a hearing that made him a partner in the grand pursuit of justice. Yet regardless, Rabbi Sacks writes, that moment when Abraham queried God's justice is a turning point in the history of the spirit. "There was nothing like this before, nor is there, to my knowledge, anything like it in any other religious literature. . . . For the first time, a human being challenges God Himself on a matter of justice."[65]

Far from softening or excusing Abraham's boldness, the Jewish people underscored it—from the Sages' notion of the principle of "audacity [*chutzpa*] toward heaven" down to Elie Wiesel's *Night*, in which he (as a devout believer) dared to explore God's presence in the horror of Auschwitz. God is a God of justice, so all God's people whose hearts cry out "Why?" and "How long, O Lord?" are free to cite God's justice in framing their claims and making their case to heaven. To all who long for justice on the earth and cry out against the sighs and tears of cruelty and injustice, this point is unique and precious. In Rabbi Sacks's words, "God rules by right, not might. . . . God is not merely powerful, but ethical, and it is precisely the pursuit of the ethical that brings God and humanity together in a covenant based on righteousness and justice."[66]

This notion of arguing on behalf of the true, the right, and the good lies behind the Bible's principle of corrigibility. We are all always open to challenge and correction. "No one is above criticism, and no one too junior to administer it, if done with due grace and humility. A disciple may criticize his teacher; a child may challenge a parent; a prophet may challenge a king" if they are doing it in the name of the right and good.[67] The God of Sinai and all who know him and live within his covenant are partners in the pursuit of justice against the evils of the world. Finally, to be fulfilled in heaven one day, justice must be fought for here and now every day, and the argument with heaven for the sake of heaven is a fruit of the covenant and a vital weapon in the human struggle for justice on the earth.

ALL BECAUSE OF LOVE

As with many spheres of life, the great mistake of politics is imperialism—which politicizes everything and acts as if politics was the be-all and end-all of life. The same is true of revolutions. Too often they become a world unto themselves and never serve any purpose but their own cause and the power of their leaders. They forget that their cause once served the higher human end of justice and transformation. Liberation should always be in the service of life. Negative freedom is only the stepping-stone to positive freedom. Prisoners, slaves, addicts, hostages, victims, and captives of any kind should always be set free to live free, and freedom is not simply a moment ("free at last") but a way of life with no recidivism or backsliding.

Exodus takes this soaring vision further than any other revolution or liberation. Those that God set free to live free were liberated to love. That is the extraordinary but often overlooked outcome of the exodus, and it stands as a challenge to all who champion freedom. It raises the question: Has the freedom of those freed issued in a broad and expansive enjoyment of life? Rabbi Sacks raises this issue in pointing to the enormous contrast between the exodus as it happened and the exodus as it came to be understood in later Jewish history. Exodus in real time was the story of an unruly bunch of slavery-hardened grumblers who rarely seemed worthy of or grateful for the remarkable rescue lavished on them. But as time went by and the truth sank in, a different picture emerged. It was nothing less than "a retelling of the story of the exodus as a love story."[68] For the prophets Hosea and Ezekiel, Sacks writes, "The Giving of the Torah at Mount Sinai has been transformed by the prophet into a marriage ceremony."[69] It was then far "more than a theological drama about the defeat of false gods by the true One, or a political narrative about slavery and freedom. It is a love story."[70]

Taken wrongly, that point could be misinterpreted to justify Jewish chauvinism, but Sacks closes off that temptation at once. Not just the exodus, but humanity, creation, and the entire universe all exist under the overarching truth of the words "God loves" or as the New Testament states, "God is love" (1 Jn 4:8).[71] To both pagan and secular cultures, that statement would be absurd, though for different reasons. For most pagans, humans were seen as the playthings of the gods, so they always needed to appease the gods. For the philosophically educated in the ancient world, it would have been unintelligible. They held that humans love because they lack, and the gods lack nothing, so the gods do not need love. For modern secularists it is self-interest, not love, that drives society, so love has nothing to do with public life and the "real world."

Yet according to the Bible, nothing better demonstrates our humanity than the freedom to love and be loved—including our neighbor, the stranger, and even our enemies. A key part of America's present crisis lies in the fact that its world-renown in public relations is increasingly contradicted by the growing infamy of its poor interpersonal relations, from political leaders down. Love has many aspects, of course, but love in the human heart is the greatest energy in the created world, and the freedom to love is the greatest freedom in the world. Set free to live free, the highest freedom is the freedom to love and to create a community where respect and love dignify all relationships.

Is such a statement mere sentimentalism and a subject fit only for Valentine's Day cards and red-heart emojis? Or is it realistic? With America increasingly espousing a culture of death, from abortion at the start of life to euthanasia at the end, and with broken families and violence scattered throughout, this question is not idle. The world waits and watches for the answer, but there cannot be an answer without the rediscovery of covenanting that is deeper and richer than simply law and due process. A *politics of life and love* may sound squishy and sentimental, but rightly understood, covenant keeping at its heart is a matter of promise keeping, trust, and trustworthiness. Without good relationships and good communication, there cannot be a good society—or real and lasting freedom and genuine patriotism.

America cannot endure permanently half 1776 and half 1789. The compromises, contradictions, hypocrisies, inequities, and evils have built up unaddressed. The grapes of wrath have ripened again, and the choice before America is plain. Either America goes forward best by going back first, or America is about to reap a future in which the worst will once again be the corruption of the best.

6

PASSING IT ON

PRINCIPLE 6: FREEDOM MUST BE CELEBRATED AND HANDED ON

"All things are mortal but the Jew; all other forces pass, but he remains. What is the secret of his immortality?"[1] Mark Twain's question to the readers of *Harper's* magazine in 1899 has puzzled many thinkers down the centuries. The Egyptians, the Babylonians, the Persians, the Greeks, and the Romans, he wrote (and we might add the Spanish, the Dutch, the French, and the British), have all come and gone. They "filled the planet with sound and splendor, then faded to dreamstuff and passed away." But the Jew has survived "and has done it with his hands tied behind him. . . . The Jew saw them all, beat them all, and is now what he always was, exhibiting no decadence, no infirmities of age, no weakening of his parts, no slowing of his energies, no dulling of his alert and aggressive mind."[2]

Mark Twain was not alone in wrestling with that question, and today we raise it even more soberly in the light of three things: the horror of the Holocaust, the reemergence of anti-Semitism in Europe and America, and the growing awareness of the indispensable contribution of Hebrew ideas to the greatness of the West. Jean-Jacques Rousseau, Nikolai Berdyaev, and others have all pondered the miracle of the Jewish survival—surviving against insurmountable odds. Most nations are held together by their land, their language, and their national institutions. For two thousand years the Jews were cut off from all these things, the land, the temple, the monarchy, and a public celebration of their festivals, but they survived. They were exiled, scattered, despised, persecuted, and powerless, but they survived. No other people in history have been persecuted so horrendously and so often, and no other people have been so scattered across the earth.

(Where I was born in Kaifeng, an old imperial capital in north-central China, there had been a synagogue for centuries.) But despite everything, they survived.

Indeed, the survival of the Jewish people is so remarkable, so near-miraculous, that it has been viewed as a "signal of transcendence"—an event that punctures purely secular explanations and points beyond itself to a divine answer that would have to be true to account adequately for what has happened. (Rabbi Sacks cites Louis XIV asking Blaise Pascal for a proof of the existence of God, and his reported reply was, "Your Majesty, the Jews!")[3] Leaving aside the possibility of a miracle for the moment, the Jews themselves have a simple explanation for their survival—their insistence on education and the importance of transmission. Their identity, their history, and their values were passed down safely from generation to generation. In Rabbi Sacks's summary, "The Mesopotamians built ziggurats, the Egyptians built pyramids, the Greeks built the Parthenon, and the Romans the Coliseum. Jews built schools. That is why we are still here. That, in answer to Mark Twain's question, is the secret of our immortality."[4]

THE SECRET OF SURVIVAL IS SCHOOLING

The secret of Jewish survival pivots on a plain and simple truth that is foundational and critical to freedom, yet one that is routinely overlooked by many democracies and by many advocates of freedom today. Rabbi Sacks puts it in two ways. First, and more generally: "The great challenges of humanity are too large to be completed in a single generation."[5] Second, and more specifically: *"If any change in the human condition takes longer than a generation, education becomes fundamental."*[6]

The logic of these two statements is simple and unassailable, but few basic truths have been ignored more foolishly by those who claim to be advocates of faith or partisans of freedom. The principle of course applies to marriage and families too—there is an unbreakable link between faith, families, and fertility. Unfashionable as it is to say in the madness of the present climate, both society and future generations are served best when mothers and fathers conceive children in a loving and lasting union of a marriage between a man and a woman. Many of the other forms of marriage are proving to be a dead end in one way or another. The American republic is therefore in the process of making a massive and historic triple blunder. The "land of the free" is foolish for switching revolutions (from the 1776 way of freedom to the 1789 way of freedom). It is foolish too for diluting marriage and families in ways that are incapable of serving the future, and it is foolish for neglecting the form of transmission without which there can be no enduring freedom at all—civic education.

I use the word *transmission* rather than *tradition* for two reasons, though the terms overlap in describing the passing on from generation to generation. First, *transmission* puts the focus on the means rather than the content. And second, *transmission* has none of the negative modern connotations of *tradition* and *routinization* as the heavy hand of the past. The bias in that connotation is of course fallacious, for the past is often the inspiration for throwing off the heavy hand of the present. But there is no question that tradition, idolized, can indeed become a ball and chain. As Rabbi Heschel notes, "Wise, essential and pedagogically useful as the principle 'respect for tradition' is, it is grotesque and self-defeating to make it the supreme article of faith."[7]

Put differently, there are two essential poles within covenantalism (and constitutionalism). Covenantalism is an ideal of *ordered freedom*, and it therefore has to balance both order and freedom, both structure and spontaneity. Each generation has its own bias toward one or the other pole. Our contemporary bias has been toward freedom at the expense of order, but that bias has created such problems that it could easily swing to the opposite extreme that is no better. As we have seen throughout this exploration, freedom without order leads to anarchy and chaos, whereas order without freedom leads to authoritarianism and control. Thus, the overall balance is easy to state but hard to sustain. As Rabbi Heschel states in a different context, order is the body and freedom is the spirit, yet that creates the challenge. "The body without the spirit is a corpse; the spirit without the body is a ghost." In sum, "He who is not aware of this central difficulty is a simpleton; he who offers a simple solution is a quack."[8]

In America the solution to this difficulty used to be civic education, the key part of schooling that is critical to the transmission of freedom. On the one hand, civic education sustains freedom by looking back. In doing so, it inducts each next generation into the understanding of who they are through the understanding of who their parents and ancestors have been, for better or worse. Transmission is therefore the key to ongoing identity. On the other hand, civic education sustains freedom by looking forward. It inspires each next generation to strive toward the ideals that remain to be reached and the work that remains to be accomplished. Transmission is therefore the key to the ongoing aspirations and ambitions that fuel free people's progress from generation to generation. The task of freedom is always unfinished, and healthy transmission keeps its agents committed and courageous.

OUR STORY IS THE STORY WE TELL OURSELVES

Once again, the Exodus Revolution shows a different and wiser way than our practices today. Consider the Passover night when the Israelites went free—now celebrated by the Jews for a hundred generations. What did Moses talk about that night? The Israelites had been in captivity for hundreds of years, and that night they stood on the verge of going free. But did Moses talk about freedom? No. They were leaving for the long-anticipated Promised Land, the land "flowing with milk and honey." But did Moses talk about their longed-for destination? No. They were about to cross the howling waste of the wilderness. But did Moses brace them with the challenge of all it would take? No. As Rabbi Sacks notes, "Moses did none of these things. Instead, he spoke about children and the distant future, and the duty to pass on memory to generations yet unborn."[9]

Three times Moses challenged the Israelites not to forget to pass on the Passover story to their children:

> When your children ask you, "What does this ceremony mean to you?" then tell them, "It is the Passover sacrifice to the LORD, who passed over the houses of the Israelites in Egypt and spared our homes when he struck down the Egyptians." (Ex 12:26-27 NIV)

> On that day tell your son, "I do this because of what the LORD did for me when I came out of Egypt." (Ex 13:8 NIV)

> In days to come when your son asks you, "What does this mean?" say to him, "With a mighty hand the LORD brought us out of Egypt, out of the land of slavery." (Ex 13:14)

Rabbi Sacks underscores the point. *"The Israelites had not yet left Egypt, and yet already Moses was telling them how to tell the story."* Why? "The simplest answer is that *we are the story we tell about ourselves.*"[10] In another commentary, he continues with eloquence,

> About to gain their freedom, the Israelites were told that they had to become a nation of educators. That is what made Moses not just a great leader, but a unique one. What the Torah is teaching is that freedom is won, not on the battlefield, nor in the political arena, nor in the courts, national or international, but in the human imagination and will. To defend a country you need an army. But to defend a free society you need schools. You need

families and an educational system in which ideals are passed on from one generation to the next, and never lost, or despaired of, or obscured. There has never been a more profound understanding of freedom. It is not difficult, Moses was saying, to gain liberty, but to sustain it is the work of a hundred generations. Forget it and you lose it.[11]

UNIVERSAL EDUCATION AND EQUALITY OF DIGNITY

The impact of the Passover night was monumental for the Jewish people, including its lessons for schooling. "Jews became the people whose passion was education, whose citadels were schools and whose heroes were teachers."[12] Whatever the precise date of the exodus, it is providential that it took place not far from the time or the place where the first alphabet was invented (the proto-Semitic alphabet, discovered by the British archaeologist Flinders Petrie in 1905). All technological revolutions make an impact—the wheel, the arch, the compass, gunpowder, the clock, the car, and so on. But the knowledge revolutions make the greatest impact of all because of the technological advancements in the way that information is recorded, stored, and passed on. Thus the invention of the alphabet (c. 1800–2000 BC) takes its place as one of the revolutionary moments in history, along with the earlier invention of writing and the later invention of the printing press and more recently of the computer and the dawn of the digital age.

Before the invention of the first alphabet (the name itself coming from the first two letters of the Hebrew script), writing in the age of cuneiform (invented in Mesopotamia), hieroglyphics (in Egypt), and ideograms (in China) was both complicated and restricted to the political and religious elites. It was exclusive to the world of the palace and the temple. Who else could master thousands of possible symbols and pictures? These forms of writing fitted the hierarchical structures of their countries perfectly. There was a simplicity to the new alphabet. With fewer than thirty letters, it was simplified, memorable, and easily portable. It was therefore revolutionary and potentially democratic because everyone who wished to could learn the alphabet. There are hints of this broadened literacy in the Hebrew Scriptures. The book of Judges, for instance, tells the story of Gideon's siege of the town of Succoth, when a young man he captured wrote down for him the names of seventy-seven of the town's leaders—small but telling evidence of the state of literacy in Israel (Judg 8:14).

Yet according to Rabbi Sacks and other scholars, this link between the Jewish faith and literacy was anything but accidental. It was providential. "The alphabet created the book that created the people of the book."[13] (John Man: "Both new God and new script worked together to forge a new nation and disseminate an idea that would change the world.")[14] Importantly, the alphabet meant that Israel was the first and only nation to receive and learn its laws before it entered its land, and Israel had a powerful additional impetus to break with the hierarchical structures of the surrounding civilizations. The alphabet was simple enough to be taught to anyone, which created the possibility of universal literacy and equal access to knowledge.

This last point, Sacks notes, is immense because it undergirds the Jewish notion of equality of dignity. "Equality is the holy grail of revolutionary politics," he writes, but for most people this has meant equality of wealth (to be achieved through redistribution, as in socialism and communism) or equality of power (to be achieved through political participation, as in direct democracy or constant referenda).[15] But these approaches are based on contested goods, in that one person's gain is always another person's loss, so the solution will never be satisfactory or final. "Knowledge is different. If I give all I know to you, I will not thereby know less. I may know more. Equality of dignity based on universal access to knowledge is the only equality likely to last in the long run."[16]

What is unquestionable is the way that this emphasis on education and literacy became the lifeline for the Jews in the time of their greatest-ever crisis before the Holocaust: the extended period of crisis under the Romans, especially AD 70 and 133, when the Second Temple was destroyed and they were even prohibited from entering Jerusalem (which the Romans renamed Aelia Capitolina). What saved them, Rabbi Sacks observed, was the creation of "the world's first system of universal compulsory education paid for by public funds."[17] In the darkest hour of the crisis, Yehoshua ben Gamla "instituted that teachers be appointed in every province and every city, and children from the age of six or seven were placed under their charge."[18]

Jewish pride in this notable achievement is warranted. It was nearly two thousand years later before England led the way in Europe, instituting compulsory education in 1870, with many American states much later still. But it was the clarity and firmness of the Jewish rationale that is striking. One instruction reads, "If a city has made no provision for the education of the young, its inhabitants are placed under a ban until teachers have been engaged. If they persistently neglect his duty, the city is excommunicated, *for the world only survives by the merit of the breath of schoolchildren.*"[19] When a young child was first brought to school, it used to be said, "It is as though they brought him to Mount Sinai."[20]

Or again, the story is told of a delegation with a mission to establish teachers in every town in Israel. Coming to a town where there were no teachers, they asked, "Bring us the defenders of the town." The military guard was brought out.

"No," the rabbis said, "These are not the protectors of the town but its destroyers."

"Who then are the protectors?" the inhabitants asked.

"The teachers," the rabbis replied.[21]

It was the same in the Middle Ages. Peter Abelard, the great eleventh-century philosopher, observed, "A Jew, however poor, if he has ten sons, will put them all to letters, not for gain as the Christians do, but for the understanding of God's law—and not only his sons but his daughters too."[22] Rabbi Sacks's summary of this magnificent record should be pondered by all leaders who love freedom. "No other faith has attached a higher value to study. None has given it a higher position in the scale of communal priorities. From the very outset Israel knew that freedom cannot be created by legislation, nor can it be sustained by political structures alone."[23] As Montesquieu reminded Europeans in the eighteenth century, the spirit of freedom is as important as the structures of freedom.

In 1931, on the last page of his magisterial study *The Foundations of American Constitutionalism*, Andrew Cunningham McLaughlin confessed what is surely the chronic failing of American lawyers and much of American law as a whole:

> I have spoken much of law and of institutional forms, of the mechanism which can help to bind the nation together, but cannot close without pointing out that a nation, if it be a nation, must have in its possession certain common beliefs and principles. . . . The compelling central thought, then, is this: the nation is held together as a living thing not by courts or armies or congresses, but by an ethical principle of justice. Without it the nation, the American nation at least, would be without the very essence of nationalism. I wonder if it is necessary in these days to emphasize the need for social ethics as the heart of a vital community, a community that would really live and be a community in more than outward seeming.[24]

Thirteen years later in World War II, Judge Learned Hand reminded Americans of the same lesson, which needs to be sounded out again in our day, "Liberty lies in the hearts of men and women; when it dies there, no constitution, no law, no court can save it; no constitution, no law, no court can even do much to help it."[25]

THE PRIMACY OF THE HEART

The reminder that liberty is a matter of the heart takes us to the very core of the challenge of freedom and to a challenge that no lover of liberty can afford to fail to appreciate—*Freedom is never stronger than its strength in the hearts and minds of each succeeding generation of citizens.* There are times when freedom requires guns and tanks, aircraft carriers and jet fighters, but no guns, tanks, aircraft carriers, and jet fighters will ever create, protect, or sustain freedom by themselves. "Make America Great Again" simply cannot and will not succeed through rebuilding the military and the economy alone. Freedom begins and ends in the human heart, in the hearts of citizens and children, and all attempts to find and fulfill it elsewhere are doomed to fail.

Because of the covenant, the primacy of the heart has always been the secret of the Jews, Rabbi Sacks writes. It stands in stark contrast to both ancient and modern thinking that either ignores the heart altogether in favor of weaponry and monuments or reduces the heart to the level of the sentimental and the irrelevant. In contrast to such errors, the Jews are

> guardians of a narrative not engraved in hieroglyphics on the walls of a monumental building but carried in the minds of living, breathing human beings who, for longer than any other people, have kept faith with the future and the past, bearing witness to the power of the human spirit when it opens itself to a greater power, beckoning us to a world of freedom, responsibility and human dignity.[26]

The primacy of the heart would not matter for either an organic society or a hierarchical society, whose national strength lies elsewhere. But it is crucial for a covenantal people such as the Jews and a constitutional society such as the American republic. America is a nation by intention and by ideas, so the health of those ideas in the hearts and minds of the people is all-important. Freedom is a vision of life designed to create a community of free people who can live freely, act freely, and speak freely as they were created and called to live. *Schooling in freedom is therefore essential to sustaining freedom because education is a matter of formation in character as well as transmission across the generations.* "What we need more than anything else," Rabbi Heschel writes, "is not *textbooks* but *textpeople*. It is the personality of the teacher which is the text the pupils read; the text they will never forget."[27]

EACH LINK IN THE CHAIN MUST BE STRONG

The knotty problem at the center of transmission is obvious: the problem of the egocentrism of the human heart and the tension between freedom and time. The covenant (or constitution) that is the foundation and framework for a free society is a matter of freely chosen consent. As we saw, this led to the important principle of the Jewish sages that "an agreement must be free to be binding."[28] That freely chosen but binding vow is easy and natural for a couple in the full flush of love at their wedding or for the generation of the Jews who were at Sinai. But what of Jews in later generations who were not at Sinai or young Americans today who know nothing of the victory at Yorktown or the miracle at Philadelphia? All later generations are simply born into the covenant or the constitution. Why should I be bound by what I promised earlier, and why should anyone be bound by promises that were made by others?

A *bat* or *bar mitzvah* has a different meaning for young Jews than baptism or confirmation for young Christians, but the overlapping purpose is the same—the initiation of adulthood and the assumption of responsibility for the ongoing guardianship of the covenant or the faith. Strikingly, there is no equivalent for young Americans and the Constitution. Today, with the collapse of civic education in the public schools, the teaching of an alternative American history and the increasing disparagement of the flag and the national anthem, young Americans lack both the education and the initiation. It is now clear that many young Americans have a serious deficiency as citizens. For no fault of their own, they are both ignorant and irresponsible. Transmission is breaking down. The responsibilities that come with birth have not been shouldered, talk of revolutions other than 1776 is in the air, and on such developments hangs the future of American freedom. What has been allowed to happen in American schools and colleges in the last fifty years is a monumental folly, and nothing short of a death wish.

The separate links in the chain must each be strong for freedom itself to be strong. The *transmission* of freedom depends on the *celebration* of freedom, which depends on *education* for freedom, which depends on *formation* in freedom, all of which depends on a *renewal* of freedom when freedom lapses or breaks down. Thus, whatever freedom means for a community or nation in terms of its declarations, constitutions, laws, courts, political institutions, and elections, these things by themselves will never guarantee or maintain freedom. Freedom begins and ends in the human heart, and that is where it must stay alive and remain refreshed.

This point is commonly misunderstood today. Many people feel embarrassed to talk about concerns about character and personal beliefs. Surely, these are soft factors in the hard-nosed world of politics and law courts. Besides, they say, private beliefs are irrelevant to the public good. Others resist the importance of the personal and the private on principle as if to stress their importance is to invite an intrusion. They hold the mistaken idea that because the government has no right to dictate to the heart and conscience of any citizen (which is correct), what citizens believe and how citizens behave are irrelevant to the public good (which is incorrect). Freedom of religion and conscience is unquestionably the first freedom and therefore inalienable and inviolable. Absolutely no one, and certainly not the government, has the right to dictate to the conscience of anyone. But private beliefs are all-important to public life. What is important, too, is that such beliefs must be formed and educated in a manner that is appropriate to freedom. The human heart is the prime factor in any consideration of freedom. Those who love freedom must never forget its primacy—and, crucially in the Bible's view, its ambivalence.

FREEDOM'S TWO FORUMS

The ambivalence of the heart is important. On the one hand, according to the Jewish and Christian understanding, the heart is central to freedom because the expression and exercise of the will come from the heart. As emphasized earlier, God has created human freedom, and he so respects the freedom of the human heart that he limits his own freedom and never invades the heart. In Roger Williams's graphic image from the seventeenth century, God grants "soul liberty." He does not "rape" the conscience.[29] For each of us too, there is inviolable integrity to every other that must always be respected, beginning with the heart and conscience of the other.

This principle is crucial for freedom and free societies for an important reason. The liberty of the heart and freedom of conscience form the *inner forum* of freedom that complements the *outer forum* of the public square in the wider community or nation. Both forums must be free, and both must be respected and guarded if society is to be truly free and to remain free. Yet the general tendency today is to forget the inner forum and focus only on the external forum.[30] But if the heart is indeed primary, that tendency will always end in diminishing freedom.

On the other hand, also according to the Jewish and Christian view, the heart may be free, but it is easily corrupted, it often goes astray, and its freedom becomes self-destructive when it insists on going its own way (the great alienation). In short, to keep the heart on course, both the heart and its way of freedom require truth, character, and a way of life. To sustain and fulfill its freedom the heart must learn to choose these framing truths and be shaped and disciplined by them, or sooner or later it will again go its own way and end in losing its way.

That is the truth served by the notion of covenant (the great constitution). Freedom that is won must be ordered. It must be ordered internally in terms of *character* and ordered externally in terms of living according to the *covenant* or *constitution*. Edmund Burke's famous "Letter to a Member of the National Assembly" is worth reflecting on in full, remembering that Burke was a self-professed Whig (or liberal) and not a conservative. He had previously defended national revolutions in America, Ireland, Corsica, and Poland, but he was the first to see that the French Revolution was quite different.

> I doubt much, very much indeed, whether France is at all ripe for liberty on any standard. Men are qualified for civil liberty, in exact proportion to their disposition too put moral chains upon their appetites; in proportion as their love to justice is above their rapacity; in proportion as their soundness and sobriety of understanding is above their vanity and pre-sumption; in proportion as they are more disposed to listen to the counsels of the wise and good, in preference to the flattery of knaves. Society cannot exist unless a controlling power upon will and appetite be placed some-where, and the less of it there is within, the more there must be without. It is ordained in the eternal constitution of things, that men of intemperate minds cannot be free. Their passions form their fetters.[31]

Self-government is what John Winthrop called law-governed liberty or federal liberty (the term *federal* coming from *foedus*, the Latin word for covenant). Un-bounded freedom is a dangerous illusion. Freedom requires its proper boundaries, and there are only two options for society: internal restraint or external constraint, and those who reject the gentle school of character condemn themselves to the harsher school of the police, the surveillance camera, and the law courts. (Dos-toevsky: "If you want to overcome the whole world, overcome yourself.")[32]

Behind that warning lie three unavoidable facts. First, freedom's greatest single temptation is to think that freedom means that we can do whatever we like. Second, free people forget that their greatest successes are their greatest danger. In Rabbi Sacks's words, "Nations face their greatest danger at the point of their greatest success. Affluence leads to overconfidence, which begets forgetfulness, which leads to decadence, which results in lack of social solidarity, which leads in the end to demoralization—the prelude to defeat."[33] Third, covenantalism's greatest single weakness is the failure of promise-makers to keep their promises. All political systems have their strengths and their weaknesses, as the classical writers explored in-depth, and the weakness of the covenantal and constitutional forms of government is plain—promise keeping. A covenant is a pledge and a promise, and faithfulness to the pledge and the promise creates trust and nourishes freedom, whether in a marriage or a republic. But we humans do not keep our promises well. God keeps his word, but we humans do not, and the outcome of a broken covenant is the loss of freedom. Thus, once again, schooling in the sense of formation for a life of freedom is essential for freedom.

AS IF THEY WERE THERE

The Exodus stress on transmission displays several salient features. Each one is important for any community or nation that desires to be free, but they are notable for another reason too. Western societies today may still trumpet their freedom, but these features are mostly conspicuous by their absence.

The first and most obvious feature of transmission in Exodus is the insistent emphasis on history. Time and death are the relentless foes of human freedom, as they are of humanity in general. Nothing lasts forever. "This too shall pass." As Nietzsche remarked tartly, "A society is not at liberty to remain young."[34] Human freedom, however, is not just a matter of the will and its capacity to engage the present, but of the imagination and its ability to soar into the future and the memory and its ability to roam back over the past. Humans enjoy these three powers—memory, imagination, and will—and do so to a degree that is decisively different from our fellow creatures, the animals. Together, these powers engage the crucial aspects of time—the past, the present, and the future—and they are therefore critical to human freedom, both in becoming free and remaining free. "The best prophet of the future," Rabbi Heschel writes, "is our past."[35]

History for many people in the West has become dry, remote, and uninteresting. What mattered for the Jews was history made memory, made personal, and made alive. Jews had longer, richer memories because individual memory expanded by merging into family memory and expanded again by merging into the memory of the nation. Each one could and did declare annually, "*My* father was a wandering Aramean" (Deut 26:5). It was the history of the Jews condensed to a single sentence. It was the single thread that, if you pulled it, would tumble out into the rich colorful saga of an entire people.

Such memory is essential to two things: a sense of identity and continuity. Without memory, we would not know who we are or where we have come from. And in the same way, the collective memory of remembered history is indispensable to the identity and continuity of a free people. If memory and a sense of history are lost, freedom too will soon be lost. Only through remembering history can unique and decisive events retain their unfading power and sustain their influence on generations who were not present to witness the events for themselves. Rabbi Heschel urged that when Jews studied the Torah, it must be as if it were given us today, and the same should be true of thinking of the exodus.

In the words of the Mishnah, "Generation by generation, each person must see himself as if he himself had come out of Egypt."[36] Exodus was an event that happened one time and also an event that happened for all time. For the intergenerational chain to remain strong and unbroken, four things must happen together, Rabbi Sacks says in expounding Maimonides. We must both "tell ourselves" and we must "tell our children," and we must "externalize" the story and "internalize" the story.[37] To recount history is to "remind and rebind"—to remind people of history and so to rebind society.

The importance of history is so obvious that its neglect is as startling as it is stupid. The full chorus of history warns of the folly of neglecting history. "He who cannot draw on three thousand years," Goethe wrote, "is living hand to mouth." "A people with no memory of its past," a French aphorism runs, "is like a mature man who has lost all recollection of his youth."[38] "Decay of libraries," poet laureate Ted Hughes wrote, "is like Alzheimer's in the nation's brain."[39] Plainly, Israel's constant call to "Remember" and "Never forget" was its safeguard and its antidote, whereas America and the West have carelessly abandoned history, and now find themselves living hand to mouth and suffering cultural dementia. This loss of history is a key reason why Americans have shifted from 1776 to 1789 almost without noticing. Those with the Year Zero mentality of the French Revolution need neither learn from the past nor take thought for the future. The angry present is all that concerns them. Once again, America's abandonment of civic education amounts to the death wish of 1776.

The Bible's stress on history grows directly from its notion of covenantal time and its invention of history as we know it. "Jews were the first people to find God in history," Rabbi Sacks writes, "they were the first to think in historical terms—of time as an arena of change as opposed to cyclical time in which the seasons rotate, people are born and die, but nothing really changes."[40] Long before the Greeks, the Jews were the first to write history and the first to see "in the chronicles of mankind something more than a mere succession of happenings—to see them as nothing less than a drama of redemption in which the fate of the nation reflects its loyalty or otherwise to a covenant with God."[41] Time for the pagan world around them and for today's posthumans and all who subscribe to the cyclical view of time is always tied to nature—and to nature looked at as the source of fertility and prosperity. The festivals of both the ancient pagan world and the revolutionary world of 1789 were tied to nature—"Mother Nature" and "cultivation" rather than "cult," as the Jacobins expressed it.

Not so the Bible's view. For a start, the Jewish celebrations looked back to creation itself rather than to nature at any later moment. But then, the Jewish year looked back to history rather than to nature. To be sure, the Jewish festivals took over celebrations that elsewhere were tied to nature, but they transformed them into a celebration of history—historical events through which God liberated and redeemed his people Israel in real-time. The Passover, for example, was originally a spring festival, but Israel transformed it to create a celebration of the exodus from Egypt. In Rabbi Heschel's words, "To Israel the unique events of history were spiritually more significant than the repetitive processes in the cycle of nature, even though physical sustenance depended on the latter."[42]

Of all historical events, exodus was the supremely important founding experience for the Jews. Far from a bare and mostly forgotten date, like AD 1066 for the English, the exodus was decisive for the Jewish identity and way of life. Rabbi Sacks explains. First, exodus became the *axiom* for Jewish thinking (remembering they were once slaves underlies the reason for many of their laws). Second, exodus represented the *alternative* they were called to be, in contrast to the surrounding nations (Hebrew freedom was to be anti-Egypt and counter-Babylon). And third, exodus was not only behind them but ahead of them as an *aspiration*. Exodus "opens out into a dramatically new vision of what a society might be like if the only Sovereign is God and every citizen is in His image. It is about the politics of the powerless and the powerlessness of power. Politics has never been more radical, more ethical and more humane."[43]

SOLIDARITY IN CELEBRATION

Along with history, a further feature of Jewish commemoration was its all-inclusiveness. The responsibility for national freedom was a collective responsibility, so the celebrations were for everyone too—men, women, and children—and they were celebrated with feasting and with joy. That meant too, and again in shining contrast to America and the West, that the covenant (constitution) and the laws were not for lawyers alone but for everyone. Not only were the people all equal before the covenant and the law, but the covenant and the law were the preserve of everyone, not just the lawyers. Rabbi Sacks remarks with pride, "Legal knowledge was never the closely guarded property of an elite. . . . Already in the first century CE Josephus could write that 'should any one of our nation be asked about our laws, he will repeat them as readily as his own name.'"[44]

Does history still matter when Google and Wikipedia allow us to look up any fact we wish and settle any dispute in seconds? When computer knowledge has expanded exponentially and human memory has shrunk or been replaced? History matters all the more, Rabbi Sacks says. "You can delegate history to computers, looking it up when you need it. But you cannot delegate memory. Memory is inherently inescapably personal. It is what makes us who we are. If you seek to sustain identity, you have to renew memory regularly and teach it to the next generation."[45]

Does the West even know its own story? Is its storytelling alive and well? Can the English say why Magna Carta matters? Can Americans expound the Declaration and the Constitution "as readily as their own name"? Can young Americans recount George Washington's crossing of the Delaware or the Battle of Gettysburg or the civil rights march at Selma, "as if they were there"? The overall impact of this multilayered storytelling, remembering, and celebration was profound. First, it gave each succeeding generation of Jews an experience of exodus and Sinai "as if they were there" themselves. Second, it allowed each generation to dedicate themselves to the covenant, all over again, and with the same freely chosen consent as the first generation. And third, it inscribed their Jewish identity on their hearts with a freshness that would not fade. Rabbi Sacks comments on such celebration and education: the result "from the very dawn of intelligence is that they are, as it were, engraved on our souls."[46] The celebration of the Passover carries the solemn double requirement: that every Jew is a guardian of the story and that memory, and deeper still that "*each person must see himself as if he himself had come out of Egypt.*"[47]

RENEWAL AND RESTORATION

When it comes to sustaining freedom, there are two equal and opposite errors often made. One error is the arrogance and stupidity of thinking that freedom will last forever and will never need renewing. And the other is to think that once freedom is lost, it can never be regained. (Rousseau: "Free peoples, remember this maxim: liberty can be gained, but never regained.")[48] In the time-torn world, nothing lasts forever. Call it entropy, call it the second law of thermodynamics, or call it the passing of time and the presence of sin. Everything from our bodies to our cars and our cities either runs down or breaks down. So too does freedom. Humans make promises and break promises, and trust and freedom break down in their wake. Both humility and wisdom therefore require a realism that takes renewal seriously if freedom is to be sustained. The Sinai vision of freedom addresses both problems—the running down and the breaking down.

Covenants need to be renewed and covenants can be renewed. Sinai's provision for the running down was for a *regular renewal*—a covenant renewal ceremony every seven years or the renewal needed when a leader, such as Moses, hands over to his successor, such as Joshua, and then Joshua to his successors in his turn (Deut 29; Josh 24). Rabbi Sacks describes Moses' original instructions to the people: "Every seven years, at the end of the year of release, the king must convene a national assembly and read the Torah to the people (Deut 31:10-13). This was, in effect, a covenant renewal ceremony, reminding the people of their past, their collective *raison d'être* and their commitments to God."[49]

Sinai's provision for the breaking down was for a *special renewal*—a national rededication and restoration after times of disaster and exile. The most important example in the Hebrew Scriptures was the dedication of the Second Temple when the nation found itself in the sorriest state in almost every way—after the trauma of the destruction of Solomon's first temple in 586 BC, the seventy years of exile in Babylon, the loss of ten of the original twelve tribes of Israel, and the near collapse of the Jewish worship and language. "Eventually," Sacks recounts, "Jewish life, and with it the restoration of the Temple as the spiritual heart of the nation, was re-energized by two remarkable leaders who had recently arrived from Babylon: Ezra and Nehemiah. Together they convened a new national assembly, one of the most important in Jewish history."[50] Crucially then, and crucially today, there was a strong link between good *leadership* and the importance of the *power to convene* or to bring people together as an assembly, a much-needed gift at the present moment.

Both these forms of renewal had the same purpose: covenantal (constitutional) renewal and the handing on of strong faith to the future. In Rabbi Sacks's words, "Civilizations that value the young stay young. Those that invest in the future have a future. It is not what we own that gives us a share in eternity, but those too whom we give birth and the effort we make to ensure that they carry our faith and way of life into the next generation."[51] Thus national identity may be restored and continuity across the generations may be renewed. The American republic and most Western democracies are deeply in need of such renewal today if they are to sustain their historic freedoms and not lose them altogether.

"The past is prologue," Americans say and carve the reminder on their monuments across their capital city. But that is taken as a boast that all roads lead to us, rather than an admission that the present may need reviving for the sake of the future. Do Americans today have any provision for national renewal and rededication? Do they show signs that they know how to use them? The leaders and citizens of the American republic and all the Western democracies should ponder Rabbi Sacks's conclusion: "The real battle faced by Israel was less military than spiritual. Jews might lose everything else, but if they kept their identity, they would outlive the mightiest of empires."[52]

In sum, Rabbi Sacks claims, *covenant renewal offers nothing less than the exception to "the otherwise universal law of the decline and fall of nations."*[53] That claim alone should arrest the minds of all who know history and all who appreciate the gravity of the present crises in America and the West. "Covenant renewal defeats national entropy. A people that never forgets its purpose and its past, that reenacts its story in every family every year, a nation that attributes its successes to God, and its failures to itself, cannot die.[54] Egypt was "the school of the soul" for the Israelites, so the retelling of the exodus was never to be forgotten. Indeed, they were warned, "if you ever forget it, you will be forced to relive it, through further exiles, other persecutions."[55]

Always follow the way of freedom, and never forget the way you have come. These two enduring principles of sustaining freedom are easily stated but rarely adhered to, and no book is more realistic than the Bible as to why this is so. People forget. *Winning freedom* and *ordering freedom* are the two earlier and highly demanding stages that make the third stage, *sustaining freedom*, look easy. But appearances are deceptive. The third stage is the hard one, though for different reasons. Escaping Pharaoh, defeating George III, or throwing off Czar Nicholas II may have been Herculean and heroic, but the hard task still lies ahead. As Rabbi Sacks writes, "You were attacked by your enemies. You may think this was the test of your strength. It was not. *The real challenge is not poverty but affluence, not slavery but freedom, not homelessness but home.*[56]

Power blinds. Prosperity deludes. Forgetfulness breeds complacence. "Affluence begets decadence."[57]

Rabbi Heschel delivered a warning to his generation when power and prosperity were breeding complacency, "Self-satisfaction is the opiate of fools."[58] He then quoted Oscar Wilde: "In this world there are only two tragedies. One is not getting what one wants, and the other is getting it. The last is the real tragedy."[59]

Again and again, Moses says to Israel, "Remember" (Deut 5:15; 8:2; 9:7; 24:9; 32:7). Keeping memory alive was to be a national duty and indispensable for national health and survival. *"Civilizations begin to die when they forget. Israel was commanded never to forget.* . . . The politics of free societies depends on the handing on of memory."[60]

CUTTING OFF THE BRANCH THEY ARE SITTING ON

There is one immense implication of the importance of the great transmission for freedom. *Schooling in the art of freedom is not a luxury but a necessity.* Civic education is essential for a free society. By ignoring the responsibility to hand on freedom, many Western societies are failing badly over the challenge of passing on the torch of freedom. This failure is especially critical to the United States because freedom is at the heart of America's self-understanding, and America faces particular challenges to freedom created by American mobility, diversity, and immigration. The failure can be gauged at several places.

First, postwar liberalism has given rise to soft and unrealistic libertarianism and the dream of a never-ending and unbounded freedom that has never been seen in history before. Broadly secular and expressly anti-Christian, such post-Christian liberals have presumed on the continuation of American superiority and wealth to advance a view of freedom that simply cannot last. Secular liberals have declared that God, religion, family, patriotism, and duty are all redundant to their vision of freedom. With a little help from the expanding market, the benevolent state, the enlightenment of the academy, and the horn of technological plenty, freedom and toleration can grow from strength to strength—if only everyone does what they like and remembers to be tolerant and to do no harm. Put humanity in the place of God, and all the freedom and generosities of God can be attained by humanity, with the sunny prospects of a better life for everyone—or so Americans have pretended.

The philosopher John Gray, an atheist himself, points out the folly of this hope. Dostoevsky, he notes, was just such a liberal when he was younger, but he came to see the bankruptcy of unbounded freedom and the outcome it leads to. Dostoevsky was not only prophetic in his critique of communism, Gray argues, but he was also no less prescient in his critique of Western liberalism. That indeed was the logic of the much-quoted admission by the revolutionary Shigalyov in *Demons*: "I got entangled in my own data, and my conclusion directly contradicts the original idea from which I start. Starting from unlimited freedom, I conclude with unlimited despotism. I will add, however, that apart from my solution of the social formula, there can be no other."[61] Unbounded freedom produces unwanted fruit. "Slaves must be equal: without despotism there's never been any freedom or equality, but there must be equality in the herd."[62]

Second, America has helped to undermine its own sense of identity and tradition of freedom by abandoning civic education in its public schools (though kept alive in private schools and in homeschooling). This matters, of course, because if America is a nation by intention and by ideas, to weaken the ideas is to weaken the identity. Once again, the abandonment is the result of the "long march through the institutions" and the triumph of 1789 over 1776. And it thrives on the recurring "blame America first" refrain that America is inherently racist, imperialistic, militarist, genocidal, and the like. Education is indoctrination, it is said, so any notion of Americanism is coercive and an imposition upon unwilling minorities.

The breakdown of civic education leads to growing uncertainty and confusion over America's identity and freedom. It is still relatively easy to obtain naturalization papers and become *an* American, but it is increasingly difficult to know what it is to *be* American. This means in turn that there is no *unum* to balance the *pluribus* of the original American motto—*E Pluribus Unum* (Out of many, one). The uniting first principles of what it means to be American have been called into question, and the balkanizing and splintering of America proceeds apace. Education is indispensable to freedom because it is both "an apprenticeship in liberty" and a "constant conversation between the generations."[63] Thanks to this crisis in public education, America has lost its freedom schools.

Third, America has allowed ideas and ideologies—above all, cultural Marxism or critical theory—to flourish in its colleges and universities. These ideas are not just unrealistic, as with libertarianism, but openly hostile to Western civilization and basic freedoms, such as freedom of conscience and speech. Watch the impact of these trends converging, and the result is an America at war with itself. The first principles of freedom have not been passed on. The baton has been dropped, and the flame of freedom dowsed. People lament the polls that show how the younger generation is not rising to defend freedom as before, but the fault does not lie with the younger generation. It lies with those who have not understood freedom well enough to know that they must pass it on.

Fourth, the breakdown in transmission has been reinforced by a constellation of other trends in American society—the general neglect of history and the past, the obsession with change and the future, the neglect of book reading, the generationalism that is a relativistic obsession with the complete separateness of each generation ("It's a generational thing. You wouldn't understand."), and so on. Americans often defend themselves by pointing to the vogue for reading about the founding generation—David Rubenstein's *The American Story* and numerous bestsellers by David McCullough, Ronald Chernow, Jon Meacham, and others. But brilliant and bestselling though these authors are, their overall effect is to shine a light on great leaders and great women and men of character, but oddly, not the nature of the American experiment, how it works, and what it requires—all of which is at stake today.

Is the resulting breakdown in transmission due simply to a lapse in attention or is it more serious? Clearly, today's more radical expressions are opposed to the very notion of handing on. Transmission itself is suspect. The desire for freedom means autonomy, autonomy means independence, and independence means pride and a cutting off—a self-chosen rupture from creation, from givens, from the past, from history, from earlier generations, and from debts, ties, indebtedness, and obligations of all kinds. But down that road lie hubris and isolation, and the mathematical certainty that freedom will not last. We are all heirs, recipients, and debtors to the very core of our being, and the heritage of freedom asks a question of every one of us. Will we choose cultural dementia and the death of freedom? Or will we love our children and our children's children as ourselves, and will we hand on to the next generations the best and highest of all that was handed down to us?

America cannot endure permanently half 1776 and half 1789. The compromises, contradictions, hypocrisies, inequities, and evils have built up unaddressed. The grapes of wrath have ripened again, and the choice before America is plain. Either America goes forward best by going back first, or America is about to reap a future in which the worst will once again be the corruption of the best.

7

PUTTING WRONG RIGHT

PRINCIPLE 7: FREEDOM MUST ALWAYS ADDRESS WRONGS, BUT IN THE RIGHT WAY—THE WAY OF THE LEFT

Simon Wiesenthal's memoir *The Sunflower* is one of the most haunting books of the twentieth century. It should be required reading for all schoolchildren in our time. At its heart, Wiesenthal, a death camp survivor, raises a question that drives a sword into the heart of the modern world and rips open a glaring part of the great divide between 1776 and 1789. While in a concentration camp in Poland, Wiesenthal and other prisoners were marched into town for a manual labor project. There he was singled out and escorted to the bed of a dying SS officer, Karl.

Hideously wounded and bandaged beyond recognition, Karl was even more hideously tortured by his conscience over what he had done to the Jews. Without the absolution of one Jew to whom he could confess, he could not die in peace. Would Wiesenthal be that Jew? The seconds ticked by. They were two men brought together by fate. One, helpless, asks the other for help. The other feels helpless in his inability to give it. Finally, Wiesenthal acted. He brushed off the hand of the dying man. "At last, I made up my mind and without a word I left the room."[1]

Years later, Wiesenthal asked, "Was my silence at the bedside of the dying Nazi right or wrong?" He then questions us all. What could he have done? What should he have done? What would we have done? What would we do in a similar situation? Anyone who has been in the presence of a death camp survivor, such as Elie Wiesel, whom I revered, knows that there is no simple answer to any of those questions. But the last question remains inescapable for all of us as moral agents and responsible citizens today. How are we to respond to wrongs of any kind, and especially to the radical evils such as slavery and racism that have been a central feature of the United States for so long?

Here once again the vision of Exodus (and the whole Bible) is radical, original, practical, timely, and a shining contrast to the attitudes of the revolutionary faith of all whose ideas have come down from the French Revolution and its heirs. This critical contrast takes us to the heart of the crisis into which America was plunged in 2020 by the horrific killing of George Floyd by a White policeman in Minneapolis, captured on video for all the world to witness.

THOU SHALT NOT JUDGE

At first sight the responses to Wiesenthal's questions seemed to suggest that the significant difference was between Jews and Christians. In one edition of the book most of the Jewish responses to Wiesenthal's questions said that he was right not to forgive, and most of the Christian responses said he was wrong. The reason, the Jews said, is that only a victim has the right and the responsibility to forgive, so by definition a murderer is unforgivable because the victim is dead. Some therefore say that even God cannot forgive a murderer (though Israel's greatest king, David, was forgiven for both committing adultery and murdering the woman's husband).

That impression of the divide is misleading. The Jewish insistence on personal responsibility and judgment as "measure for measure" may sometimes sound chilling, but equally the Christian emphasis on automatic and indiscriminate forgiveness can easily become a form of Dietrich Bonhoeffer's "cheap grace." But in truth, the chief division is not between Jews and Christians. They both have a high and distinctive place for forgiveness as central to rigorous remediation for the sins of the past. The real division is between the members of the biblical family of faiths and those of other worldviews and political philosophies, including the progressive left, who have no real place for forgiveness and reconciliation at all.

A choice to retaliate rather than forgive seems instinctive and natural in human experience, though it has never been the way of societies shaped by the Bible. Andrew Carnegie, the legendary industrialist, philanthropist, and atheist was proud of his revised edition of the Scripture: "If a man strikes you on the cheek, turn unto him the other also, but if he strikes you on that, go for him." But Carnegie himself was not a man to nurse grievances, so he was surprised when his former business partner Henry Clay Frick refused the olive branch that he held out to him after a major argument. "Tell Mr. Carnegie," Frick responded, "I'll meet him in hell."

In the same way, President Trump always took great pride in his ability to counterpunch. ("He's a Queens boy," one of his friends said to me as an explanation when he was elected. "If you punch a Queens boy, he will punch you right back. That's what they do.") The president's habit, unleashed on Twitter, led to the insults and ad hominem invective that the Torah calls "evil speech," and became one of the worst features of his presidency—though abundantly reciprocated by his enemies as time went on.

INDISCRIMINATE FORGIVERS

The trouble is that as the West slips further from its Jewish and Christian roots, retaliation is going mainstream and with damaging results. The West is spurning notions such as repentance, forgiveness, mercy, reconciliation, and turning the other cheek, and there is an increasing tendency to go to the extremes in responding to wrongs. Take the two extremes we have seen in the last generation, one representing the dying vestiges of the Jewish and Christian faiths and the other demonstrating the power of the new post-Christian faiths. On one side, and not so long ago, there were the "indiscriminate forgivers." These were people who were soft on wrongs. Today, such attitudes seem naive and quaint, but the very strangeness shows how much America has changed in a short time. Such people were more sentimental than ethical, they stressed grace without judgment, and they had a thousand ways of showering down forgiveness that was too easy and quite ineffective in dealing with genuine wrongs. "Love means never having to say you are sorry," Erich Segal trumpeted in the film *Love Story*, but later, when asked to explain the celebrated line, he admitted that its significance had long escaped him.

It may seem hard to believe that this softer extreme was ever in vogue. In fact, it was the product of the decaying Jewish and Christian culture and depended for its force on the soft remnants of the biblical ethic. Harvard Law School professor Mary Anne Glendon skewered it as contrition chic, and there were reasons why it became fashionable for a time. For one thing, there was a vogue for nonjudgmentalism. Vacuously tolerant, the idea was bandied around that "Thou shalt not judge" was the "eleventh commandment." It even led some to the dangerous nonsense that, as one Yale student argued to me, it was worse to *judge* evil than to *do* evil. Talk of forgiveness for everyone, for everything, became easy and automatic. Not to judge at all was said to be next best to understanding all, and since to understand all is to forgive all, there was nothing to be forgiven because all could be understood. Thus all was forgiven because nothing was to be judged, and no one really cared—a recipe for moral indifference and becoming uncaring.

Another factor in the softer extreme was the vogue for confessing the sins of others rather than our own and apologizing for the sins of the past but never the present. Thus President Bill Clinton apologized to the African people for slavery. French President Jacques Chirac apologized to the descendants of Alfred Dreyfus for the "judicial error" that sent him to jail in 1898. British prime minister Tony Blair apologized to the people of Northern Ireland for the massacre of fourteen civilians in 1972. Japan apologized to Korea for the atrocities committed by its troops in World War II. And Switzerland apologized to Jews whose money was taken and kept by Swiss banks during the same war. Doubtless, the evils were evil and the apologies were sincere. But never in history have so many archives been ransacked, so many witnesses deposed, so many hearings held, so many testimonies plumbed, and so many statues torn down—all on behalf of exposing "the sins of fathers" rather than our own.

Yet another factor was the modern penchant for image makeovers that reduce confession to a carefully staged step in the process of public rehabilitation. Following the shift from *character* to image, the world was awash with what was called the useful apology or mea-not-really-culpa. This is the calculated acknowledgment of personal weakness, carefully designed to address a political or financial problem without making any concession that could attract further harm.

In most cases no one listening to the apology has the slightest idea whether the scripted words were sincere or not. But who cares? The modern apology is not really an apology from the abuser to the victim. It is for public consumption, a plea bargain with fans, supporters, and critics and a required step on the path back to social rehabilitation. Whatever passes for repentance is an early move in the healing process. The happy ending is "achieving closure," capped by the announcement that it is time to move on and time for the tabloids and paparazzi to stalk someone else.

In sum, this first extreme trivialized evil, guilt, responsibility, confession, and restoration simultaneously. In a guilt-free, sin-lite era, few statements were emptier than "I take full responsibility." That was especially so in America where full responsibility was rarely accompanied by the responsible act of resignation. It may be a far cry from Henry Ford's maxim, "Never apologize, never explain," but in fact it is the equal and opposite error. Offering a hollow comfort without any challenge to moral change, cheap-grace forgiveness is a powerful collusion with the pretense that all is well because nothing is really wrong. It papers over wrongs rather than fixing them and is completely bankrupt as an answer to the present levels of conflict and hate and as a remedy for radical evil.

There can be little disagreement that this first extreme was wrong. Indifference toward evil becomes evil itself because the evil that is an exception, when left unchallenged, becomes evil as the norm, and a norm is normal, so nothing need be done. Those who turn a blind eye to evil and injustice done to others have signed on as accomplices to evildoers and evildoing.

INTRANSIGENT UNFORGIVERS

Since that time, which was not so long ago, America has lurched sharply from the extreme of the "indiscriminate forgivers" to the opposite extreme—that of the "intransigent unforgivers." These are the left-wing radicals who fight against injustice rightly, but with a merciless notion of justice that is destructive. The mercilessness stems from the heart of their ideology and allows no place for any forgiveness for the sins of the present (called out) or the past (with its heroes cut down and its history rewritten). Both their short-term tactics and long-term objectives make them ruthlessly hard in responding to wrongs—deliberately exploiting wrongs to promote their own cause rather than remedy the problems.

The problems of this second extreme are often masked for a simple reason. The inequalities and the injustices the radicals confront are so real and so blatant that it is impossible for people not to be stirred and easy for people to step forward in support without asking questions. Yet there need to be questions. Take, for example, the widespread conflation of the slogan "Black lives matter" with the organization that goes by the same name. No one should be deceived. The claim in the slogan is undeniable as a statement of human worth, but it is contradicted by the character and ideology of the organization that is also un-deniable for those who investigate. No version of Marxism in any form has ever been the champion of the truth that lives truly matter. And in practice it is clear that the pent-up rage of many BLM and antifa radicals is so great that their demands must be met or the system must be burned down. Destruction, not life, is in their hearts, and the old cry of insatiable justice flares out again: "Let justice be done, though the world perishes" (*Fiat justitia, pereat mundus*).

How can a fight against genuine injustice grow into such destructive rage? The truth is that hate is often legitimate outrage blocked or misdirected and then turned murderous—either frustrated externally by the stubborn perpetuation of the injustice or distorted internally by the faulty response of the person outraged. An early Chinese convert to Marxism aptly expressed such rage and hate. His outrage at the gross inequalities of wealth that he saw had swollen into such consuming hatred that he passionately desired to destroy anyone anywhere who had excessive wealth. Then, he said, he swore "to kill every person in the world if there was a chance, and then because the world is not right, he determined to go to heaven and kill God himself!"[2]

Resentment-fueled radicalism is the perfect outlet for envious rage, and its fist-shaking, building-burning, shop-looting, statue-toppling anger erupts in the radical wing of the progressive left. But what really matters is not the barbaric face of the extreme left, which truly is extreme. What undermines the republic is the revolutionary ideology behind it and an ideology that is far more sophisticated and far harder to combat than the arson and looting in the streets. Rioters can be curbed by law and order, but the spreading contagion of dangerous ideas is harder to contain than a pandemic. In the end it will be the ideas that subvert the law and disrupt the order even more than the rioters.

As mentioned in the introduction, what America is now beginning to see and American leaders must face up to is the third major stream of revolutionary faith flowing out of the French Revolution. The first two streams were the *revolutionary nationalism* of the nineteenth century and the *revolutionary socialism* of the twentieth century. This third stream is *revolutionary liberationism*, which is also called neo-Marxism, Western Marxism, cultural Marxism, updated Marxism, and even "user-friendly Marxism."

Naming the movement and defining its ideology are a challenge because there is no agreed definition of what they are. My own term *revolutionary liberationism* is an attempt to do justice to many of the diverse components. Many of the advocates of the movement seem to delight in impenetrable jargon, and perhaps deliberately, they call themselves different names as if to throw their critics off the scent. Thus the radicals call themselves the "left," the "progressives," the "resistance," the "social justice warriors" (and social scholars), the antifascists, the antiracists, the woke movement, and often anything but open Marxists. Yet in a 2015 interview on the *Real News Network*, Patrisse Cullors, one of the co-founders of Black Lives Matter, stated, "We are trained Marxists. We are super-versed on ideological theories."[3] And in a major text on the ideology, its proponents insist that while they are *post*-Marxist in one sense, they are definitely post-*Marxist*.[4] In other words, they have broken with classical or orthodox Marxism over the failure of such concepts such as *economic determinism* and the need for a *general strike*, but they are still Marxists and they should not be mistaken for liberals or even moderate socialists.

MADE IN EUROPE, FLOURISHING IN THE UNITED STATES

The distinctive strength of revolutionary liberationism is a blend of neo-Marxism and postmodernism. It was born in continental Europe, but now flourishes above all in the English-speaking world. It owes everything to five particular moments in its development as a movement or as a loose coalition of radical ideas. The first phase was the work of Antonio Gramsci, writing (and dying) in jail under Mussolini in Italy in the 1920s. His contribution was to pioneer a revised understanding of Marxism. Revolution had not happened as Marx predicted, even in Russia in 1917, and it never would under the conditions of the advanced modern world. Gramsci therefore revised Marxist theory to suit the challenges of revolution in the highly developed societies of the West—shifting the focus from economic determinism to cultural dominance, from the working class to the cultural elites, and so on.

The second phase happened when Gramsci's ideas were picked up by the Frankfurt School. Starting in Germany but writing across Europe and the United States from the 1920s to the 1960s, the scholars of the Frankfurt School were diverse—Theodor Adorno, Max Horkheimer, Erich Fromm, Walter Benjamin, Herbert Marcuse, and others. They often gave the impression of a quarrelsome group of Marxist intellectuals who couldn't agree with each other, and they too seemed to delight in their obscure jargon. But for all their cantankerousness, their recurring themes struck a wider chord on the left and with the young, above all with the New Left in America in the 1960s. Their ideas resonated with the growing feeling of human "alienation" (following the young Marx), the sense of "dehumanization" created by bureaucracy, the fears and unease aroused by the "totally administered state," and the coercive conformism of the "culture industry," and so on. Such ideas were all in the interest of liberation, transformation, revolutionary change, and what André Breton called "the Great Refusal," a slogan that summed up the 1960s counterculture to perfection.

The third phase came at the close of the 1960s. Herbert Marcuse, a leading member of the Frankfurt School in California, and Rudi Dutschke, the leader of the Red Brigade in Germany, each called for "a long march through the institutions." For all the success of the civil rights movement, the ferment of the counterculture, the power of the resistance to the Vietnam War, and the disruptions of the decade of "drugs, sex, rock and roll," the radicals knew that the revolution could not win in the streets. They needed to penetrate and prevail in the thinking of the "cultural gatekeepers"—in the colleges, universities, and secondary schools, in the press and media, and in the so-called "culture industry," the worlds of Hollywood and entertainment. The long march was launched, and the success of their penetration of the heights of American society over the next fifty years was astonishing.

The fourth phase came in the 1980s and 1990s with the convergence between the neo-Marxism of the Gramsci-Frankfurt School and the postmodernism that rose in post war France. Postmodernism, with its celebrated rejection of all "grand narratives" and its commitment to "deconstruction," was the work of philosophers such as Michel Foucault, Jacques Derrida, and Jean-François Lyotard. In its early phase postmodernism was almost entirely a theoretical exercise and showed little interest in transforming society. But when it converged with the objectives of neo-Marxism, it took a decidedly political and practical turn. Since then, critical theory, or simply Theory, has been the ideological force driving the progressive left. Countless campuses now have been influenced by critical women's studies, critical race theory, queer studies, environmentalism, veganism, fat studies, and the like—all of which in turn spawned the political correctness, the speech codes, and the cancel culture that has become so controversial and damaging.

The fifth and final phase of the movement is the least understood. It brings the story of revolutionary liberationism to the present moment and deserves far greater research and debate because it raises in a new form the old questions of freedom, democracy, and money. It came early in the twenty-first century when billionaire superfunders such as George Soros and others decided to use their immense wealth to give a powerful financial boost to the organizations of the radical left. The effect has been incalculable, and unless wisely understood and responsibly countered, it may well prove to be not just a nail but a whole chest of nails in the coffin of republican self-government. With literally tens of billions of dollars now put behind their causes, the radical and progressive left has become an ever-swelling, ever-morphing, ever-rebranding hive of swarming, collaborating organizations that carry forward a myriad of left-wing causes on a thousand fronts. Mao Zedong's "Let a thousand flowers bloom" now has its American counterpart in the superfunded pop-up protest movements of the progressive left. The neo-Marxist revolution, also known under an infinite number of aliases with newly invented names and slogans such as "No justice, no peace," is now brought to you courtesy of Wall Street and Silicon Valley. The naivety of financiers and business leaders boggles the mind.

In 1960, and influenced by the Frankfurt School, Cyril Wright Mills called on academics to transform "private troubles into public issues" or to "problematize issues," which many have studiously done ever since.[5] So the radicals of the progressive left stand as torchbearers for a worldwide revolutionary movement working to liberate victims of all forms of oppression—racism, sexism, colonialism, White privilege, patriarchy, heteronormativity, and imperialism and striving for the freedom of women, Black people, brown people, LGBTQIA+ people, minorities, animals, and the environment. The *rainbow coalition* has steadily expanded, and now through *rainbow combustion* it has exploded into a broad radical movement that threatens to dismantle the American experiment and transform America forever. One moment, the cause is Occupy Wall Street, and the next moment it is Black Lives Matter, and then climate change or whatever is the issue du jour. They are all linked by their underlying ideas. And the plus sign at the end of LGBTQIA+ movement stands for the open door for any as-yet-unknown cause on behalf of any oppressed group yet to be identified in the future. After all, as Tom Paine argued in *An Age of Reason* in 1794, it is the age of revolution, in which everything may be looked for. Or as the radicals say today, everything must be questioned and everything must be changed because "it's a humanity issue."

UTOPIA NEVER COMES, OPPRESSION NEVER ENDS

By the radicals' own admission, the two watchwords of revolutionary liberationism and critical theory are *hegemony* (or dominance) and *antagonisms*. For all the soaring dreams and the dense thicket of the doctrines behind the progressive left, their theoretical and practical components converge at a single point: *hegemony* or the dominance of power.[6] Their proposed dynamic of liberation is therefore to analyze and engage society in two broad ways. First, the social justice scholars set out to examine a society's discourse or the way in which speech is used throughout a society to express what the society takes for granted as truth and knowledge. This analysis is based on what Helen Pluckrose and James Lindsay call the "postmodern knowledge principle"—a radical skepticism as to whether objective knowledge or truth can be known at all.[7] In the absence of truth and objectivity, what is being looked for is the "dominant discourse," the power that decides which so-called truths and which so-called values are to be believed. Like a script given to actors to perform on stage, a script is given to everyone born and growing up in any society. That script, which covers what their society tells them is "right" and "true" and "good," shapes how they are to think and how they are to see the world and act in it.

Second, the social justice warriors then examine the society's "pyramids of power," the power relationships between groups in the society—always seeking to identify the superior and the subordinate, the majority and the minority, the officers and the subalterns, and above all the oppressors and the oppressed. This analysis is based on the postmodern power principle—the belief that society is composed of systems of power and hierarchies that determine what knowledge can be known and how.[8] As Pluckrose and Lindsay remark, critical theory is difficult to appreciate from the outside because it sounds like a gigantic conspiracy theory at the expense of the victims. Yet we are all involved unwittingly, so what it really is, is "a conspiracy theory with no conspirators."[9]

These two explorations are used in turn to assess the power relations of the different groups in a society—men and women, old and young, Whites and Blacks, Europeans and indigenous peoples, straight people and gay people, slim and obese, and so on. The goal in each case is to identify the "victim," and then to weaponize the oppressed party as the means toward liberation and revolution. Regardless of whether grievances are real or imagined, recent or ancient, victims are all who are in a minority, especially those who experience *intersectionality* (such as the Black queer trans person, who belongs to more than one oppressed group at the same time). Hence the term *grievance studies*. Thus social justice scholars identify the hegemony (or the dominance in the power relations), the social justice warriors exploit the antagonisms between the groups, and together they weaponize the "victims" and use them to thrust forward the impetus toward change and transformation.

The drawbacks and dangers of this dynamic are obvious, but the bottom line is plain: Revolutionary hope may spring eternal, but no Marxist revolution has ever worked. The revolutionary dream is never fulfilled, and the revolutionaries' oppression never ends. Better far to start with realism from the start and be aware of the dangers.

First, revolutionary liberationism is based solely on power, and inevitably it emphasizes might over right. Nothing is more central to both Marxism and postmodernism at their core. God is dead, truth is dead, and all that is left is power. The post-truth world is the post-rights world, and everything is understood in terms of power. Power is the god of the radical left. Power is their compass, their sword, their bullhorn, the field they play their game on, and the sole rule they play by. And power, of course, is a zero-sum game. Lenin's "Who? Whom?" means that someone always has power over someone else. There is no other possibility. If I have power, you don't, and if you have power, you are the oppressor and I am the oppressed—and I can cry victim.

With the weakening of religion, the marginalizing of morality, and the forgetfulness over history, power is filling the vacuum across American politics as a whole. Witness the recent threats of impeachment as power plays. But the absolute idolatry of power and the devilish exploitation of inequalities and resentments are the perfect expression of both neo-Marxism and postmodernism. They have been at the heart of the revolutionary faith of the left ever since the French Revolution. And they link the myriad of radicals who, in all the recurring revolutions and attempted revolutions, have mounted the barricades as the children of 1789. No one should ignore the progressive left's reliance on power. It is the same idolatry of might that has been the fountainhead of brutality and cruelty throughout history. In his majestic book *The Prophets*, Rabbi Heschel raises the question that links all the tyrants, butchers, and bullies of history. "Why were so few voices raised in the ancient world against the ruthlessness of man? Why are human beings so obsequious, ready to kill and ready to die at the call of kings and chieftains? Perhaps it is because they worship might, venerate those who command might, and are convinced that it is by force that man prevails."[10]

Second, the analysis depends on highlighting groups and categories, and it has no eye for individual persons, except as props and pawns. When the pyramids of power are drawn, people are viewed only as samples of tribes, interest groups, or categories that are desirable or undesirable. People are always male or female, young or old, White or Black, straight or gay, boomers or millennials, thin or obese, or whatever. They are never Tom, Dick, or Harry, let alone Maria, Zeynep, or Miriam. They are nouns and not names, categories and labels and not individuals, and that is all that matters. Winston Churchill, for example, may have been a colossus of a wartime leader, a Nobel prize-winning author, an incomparable orator and wit, among other things. But for the social justice warriors, none of that mattered. He was an imperialist, and his statue must come down. The man himself, let alone the nuances and shades of gray of his character in his times, was irrelevant.

The ultimate poison of the stress on groups should be obvious, for in an alienated and unraveling society it triggers the dangerous madness of crowds. When individuality becomes a recipe for loneliness, there is only a short step from a loneliness that cannot be assuaged to a lockstep that cannot be answered by reason, to a loss of individuality and integrity that cannot be remedied and is difficult to resist. In terms of logic the cult of crowd sameness that grows from the emphasis on groups and equality is dangerous whether it is exploited by Lenin, by Hitler, by Mao, or by the organizers of Black Lives Matter.

Third, like the Roman dictum *Divide et impera*, "divide and rule," critical theory sets groups against other groups in ways that not only reveal disharmony but puts true harmony beyond reach. The antagonisms are said to be elemental, constant, insuperable, and in our DNA. We are all sexist and racist now, and biased in a thousand irremediable ways. But how does making something omnipresent and unavoidable help us to overcome it? What would it be like for any of us to live in a community in which, if our eyes were really open, we would know that everyone is dead set against everyone else, and they cannot help it and can never be otherwise? Yet the consequence of certain critical studies is that every man is now every woman's potential assailant, and every woman is every man's potential accuser—and that is all that men and women can be.

It is one thing to be aware that we are all liable to bias and prejudice of one sort or another, but quite another to be told that only Whites are guilty of racism and only men are sexist. Marx deliberately sought revolution through exploiting the contradictions between the classes, and the progressive left now exploits antagonisms by setting sex against sex, race against race, and generation against generation. "Workers of the world unite!" was the cry of the old-line Marxists on behalf of the proletariat. "Our motto," the progressive left declares frankly, is "Back to the hegemonic struggle."[11]

Fourth, whatever the declared objective, the final state of the purported victims is usually little improved, if not almost as bad but in a different way. All too often victims become the new "useful idiots" for Marxism and neo-Marxism. History's ultimate victims have been the Jews, but to their credit Jews have refused to play the role of victims. Those who play the victim, as they know, eventually perceive themselves as victims, and in the end to paralyze themselves as victims. Sadly, that condition has become the state of racial groups who were encouraged to see themselves as victims. Perpetual political dependency on their "saviors" is only a little better than slavery.

Fifth, critical theory insists that everything, without exception, is culturally relative. Claims to universal ideals and methods are therefore suspect as the potential source of bias and oppression. Some of Theory's proponents therefore diminish, if not reject outright, the highest fruits of human thinking, which may have developed in the West but are universal and vital for human progress and development—such as reason and science. Official race guidelines issued by the Smithsonian Museum in Washington, DC, in 2020 argued that "objective, rational, linear thinking" and "hard work before play" were all aspects of "Whiteness."[12]

The logic of such claims is mind-spinning. Not only does it undermine what brought the West to where it is, but it blocks other parts of the world from following. If absolutely everything is relative, as standpoint theory asserts, who gets to say if any answer is right? Is the assertion that something is true or false merely the privilege of "privilege" based on social power? Are human rights universal or Eurocentric? Is it racist to say that two plus two equals four? Is it a hangover from colonialism to teach the scientific method to Zambians and Vietnamese? Is it anything other than nonsense to insist that science and mathematics be uncoupled from racism, capitalism, imperialism, and oppression? Is there no difference between teachers requiring their students to learn logic and their students requesting their teachers to listen to their generation's music? For all their high-minded intentions, social justice warriors who insist on such absurdities will only keep people backward, while they become the patronizing paternalists of our day, lacking only the pith helmets and Victorian paunches of those they despise.

Sixth, the outcome of the activism of the progressive left has been the steady curtailing of independent thinking, open-ended inquiry, two-sided hearings, civil debate, rational persuasion, respect for differences, and freedom of expression. The difference between true liberalism and the illiberalism of the left grows clearer by the day. According to critical theory, even notions such as truth, objectivity, and persuasion are instruments of power. If you are on the side of power, you must "check your privilege," and if someone you are talking to is on the side of the "oppressed," you must "never speak, simply listen." The words of the oppressed are "their truth" and therefore "true" regardless of truth. Those who are not watchful or brave soon find themselves silenced or swept along with the current until they find themselves asked to believe the unbelievable, agree with the disagreeable, and stay mute before the highly objectionable.

To be sure, silence is complicity, but a complicity that is the fruit of confusion and uncertainty as much as cowardice. Political correctness, speech codes, charges of microaggression, sensitivity to triggering, and the provision of safe places all mean that in the name of liberation freedom is being shut down. Revolutionary liberationism is proving to be the fast track to George Orwell's "thought crimes" and "newspeak," and no true liberal can afford to stay silent.

Seventh, many of the arguments of neo-Marxism and critical theory are illogical and manipulative. The old postmodern maxim "There is absolutely no such thing as truth" has long been seen to be self-contradictory or meaningless. As philosopher Roger Scruton often used to say, someone is saying to you in effect, "Don't believe what I am saying. So don't." In the same way, an antiracism that sees racism in everyone, everywhere, and in everything, cannot help becoming racism by another name, and it does. The charge that all is racist is bound in the end to become racist itself. The same people who reject all binaries when it comes to sex are the very ones who say that racism is binary—"There is no such thing as a nonracist," they say. "There are only two types of people: racists and antiracists."

In the same way, people are shouted down for saying that "All lives matter." But either "Black lives matter" *because all lives matter, including Black lives too* (because, for example, all people are made in the image of God) or "Black lives matter" inevitably becomes a cover for racism itself. Yusra Khogali, a Black Muslim who is a Black Lives Matter leader in Toronto and another self-professed "trained Marxist," openly demonstrated her choice. She prayed, she said, that Allah would give her strength not to "kill subhuman whites." "White ppl," she texted, "are recessive genetic defects. this is factual."[13] The gap between the meaning of the words "Black lives matter" and the mission of the organization by the same name is glaring. Most disturbing of all, many of the BLM activists are using slogans that converge with those of Louis Farrakhan and the Nation of Islam, and are rabidly anti-Semitic.

All too often the charge of racism is expressed in the form of a "Heads, I win. Tails, you lose" type of argument. Sensitivity training seminars are designed expressly to browbeat people into submission. As Helen Pluckrose and James Lindsay point out, "Worst of all is to set up double-binds, like telling them that if they notice race it is because they are racist, but if they don't notice race it's because their privilege affords them the luxury of not noticing race, which is racist."[14] Such tactics and attitudes, the two authors conclude, "tear at the fabric that holds contemporary societies together."[15]

Eighth, politically correct language often ties itself in knots of its own making. Like the courtiers afraid to tell the king that his fashionable new clothes were a fiction and he was parading in the buff, many of the contorted theories of critical theory lead only to absurdities that people are afraid to blurt out. The reason lies in the lengths to which language and even reality has been distorted, above all in queer theory. Queer theory is the deliberate subversion of all that is considered normal, even the norms of biology and science. After all, there is no such thing as truth and objectivity. That is the fallacy of essentialism, they say. Everything is socially constructed, and what can be socially constructed can be deconstructed and reconstructed—at will. No one is any longer who they *are*, for there is no essence or core reality of who we are. We are each free to be what we choose to be. What we *do* is more important than what we are.

What matters, then, is no longer the reality, say, of biology and the body a person is born with, but how people feel, and feel now rather than five minutes ago. Are you male or female? Straight or gay? You can be one or the other or neither, depending on how you feel and what you prefer. And tomorrow you can shake the kaleidoscope again and begin all over. All essences are gone, all binaries are abolished, all boundaries are blurred, and all choices are malleable and changing. The possibilities then are infinite. But then of course the chaos begins as there is no resting point anywhere for anyone and no identity or character. What looks like infinite freedom soon becomes dizziness, nausea, paralysis, and madness. The American Cancer Society is afraid to use the term *woman*, so it refers to "individuals with a cervix," and the wise nod gravely.

The net result is a topsy-turvy world that is sometimes funny, sometimes absurd, and sometimes tragic, but such an upside-down world is not new. The Hebrew prophets saw it as a mark of decadence that truth had been turned into lies and lies into truth. G. K. Chesterton saw it beginning again a century ago. The time was coming, he wrote in 1926, "when a man may be howled down for saying that two and two make four, in which furious party cries will be raised against anybody who says that cows have horns, in which people will persecute the heresy of calling a triangle a three-sided figure, and hang a man for maddening a mob with the news that grass is green."[16]

Where is Monty Python when we need him? It may soon be as dangerous to declare that two plus two equals four as to argue that men are men and women women, and there are only two genders. To *queer* is now a verb. It means to disrupt the normal ways of seeing something and to open up the possibilities of new and unusual ways. But where does anyone stop? The daring, risk-taking, liberty-loving sound of the verb makes the noun inherently unstable. By definition the queer, if truly queered and queering, becomes the person who is at odds with all essences and all norms, and even with a firm view of what was once himself or herself—which means that *there is no one there.* "I doubt, therefore I am," Descartes declared in the seventeenth century, but doubt became skepticism, became complete uncertainty, became incoherence, and finally nihilism and insanity—and will again with the extremes of critical theory unless small boys dare to tell the emperor he has no clothes on.

Ninth, the accusations of the progressive left often mask their hypocrisy. They repeatedly charge, for example, that in the name of freedom Americans perpetrated terrible evils on a whole series of defenseless victims, from the Native Americans in New England to the rural peoples of Vietnam and Afghanistan. Needless to say, there is truth in the charge. Imperialism and colonialism in all their forms are the abuse of power writ large. But the hypocrisy in the charge is blatant, for behind the accusing finger, three fingers point backwards. Wherever there was genuine evil, and there was too much, it was wrong, egregiously wrong. But the evils were also hypocritical, un-Christian and un-American because they represented might riding roughshod over right, rather than right over might as Sinai advocated and the Declaration of Independence promised.

In other words, the progressive left accuses America of its own cardinal sin— the abuse of power. The very evils the past is accused of were carried out in the same power-driven manner that postmodernism advocates as realistic and natural and that all left-wing revolutions, from 1789 on, have practiced as basic policy. The result is reminiscent of Seneca's comment on the peace won by Caesar Augustus. A certain peace came when Octavian had no more rivals, but "I am reluctant to call mercy what was really the exhaustion of cruelty."[17] Tacitus made a similar comment on Rome's insatiable drive for expansion: "To ravage, to slaughter, to usurp under false titles, they call empire; and where they make a desert, they call it peace."[18] Pax Romana, it was said, was never true peace. Rome formed its peace on the tip of the spear and the edge of the sword. In the same way, much of America's continental and global expansion grew from the barrel of a Colt revolver or the bomb bays of a B-29. And when it did so, it flouted America's "better angel" and contradicted the logic of America's founding. Yet such wrongs should be seen as an aberration and not the norm. They should have been addressed and corrected by the ideal rather than tolerated and celebrated to the point of undermining the ideal.

Tenth and last, if the sole determinant of history is power, then the sole outcome can only be conflict without end or the final dominance of a power that is irresistible. Marx predicted that with the success of the revolution, the state would wither away. But as the history of Marxism shows, all that has withered away is the myth of the state withering away. That claim was Marx at his most utopian, and few Marxists bother to repeat his foolish hope today. Neither logic nor history offers such an alternative. In the short term, coercion and violence are the price to be paid for relying on power. "You have to break eggs to make an omelet," revolutionaries say. "Pride began in a riot," left-wing radicals remind us. This is no time for "respectability politics." But by the same logic, the long-term prospect is endless conflict—or authoritarianism. The left is disarmingly candid about such a conclusion. One bestselling radical manifesto admits, "The central role that the notion of antagonism plays in our work forecloses any possibility of a final reconciliation, of any kind of rational consensus, of a fully inclusive 'we.'"[19]

From the perspective of postmodernism and critical theory, there cannot be any resolution to the clash of power against power. Hegemony is all, and antagonisms are everything, so *might* conquers *right*. There can be no lasting victory for any party except the "peace" of domination and despotism. Short of that, each exploited antagonism and each power-based victory will be only a temporary reversal of their former oppression and yet another swing in the grand merry-go-round of power through which losers unseat winners, minorities upend majorities, and victims overturn oppressors until each is overthrown in its turn. Only Leviathan can quell the war of all against all, and only a global Leviathan can dominate the global stage. But once again, such a "peace," whether *Pax Americana* or *Pax Sinica* would be the appalling prospect of the peace of a dominance beyond any resistance by the rest of the world.

ARGUMENT NOT FOR THE SAKE OF HEAVEN

All these dangers are inherent in revolutionary liberationism, but other arguments can be added. We saw earlier (see chap. 5) that covenantalism makes possible the characteristic Jewish notion of an "argument for the sake of heaven." That argument provides a powerful moral impetus toward activism on behalf of justice. But as Rabbi Sacks points out, the Jewish sages also had the notion of an "argument *not* for the sake of heaven."[20] The argument for the sake of heaven is a stand on behalf of truth and justice, whereas the argument *not* for the sake of heaven is a stand on behalf of power and self-interest. Such a darker and dangerous argument, Sacks warns, often betrays its underlying resentment. As a rule of thumb, "if you want to understand resentments, listen to what people accuse others of, and you will then know what they themselves want."[21]

Sacks illustrates his understanding from the Torah, with Korah's rebellion against Moses. He then demonstrates how this tactic (the psychological process known as "splitting-and-projection") is at the heart of anti-Semitism, and it applies to the progressive left too. Thus accusations of "male privilege" and "White privilege" are often leveled when the privileges in question are actually at their weakest. But truth and fairness are not the point. The accusations of privilege work as a resentment-fueled bid for the power of those who currently have the power. Destroy the standing and credibility of those accused. Reduce them to nonpersons and they can be called out, devoiced, and canceled. And if the accused are in the past, their fame can be besmirched and their place in history rewritten. *Privilege is simply the target the progressive left paints on the back of those whose power they want.* Neither the truth of the issue nor the justice of the outcome is their concern. What matters is power, and the accusation is the way to replace *their* power with *our* power, *their* hegemony with *our* hegemony.

TAKING UP THE CAUSE OF THE WOUNDED AND THE DEAD

It is worth repeating that the trouble with criticisms of the progressive left is that more than critique is needed. Many of the injustices and inequalities are genuine, and they require genuine resolution. The advanced modern world is rife with almost daily instances of injustice and inequality, many of them egregious and some of them institutional. And with the ever-watching eye of the cell phone and video camera, the fuses that set off widespread outrage are short. Thus, in all too many cases the initial justification for outrage is unarguable. Cases of violence such as the killing of George Floyd in 2020, are real, vile, wrong, and all too common. They stand to the progressive left as the murder of Archduke Ferdinand in Sarajevo in 1914 did to the outbreak of World War I.

Justice has to be done to the legitimate and understandable element of outrage against injustice. Both Michael Ignatieff and Rabbi Sacks rightly remind us that the impulse to retaliation is not only an emotion but an ethic. The *emotion* of revenge is obvious, and all too often it is ugly, easily condemned, and counter-productive. But the emotion is only half of what drives retaliation. The *ethic* of revenge is less obvious but nobler, and the ethic is what fires and sustains the avenger—their passion for justice for the oppressed, the wounded, and the dead. It needs to be recognized. Ignatieff explains, "But revenge—morally considered—is a desire to keep faith with the dead, to honor their memory by taking up their cause where they left off. Revenge keeps faith between the generations."[22]

All who love justice must do justice to the genuine moral outrage that flares up against injustice. *Impartiality toward people is a virtue in a judge or an umpire, but indifference toward evil is a vice in neighbors and citizens, and a vice that reinforces evil by turning it from an exception into an accepted way of life.* But, and this but is all-important, the genuinely ethical component in anger is not a blank check to justify all responses to injustice. The problem of the left is not the injustice they confront but the injustice they compound—through their response. Both Sinai and Paris stand united in the conviction that there are egregious wrongs in the world and that they must be righted. But whereas Sinai works to right the wrongs and reconcile the wronged and the wrongdoer (as we will see in chap. 8), Paris counters wrong with retaliation in a manner that perpetuates the wrongs and serves the interests of the activists rather than the victims.

THE NEW EMPEROR HAS NO CLOTHES

For all their rhetoric of freedom, the progressive left could hardly be further from the responsible freedom of Sinai and the covenantal/constitutional republic of the American founders. Surely by now there is no excuse for anyone to be fooled by the propaganda and tactics of the progressive left. Their tactics and slogans vary, but the recurring features are plain. In earlier days and with clearer sight each would have been seen as un-American and illiberal—the blaming that helps people escape from freedom and responsibility under the guise of grievance, the doublethink that enables activists to excoriate the enemy and defend their own side against the same charges, the shibboleths and speech codes that police politically correct thinking, the safe places and cancel culture that insulate the sensitive and the offendable from free thinking and heresy, the historical scouring that alerts the mob to new villains to attack and new statues to demolish, the generational shaming that smears one generation by association with another, the verbal triggers and tripwires that booby trap debate and help snare all opponents in the minefield of ever-changing faux pas, the cultural cleansing that ensures strict ideological orthodoxy and uniformity, and the po-litical corralling by which cultural minorities are forced to remain victims and kowtow to their rescuer-masters.

Through tactics such as these, the partisans of the progressive left have de-generated into American Jacobins, the new *sansculottes* ready to follow the siren call of the latest Twitter Robespierre. Too many activists have become the new ambulance chasers, with each new violation a media op and a fundraising moment. Too many social justice warriors are those who are fired up around the clock by the thought that someone somewhere may be traumatized, and therefore a new victim to be weaponized. They are all zealous prosecutors now, and the culprits they find are guilty at once, with no trial or jury of their peers and no appeal to any court but the thumbs-up or thumbs-down of the social media emperor mob.

The American left has become a toxic blend of utopianism, hypocrisy, stupidity, and catastrophe—*utopian* because none of us is perfect, so the purity campaigns are unending; *hypocritical* because such tactics are bullying and oppression by another name; *stupid* because future generations will marvel at our generation's blind spots and evils just as we marvel at those of earlier times; and *catastrophic* because there will be no end to the wrongs that must be avenged in the same ruthless, scorched-earth manner.

Today's incidents have a nasty habit of flaring suddenly. They jump from reasonable statements on behalf of freedom and justice to preposterous claims to which the mob allows only one answer. Yet the real answer is, "This new emperor has no clothes!" But who are willing to risk their necks to say so? Or again, the trends may start with a tweet and a countertweet, rise rapidly to a barrage of legal and political punches and counterpunches (and death threats, impeachments, and impeachment hearings), and reach a crescendo in a wave of protests that become a riot of arson and looting. But in every case, the left's approach can only end in a grand Corsican blood feud writ large.

Rabbi Sacks warns, "There is no natural end to the cycle of retaliation and revenge. The Montagues keep killing and being killed by the Capulets. So do the Tattaglias and the Corleones and the other feuding groups in history and fiction. It is a destructive cycle that has devastated whole communities."[23] The only firm barrier against riots and revenge is the rule of law, but if the rule of law is itself weaponized, then it will no longer be trusted, and its barriers will be broken down. Violent reciprocity may reach a hurricane-force level that cannot be halted by anything short of scapegoating and assassination or by the imposition of dictatorship.

LA REVOLUTION SANS MERCI

Americans, including many on the progressive left, pay homage to Dr. Martin Luther King Jr., but the chasm between Dr. King and the progressive left has grown vaster by the year. His ideal of the "content of your character" matters little today. The highly racist color of your skin (or the sexist combination of your X and Y chromosomes and the ageist date of your birth) is everything. But the greatest contrast is where we began this chapter. The left has a full catalog of "sins" but no forgiveness for sin. Like Keats's poem "La Belle Dame sans Merci," the revolution is pitiless and the revolutionary merciless. The contrast with the way of Sinai is astonishing. The left constantly castigates its enemies for their flagrant sins, such as racism, sexism, and homophobia, *but it offers no mercy and no forgiveness.* There is no way back from any of their sins.

To anyone charged with one of the left's deadly sins, the agitators and the social media mob are ruthless. They mete out instant convictions and roadside sentences with unsmiling severity and hurry the hapless victims toward Madame Guillotine with summary dispatch—unless, of course, the accused is one of their own, in which case they are spirited to safety. For all others, public confession and recantation lead not to a change of life and a second chance but to execution. When someone has transgressed the taboos, forgiveness is unthinkable and impossible. The "justice" of the baying Twitter mob is insatiable. After all, the sin exposed for all to see is "systemic," "ineradicable," and in the enemy's DNA. And for those who operate solely on power, forgiveness is beyond their ken. Forgiveness is a matter of principle and freedom, not power. Before the kangaroo court of power, atonement makes no sense. The sole options are appeasement, abasement, or annihilation.

The end of that line is the searing dismissals such as those Sigmund Freud meted out to one-time disciples who disagreed with him. He would quote Heinrich Heine, "One must forgive one's enemies, but not before they have been hanged."[24] (To which one historian commented, "There is much evidence of hanging, none of forgiveness.")[25] Needless to say, what sounds natural for today's unforgivers is tragic for the unforgiven. For when no apologies are accepted and no forgiveness is given, not even appeasement will satisfy. All that is left is abasement, groveling, and a forced confession. It matters little whether it is before a communist apparatchik, the "furies" of the press, the social media, or a politically correct mob. Abasement is abasement—and serfdom if not extermination.

Are these comments overwrought? I could cite chapter and verse, but the incidents pass quickly while the patterns persist. For many outside observers, America has already changed beyond recognition, and you will remember that my parents and I were witnesses to the climax of the Chinese Revolution and the beginning of a reign of terror. These warnings are not about the future. They are about the dangers already evident in America's culture warring in a post-modern, progressive, and power-based style. Examples come and go almost daily. When trust breaks down, suspicions, rumors, and conspiracy theories are stoked incessantly, and power is the sole coin of the realm, then Hobbes's "war of all against all" becomes a form of "hatred of all against all." Rabbi Heschel called such cynicism "the sneering doctrine," and the pages of the mainstream press and the logic of the Twitter world are the evidence for it.[26]

At its most damaging, rampant suspicion hardens into cynicism and then malice and becomes the implacable hatred of leaders, when they are disliked so much that they are utterly, totally, and forever wrong and can say no right and do no right. The Roman historian Tacitus wrote of Emperor Galba, "Now that Galba was detested, everything he did, whether right or wrong, brought upon him equal detestation."[27] That is a perfect prefiguring of the Never Trumpers and the so-called Trump Derangement Syndrome that has so disfigured the American press and public alike.

FREEDOM AND HATE ARE CONTRADICTORY

Unquestionably, this second extreme of the intransigent unforgivers is the clear and present danger in America today, and its logic must be faced squarely. There is a glaring irony at the core of critical theory. Its advocates set out claiming that liberation begins with critique, but they end as yet another power group that stifles freedom and prohibits all criticism. The critical theory critics fail to criticize themselves, and they do not allow others to criticize them. Freedom of conscience is dismissed as a code word for bigotry, and freedom of speech is silenced. But for the purposes of this chapter, there is an overarching reason why the progressive left is dangerous to freedom. The way the left addresses wrongs is lethal for freedom because they arouse passionate emotions on behalf of justice, but only to exploit the emotions and the injustices and keep themselves in power rather than seeking to remedy the conditions that gave rise to them. Too often the result is rage and hate.

It is quite simply impossible to hate and to be free, whether the hatred is on the left or the right. It is also impossible for a society to indulge hatred and claim to be free. Those who hate and those who engineer resentment condemn themselves and their societies to a life sentence as prisoners of the past. That was the reason, Rabbi Sacks explains, behind Moses forbidding the Israelites to hate the Egyptians, who had oppressed them.

> If the people had continued to hate their erstwhile oppressors, Moses would have taken the Israelites out of Egypt but would have failed to take Egypt out of the Israelites. They would still be slaves, not physically but psychologically. They would be slaves to the past, held captive by the chains of resentment, unable to build the future. *To be free, you have to let go of hate.*[28]

No one should miss the danger and the meaning of this aspect of the current American crisis. The danger is that, beyond all question, hate is the expression of malice and the most evil and destructive force in human history. Destructive hate is now coursing through America. Hate is being stirred up by the progressive left, echoed by the reactionary right, exploited by leaders who should know better, reinforced by the social media, and left unanswered through the lack of Lincoln-like leadership and the failure of religious leaders on all sides.

If that is the danger, the meaning of the crisis lies in the fact that the present situation is yet another demonstration of the great divide between the way of the prophets and the way of the left:

- Where Sinai stands for right, the left (in the form of postmodernism and the progressive left) stands for might.

- Where Sinai has a vision of *good* and therefore a clear contrast to *bad*, the left talks endlessly of the bad with no alternative good except a radical leveling in the name of equality.

- Where Sinai addresses inequality in the name of the equal dignity of all, the left exploits inequality to arouse resentment and redress injustice through reparation, redistribution, and retribution.

- Where Sinai relies on persuasion and open debate, based on its respect for freedom of conscience, freedom of speech, and freedom of association, the left uses coercion and imposition, based on its sole reliance on power.

- Where Sinai emphasizes *innocent until proven guilty* and thereby builds trust, the left stresses *guilty until proven innocent* and thereby deepens alienation.

- Where Sinai pours balm into wounds, the left searches for grievances and pours in vinegar.

- Where Sinai works for reconciliation, the left works for retaliation—and always and only on behalf of its own interests and its own continuing power.

- And, most astonishingly of all, where Sinai (and Jesus of Nazareth and his followers down through Rev. Martin Luther King Jr.) stand for love that drives out hate, just as light drives out darkness, the left perpetuates and exploits the hate and the darkness as its instruments of power.

The progressive left is deforming America, just as the logic of their concept of force and violence has long been a twisted feature of earlier revolutionary movements. Nineteenth-century Russia gave voice to the concept of violence as the "ministry of justice of the revolution," and described terrorism as "the most just of all forms of revolution."[29] Trotsky picked up the same language of violence in the Russian Revolution. "I tell you, heads must roll, blood must flow," he told the sailors in the Kronstadt garrison. "The strength of the French Revolution was in the machine that made the enemies of the people shorter by a head. This is a fine device. We must have it in every city."[30] Such revolutionary language can be heard only at the extremes in America today, but it can be heard on the anarchist left among the supporters of antifa, on the Marxist left among the supporters of Black Lives Matter, some of the supporters of Senator Bernie Sanders, and even in the US Congress among the "Squad," who have called for a dismantling of the system. More commonly, social justice warriors are causing divisions at the deepest levels of society, using the tools and tactics of critical theory to restructure American universities, politics, corporations, Christian denominations, and churches, and disrupting traditions of all kinds. When all are woke, they will have won.

Hate is the denial of freedom, and revenge is the denial of justice. Resentment, hate, and revenge are all personal emotions. They represent the I-Thou relationships gone badly wrong. They are therefore highly toxic when they seep into public life, whether poisoning journalism in the form of rank bias that degenerates into propaganda and fake news or poisoning justice in the many forms of weaponizing law that turns justice into a tool of power. As Rabbi Sacks reminds, "Retribution is not revenge. Punishment is not hate. Justice is not vindictiveness." Justice is "the principle refusal to let I/Thou relationships determine the fate of individuals within society"—whether defending paupers or defending presidents.[31]

Rabbi Sacks quotes Martin Luther King Jr., "Darkness cannot drive out darkness; only light can do that. Hate cannot drive out hate; only love can do that. Hate multiplies hate, violence multiplies violence, and toughness multiplies toughness."[32] He then drives the point home with unmistakable clarity for our day:

> To be free you have to let go of hate. . . . You cannot create a free society on the basis of hate. Resentment, rage, humiliation, a sense of injustice, the desire to restore honor by inflicting injury on your former persecutors— these are conditions of a profound lack of freedom. You must live *with* the past . . . but not *in* the past. Those who are held captive by anger against their former persecutors are captive still. Those who let their enemies define who they are have not yet achieved liberty.[33]

"To be free," he repeats, "you have to let go of hate."[34]

BUT NOT THROUGH US

It is time for Americans who love freedom, who understand the uniqueness of ordered freedom, and all who realize the disastrous logic of revolutionary liberationism to stand across the path of the progressive left and their mini-Lenins and self-styled Torquemadas and say, "No. You may be talking justice, but we are not deceived. You may try to spread your fanatical and insatiable views of radical justice and resentment through sphere after sphere of society, *but not through us*. Ours is a completely different vision of justice and freedom."

The record of history permits no doubt as to how civil wars and culture wars are resolved in the end if there is no good leadership. The Roman Republic of

Cicero, for example, was short-lived. The specter of monarchs and dictators loomed over it at every stage. During the civil wars that wracked Rome, every leader and every party claimed in their turn to be defending the cause of liberty and peace. But none of them could or would bring the two ideals to work together. The result was captured in the weary comment of the Roman historian Lucan: "When peace came, it was the peace of despotism."[35] Rome's brief republican revolution ended in the Caesars, just as France's revolution ended in Napoleon Bonaparte, Russia's in Stalin, and China's in Mao.

In America today the blend of the three *Is* is growing toxic—inequalities, injustices, and ideology. Liberty and peace are again in open tension, and the lure of Leviathan can be heard in the land. The revolutionary left has never proceeded any other way—peace through domination. Almost humorously (though chillingly), Billington comments:

> The subsequent history of armed revolution reveals a seemingly irresistible drive toward a strong central executive: Robespierre's twelve-man Committee of Public Safety (1793–94) gave way to a five-man Directorate (1795–99), to a three-man Consulate, to the designation of Napoleon as First Consul in 1799, and finally to Napoleon's coronation as emperor in 1804.[36]

From 12 to 5 to 3 to 1, the warning is as clear as the math.

Unquestionably, the way of Paris, like all unprincipled power-driven movements, will lead only to authoritarianism and history's bookend of the world of order without freedom. The story of history is the story of the way power is used. For those with no principle but power, the end is clear: oppression of the weak, corruption of the powerful, and the inflation of pride that comes before a fall. As so often in history, brave cries of freedom and justice may fill the air at the start, but the final chapters are too often littered with angry mobs, kangaroo courts, torture cells, concentration camps, tumbrils, guillotines, firing squads, and dictatorship. There must be, and there is, a better way—the Sinai way.

America cannot endure permanently half 1776 and half 1789. The compromises, contradictions, hypocrisies, inequities, and evils have built up unaddressed. The grapes of wrath have ripened again, and the choice before America is plain. Either America goes forward best by going back first, or America is about to reap a future in which the worst will once again be the corruption of the best.

8

PUTTING WRONG RIGHT

PRINCIPLE 7: FREEDOM MUST ALWAYS ADDRESS WRONGS, BUT IN THE RIGHT WAY—THE WAY OF THE PROPHETS

For two hundred years "Mother Emanuel," as the African Methodist Episcopal Church in Charleston, South Carolina, was known, had stood strong. Founded in 1816, it is the oldest Black church in the South and a center of faith, hope, and resilience through all the troubled racial history of the city, including its leadership in the civil rights movement. But it never stood stronger and prouder than in the summer of 2015, after a mass shooting of nine of its members at the Wednesday Bible Study in June. Dylann Roof, a twenty-one-year-old White supremacist had joined the study, sat next to the pastor who led the evening, and joined in the discussion for more than an hour. Suddenly, Roof pulled a gun out of his pack and opened fire—killing the pastor and all but three of those attending. He then turned the gun on himself, but he had run out of ammunition, so he fled.

Roof was a self-professed White supremacist. He had intended to spark a race war. The wounds were still raw, and the atmosphere at his bond hearing crackled with tension. Would the cold-blooded slaughter of nine innocent Blacks set off riots as similar incidents have done in other cities? It was only forty-eight hours after the murders when the families of the slain were offered the chance to speak to the murderer. But the first one stepped forward and changed the atmosphere entirely. She had lost her mother. "I forgive you," she said, fighting back tears as she spoke. "You took something really precious from me. I will never talk to her ever again. I will never be able to hold her again, but I forgive you and have mercy on your soul."

One by one, and with no coordination, almost all the others did the same. One mother forgave Roof while showing him the blood-stained pages of her son's Bible, reminding the killer of one who had died for him. One was a minor-league baseball player who had lost his mother. He said later, "I've realized that forgiving is so much tougher than holding a grudge. It takes a lot more courage to forgive than it does to say, 'I'm going to be upset about whatever forever.'" Far from fulfilling the murderer's hopes, forgiveness brought the city together and averted the violence that had erupted elsewhere. The killer was still convicted, racism still persisted, and some scorned the Christians for being soft, but retaliation and revenge were stopped in their tracks. Combined with the strong stand against the Confederate flag by Governor David Beasley and Governor Nikki Haley, both of whom are people of deep Christian conviction, the crisis was averted. There could be no clearer demonstration of the Sinai (and Calvary) way of responding to wrongs.

The Sinai (and Calvary) way of addressing and righting wrongs is decisively different from that of the left and the main contours of the differences need to be explored all over again for our time. The contrast begins with Sinai's basic reliance and it continues with sharp differences from the progressive left in how it responds to wrongs. The striking differences stem from Sinai's rejection of the primacy of power and its essential reliance on right over might. The problem with the left's reliance on might over right is its inevitable abuse of power, which leads on one hand to arrogance and on the other to cruelty—and then to the desecration of the image of God in a fellow human being. All power corrupts, and all political, military, national, or revolutionary power that is not morally accountable is potentially evil and cruel in that way.

In this basic realism toward power, Sinai breaks not only with the left and current authoritarian powers of all kinds but with a stubborn feature of human thinking down the centuries. "The gods are on the side of the stronger," Tacitus wrote, in an apt comment on the Roman Empire.[1] "Political power grows out of the barrel of a gun," Mao Zedong declared in our own time.[2] The overwhelming chorus of voices in history would agree with them, *but not Sinai and not Calvary.* "The prophets were the first men in history," Rabbi Heschel insists, "to regard a nation's reliance on force as evil."[3] Unbounded power is destructive because of its arrogance and spurious sovereignty as well as its eventual cruelty. In the words of the Hebrew prophet Isaiah, when there is no righteousness, the powerful person becomes a destroyer: "He has no regard for man" (Is 33:8). Power requires righteousness. Power requires respect for the inviolability of fellow humans, and power requires accountability. Might must always be held in check by right. The ancient and modern gods may be on the side of the stronger, but the God of the Bible is on the side of the weaker and those unable to defend themselves. Justice, not power is the final determinant of history. There is a principled providence in history that the prophet Isaiah called "a sword not of man" (Is 31:8).

Starting from this foundational reliance on right over might, Sinai's differences from the left shine out in its response to wrongs. There are five salient differences. First, because of sin, Sinai insists on realism and responsibility or fallibility and accountability. We are all, without exception, prone to go wrong and do wrong. There is no Rousseauesque utopianism in the Bible. There is no system so perfect that humans will not make it go wrong. When it comes to humanity, the expectation is not a matter of *if* we go wrong but *when* we go wrong. All humans make mistakes, and all humans sin—leaders included. (Rabbi Sacks points out that the Torah uses the word *if* of the people's sins, but *when* of the leaders' sins.)[4]

All means all. *All* means us. *All* means me. The judge as well as the defendant, the reporter as well as the subject of the story, and the president as well as the death-row inmate. To be realistic, both social and political life must assume that things will go wrong and provide mechanisms for holding people accountable when they go wrong and providing a way to deal with it when they do. Such realism is at the heart of the necessity for the separation of powers, and such accountability is at the heart of the notion of covenant and promise keeping. Everyone has given their word, all are accountable, and no one is immune to challenge and correction. Utopianism is always cruel in the end, but in this realism about human nature there is mercy and moderation.

To be sure, it is important that in a free society, character, and personal accountability are not the business of the government, but they are essential as the precondition for public accountability. As creator of the universe and the ruler over history, God is the only authority higher than humans before whom we humans can truly be held accountable. "Under God" is neither a cliché nor a symbol of religious establishment, but a statement of accountability.

Without God, might will prevail over right, and "wrongs" will always be decided and dealt with according to the will of the powerful. As the Athenians brutally reminded the tiny island of Melos, "You know as well as we do that the right, as the world goes, is only in question between equals in power, while the strong do what they wish and the weak suffer what they must."[5] If that is the case, there must be genuine moral scrutiny and accountability higher than our own, or justice will never prevail on the earth.

Socrates declared that "the unexamined life is not worth living." Modern people often say, "Follow your heart" and add an emoji or two. But the biblical view of the heart is more realistic. The Bible counters this sentimental attitude by, in effect, adding a warning to Socrates's excellent advice: *the unexamined heart is not worth following.* According to the realism of the Bible, all who desire to confront the wrongs of the world must begin by acknowledging the deceptiveness of their own human hearts, our own as well as those of others. In the words of the prophet Jeremiah, "The heart is more deceitful than all else; . . . Who can understand it?" (Jer 17:9). Those who allow their hearts (or the will of the leader, the party, the majority, or the revolution) to be the arbiter of right and wrong will inevitably go astray and end in reinforcing, not remedying injustice.

For Jews this personal accountability before God as the highest judge is experienced most strongly in the "Days of Awe," the ten days beginning on Rosh Hashanah and leading to Yom Kippur. (Rabbi Heschel: "For the sins we have sinned in not knowing how much we have sinned, we cry for forgiveness.")[6] For Christians the same accountability is at the heart of the weekly prayer of confession and in the season of Lent. Rabbi Sacks's description of what it means for each individual to stand before God is powerful and moving.

> It is as if the world has become a courtroom. God himself is the Judge. The shofar announces that the court is in session, and we are on trial, giving an account of our lives. Properly entered into, this is a potentially life-changing experience. It forces us to ask the most fateful questions we will ever ask: Who am I? Why am I here? How shall I live? How have I lived until now? How have I used God's greatest gift: time? Whom have I wronged, and how can I put it right? Where have I failed, and how shall I overcome my failures? What is broken in my life and needs mending? What chapter will I write in the book of life?[7]

Personal accountability must be firmly linked to public accountability in politics. The two principles are addressed generally in the notion of *the rule of law* and more specifically in the notion of *the separation of powers* and *checks and balances*—whether in the three crowns of Jewish governance (king, priest, and prophet), the separation of powers discussed by Montesquieu in *The Spirit of the Laws,* or the intricate system of checks and balances set in place by the American founders. James Madison, who had been a student of the Presbyterian pastor John Witherspoon at Princeton, wrote famously in Federalist 51,

> It may be a reflection on human nature that such devices should be necessary to control the abuses of government. But what is government itself, but the greatest of all reflections on human nature? If men were angels, no government would be necessary. If angels were to govern men, neither external nor internal controls on government would be necessary. In framing a government which is to be administered by men over men, the great difficulty lies in this: you must first enable the government to control the governed; and in the next place oblige it to control itself.

The realism of these notions of fallibility and personal and public accountability is essential to any community or nation concerned for freedom and justice. It is central to the Hebrew Scriptures, Rabbi Sacks notes, which record Israel's failings, its shortcomings, its sins, its faults as "a literature of unparalleled self-criticism."[8] The realism is also central to the long-running courtroom drama of the extended argument between God and humanity over the state of justice in the world. Sometimes God is in the dock ("Shall not the Judge of all the earth deal justly?" [Gen 18:25]). More often we humans are in the dock. But as Sacks notes repeatedly, the covenantal notion of personal and public accountability before an absolute standard is essential to the passion for justice that characterizes the Jews and humanity at its best. Several times Sacks cites Albert Einstein, who was grateful for that "almost fanatical love of justice" that made him thank his stars he was born a Jew.[9]

The sting in the tail of this realism is obvious. It is not just about the Nazis, the communists, the sex traffickers, and the child molesters. It is about free societies and middle-class people too. It is about each of us and our friends. But that is not what we each want to hear, so denial kicks in, and the dynamics of "Never again" recur all over again. As Rabbi Heschel reminds us, "There is nothing we forget as eagerly, as quickly, as the wickedness of man. The earth holds such a terrifying secret. Ruins are removed, the dead are buried, and the crimes are forgotten. Bland complacency, splendid mansions, fortresses of cruel oblivion, top the graves. The dead have no voice, but God will disclose the secret of the earth."[10] Or as the prophet Isaiah said centuries earlier, "The earth will reveal her bloodshed, And shall no longer cover her slain" (Is 26:21).

LET JUSTICE ROLL DOWN LIKE WATERS

The next component in the Sinai way of addressing wrong is justice. There are at least seven striking elements in the biblical view of justice that make it deeper, richer, and more balanced than other views in history, and the combination makes it sharply different from the alternative views of justice today.

First, justice is centered in God himself. God is a God of justice who hates injustice as a perversion of truth, goodness, and human worth. Thus human justice is rooted and grounded in the character of God—and doubly so: God loves justice and God hates injustice, and all who love justice must equally hate injustice. Seen this way, justice is not an external standard, a mere norm, or an autonomous abstract ideal higher than God. It has no objective meaning apart from God. But equally, justice is not a positive virtue only. It includes the needed outrage against injustice and wrong that is both natural and right. Thus questions about justice begin and end with God. Justice concerns God's heart for humanity because justice comes from the heart of God. "For I, the Lord, love justice," the prophet Isaiah declares (Is 61:8).

Second, human justice is essentially personal and individual, and personal and individual before it is institutional and systemic. Justice begins and ends with individuals and how individuals behave and how individuals treat their fellow humans. It is a matter of how people made in the image of God treat other people made in the image of God. Thus justice is more than simply negative— avoiding breaking the law—and it is more than a specialized matter of law, law courts, and professionalized department in society (the Department of Justice or the Ministry of Justice). Rabbi Heschel notes that when Cain committed the first murder, God does not say, "You have broken the law, and are guilty of first-degree murder." He stresses the personal: "The voice of your brother's blood is crying to Me from the ground" (Gen 4:10). First and last, both justice and injustice are personal.

God commands all humans to be just and to act justly throughout the whole of their lives—to be true, honest, fair, and kind in all their communications, relationships, and dealings with others. Justice is a matter of character, behavior, and relationships. As such, it is an imperative for each of us without exception. Whether we are dispensing justice or striving for justice, we ourselves must be just. We can and must fight for justice for others, but no one can be just in the place of anyone else. Justice and injustice will grow to be institutional and systemic because humans are social, and create and live in societies and systems. But justice and injustice are still never other than rooted and demonstrated in personal behavior and personal relationships.

Alfred North Whitehead famously claimed that religion is what people do with their solitariness. That may describe much modern religion, with its devotees taking to their yoga mats and their daily meditation exercises. It also fits in well with ancient paganism in which relationship to the gods and relationship to other human beings were two entirely different things. But what we do with our solitariness is not the way the Hebrew and Christian Scriptures understand faith—or justice. On the contrary, in the Bible's view, the way we see God determines the way we see and deal with our neighbors, and the way we deal with our neighbors is the true index of the way we see God. God is just, through and through, and all our thinking, speaking, and acting must be just, through and through. We are each made in the image of God, and the way we treat our fellow image-bearers demonstrates what we really think of the image of God and what we think of others.

DOUBLE-BARRELED JUSTICE

Third, this emphasis on justice as personal is double-barreled. It contains two distinct aspects of justice that are captured in two words for justice that run through the Scriptures. The two words are first heard in God's explanation of why he called Abraham. "I have chosen him that he may command his children and his household after him to keep the way of the LORD by doing righteousness and justice" (Gen 18:19). These two parts are then repeated endlessly, and they become the imperative for everyone: "Do justice and righteousness" (Jer 22:3).

Human justice, or justice lived out by individual human beings, must always be double-barreled. Both Hebrew words mean justice, and the combination of their separate meanings and the way they blend demonstrates the distinctiveness of the Sinai and biblical view of justice. The first word, *right* (*tzedakah*), means personal justice as righteousness and integrity, and the second word, *just* (*mishpat*), means public justice in the sense of fairness and equality before the law and before our fellow humans. The two words are repeated together constantly in the Hebrew Scriptures. They are distinct but never divorced.

One word, *mishpat*, as Rabbi Sacks explains, is justice as "public justice" or the rule of law in society. This form of justice gives people justice as "their due," and in doing so it ensures that right prevails over might in society at large. It is a form of retributive justice by which citizens receive their due according to whether they are innocent or guilty before the law. Public justice and the rule of law are essential as the framework for a good society, but by themselves they cannot create a good society. They form the boundary against injustice and are essentially negative and limited. They are what David Hume called the "cold jealous virtue of justice."[11] By itself the law as public justice is too clumsy and unwieldy to deal with all the small injustices that grow in any society. Often, it is too remote to notice the injustices done to those marginalized by the vicissitudes of life (the poor, the widows, the orphans, and the immigrants). And always, it is far too distant and narrow to cover the countless incidents in word and deed that make up daily life in any family, community, or business.

The full Sinai view of justice also required the other and more positive principle of justice: *tzedakah* or "personal justice" as opposed to public justice. *Mishpat* means "retributive justice," delivered in the interests of the ideal of equal justice under law. *Tzedakah* means the balancing principle of "distributive justice," delivered in the interests of a fair and equal society. But even the connotations of *distributive* are too narrow. Personal justice was something to strive for, to seek and pursue *actively*. "Pursue righteousness," "seek righteousness," the prophets say (Is 51:1; Zeph 2:3). Injustice may be avoided, almost passively, by not doing certain things, but justice as righteousness must be pursued actively, energetically, and passionately. Hence the famous and much-quoted call to justice in the prophet Micah:

> What does the LORD require of you
> But to *do justice* and to *love kindness* [*ḥesed*, "covenant faithfulness"],
> And to *walk humbly* with your God? (Mic 6:8; emphasis added)

Justice is not an incident but a way of life.

The Sinai view of personal justice is demanding. Justice is about the way people treat people, so it covers all human attitudes, communications, and actions toward others: the practice of respect, caring, generosity, truthfulness, and not just the obvious avoidance of flat-out lies and flagrant crimes. Justice includes the politician's tweet and the journalist's reporting as well as the corporation's hiring and firing. And the family's quarrels. If public justice ensures that right prevails over might throughout society, personal justice ensures that justice in the sense of integrity, generosity, and kindness permeates society for good in every relationship and at every level.

This double-barreled view of justice emphasizes what modern society often forgets. Justice and injustice are a matter of I-Thou and We-Thou. They begin and end in interpersonal relationships. The vast majority of cases of injustice never reach the law courts, and they shouldn't. There is an added problem in the current focus on law and law courts—the perversion of lawyers easily become hired guns for injustice. The corruption of the powerful means that those who are wealthy and unjust have the money and the skills for hire to evade justice in the courts, while those who most need justice have neither the resources nor the competence to bring their case to court and make their voices heard.

ALL FOR ONE, AND ONE FOR ALL

Fourth, justice, being essentially personal and interpersonal, is covenantal and thus a key part of living together freely and peacefully in community. Justice is a matter of what a person deserves or is due, whether that is positive, like respect or safety and protection, or negative, like a speeding ticket or a prison sentence. Justice therefore always assumes a double claim, a right and a responsibility, which each person pledges to all others simply by being members of the community together.

Covenantal justice emphasizes responsibility as well as rights and duties as well as claims. Each requires and reinforces the other, and neither stands alone. There can be no rights or claims without responsibility and duties. The reciprocal responsibility of the covenant/constitution means that the rights and responsibilities are mutually reinforcing. The stronger the covenantal commitment to responsibility, the stronger can be the claim to rights; and the stronger the claims to rights, the stronger must be the covenantal commitment to responsibility. Justice in society begins with the personal justice of each member of society. It is a matter of character, and therefore it is truly individual, but it then spreads out to be a matter of the community, and it is therefore truly social. Unbounded capitalism, for example, will inevitably be unjust. It ends with savage inequalities and a financial den of thieves and stokes its own repudiation. But as Bruno Roche and Jay Jakub have demonstrated in *Complementing Capitalism*, market economics and business conducted with an eye to justice can create a win-win partnership and an "economics of mutuality."[12]

The truth is that none of us is a Robinson Crusoe, and Western individualists who live as if they are skew justice horribly. When the clamor for rights is pursued solely in the name of individuality, there will be an even greater proliferation of claims and a weaker response to any of them, and the end will be conflict and lawsuits without end. Some people react against this extreme and go to the other extreme, arguing that the Bible has no place for rights, as if all rights were selfish. That too is wrong. The Torah says, for example, "He executes justice for [or establishes the rights of] the orphan and the widow" (Deut 10:18). A healthy society, within a covenantal/constitutional order, guarantees justice in which rights and responsibilities are one.

Is our current view of a just society as wide and rich as this? If justice is wider than law courts, then generosity and caring must be wider than welfare, and integrity, fairness, and kindness must have the widest reach of all. Mention of distributive justice inevitably suggests the welfare state and all the attendant problems surrounding dependency. But as Sacks explains again, the Sinai vision was different. First, the caring and generosity of the charity began with the voluntary rather than the compulsory. Second, it fostered a "welfare society" rather than a "welfare state." It was the direct and natural expression of collective responsibility and caring, the reciprocal responsibility of everyone for everyone. And third, it was the direct expression of the biblical principle of stewardship that is common to Jews and Christians. For the Romans and many modern people, property and money are a matter of absolute individual ownership. For the Bible, and for Jews and Christians by contrast, property and money are a matter of *possession* here and now but not ultimate *ownership*. Humans are merely trustees and stewards of what is ultimately God's but ours to take care of with fiduciary responsibility to him.

Behind the rise of Western philanthropy two thousand years ago lay distinctive Jewish and Christian answers to three questions: "Money, whose is it?" (A matter of ownership or trusteeship?) "Why Give?" (Give in order to get or give because given to?) And "Who should we care for?" (People like us or the neighbor in need?) These questions and the answers we give to them are still crucial today, and in each case the second answer is the Bible's answer, and these answers are both unique and fruitful. They make the difference between a free people, with a vital place for generosity and a robust civil society, in sharp contrast with a state-controlled society with endless conflict over zero-sum resources and dependency on government welfare. The Sinai vision of justice is therefore foundational, but again it is far more than procedural justice. It includes justice, compassion, generosity, righteousness, integrity, truthfulness, fairness, caring, and plain and simple human decency. In short, as we saw with covenant earlier, so now with justice: it is a serious and consequential mistake to shrink down justice from its rich deep significance in human relationships to the size of law courts, lawyers, and judges.

Israel's calling and mission was to be a protest people, the anti-Egypt of the world (just as Christians are called to be *in* the world but *not of* it, and thus the counterculture of history). Israel's covenantal and horizontal society was to be the opposite of the hierarchical society of Egypt, where the gap between rich and poor was vast and irremediable. But Israel's way of life was neither socialism nor communism, where equality depended on coercive leveling and redistribution. Rabbi Sacks makes that clear: "Judaism is not socialism or communism. It distrusts the power of governments and sees private property as one of the primary safeguards of liberty. But deep-seated economic inequity offends against the fundamental values of *tzedakah* and *mishpat*, social and legislative justice, deemed by God Himself to be the way of the Lord."[13]

The exodus principle of justice as mutual responsibility is most prominent in the famous command to "love your neighbor as yourself" (Lev 19:18) and in the repeated mention of care for the vulnerable and easily marginalized, the widow and the orphan. But as Rabbi Sacks points out, covenantal responsibility is most striking and most suggestive in the command to care for the stranger. "Do not wrong a stranger, for you were strangers in the land of Egypt" (Ex 22:21).

This command to "love the stranger as yourself" is striking. It flies squarely in the face of the human tendency to care only or above all for "people like us" (in Aristotle's famous phrase). In other words the command to love the stranger flatly contradicts the age-old and the supermodern human tendency toward stereotyping, tribalism, xenophobia—and eventually extermination and genocide. As Sacks writes, "Dislike of the unlike is as old as mankind."[14] Love of the stranger therefore takes its place in the Hebrew and Christian Scriptures alongside other vital stands on behalf of human dignity and freedom—against hierarchical power and its inequalities, against the dehumanization of mass enslavement in the service of monumental national projects, against the false exploitation of the other in identity politics, and against the degrading brutality of power in war.

"To be a Jew is to be a stranger," Sacks remarks.[15] That may be why Abraham was commanded to leave his country, culture, and kin and break from the surrounding pressures to conform—"Go forth from your country, and from your relatives, and from your father's house" (Gen 12:1). He was told that his descendants would be strangers in a land that was not their own. To be a stranger was in their history, and to care for strangers was in their DNA. Does this mean support for a borderless world and a "y'all come" policy of indiscriminate welcome in the global era? Not at all, for the love of the stranger was balanced by the clarity of the covenant and its commands. Closed borders and high walls with no room for human compassion or genuine refugees are heartless, but open borders with no boundaries, no American identity, no civic education, and no citizenship requirements are foolish and suicidal for a free nation.

By definition, no stranger is in our image or they would not be strangers. But by the same token, even the stranger is in God's image and therefore within the circle of our care.

Fifth, and perhaps obviously but importantly, covenantal justice is equal justice under law, for everyone without distinction and without exception—the commoner as well as the king, and the poor man as well as the rich man. And with the addition of the separation of powers and the three crowns of government, there are moral limits to the power of leaders such as kings and priests, and the prophets as social critics are guardians of the covenant and the watchdogs against the abuse of power.

A VOICE FOR THE VOICELESS

Sixth, since justice is about persons, it must always be tempered with mercy, and it must always be accompanied by passionate advocacy on behalf of those who are unable to speak for themselves—justice for the weak, the poor, and the vulnerable. Justice may be portrayed as a blindfolded virgin, unseduceable with respect to bribes and preferential treatment. But law that forgets the personal and the human can easily become inhuman and idolatrous. Justice is for the sake of humanity and not humanity for the sake of justice. The passion of this third point breathes fire into the two previous points and calls for a proper moral outrage against injustice that more than matches the outrage of the progressive left, whether genuine or weaponized.

In the ancient world it was customary for friends and relatives to speak up for their friends and relatives and avenge, for example, the murder of a family member. But who would speak up for those unable or too weak to speak for themselves—and especially for the poor who had neither the means nor the skills to stand? The ancient world was generally suspicious of outside advocates and those who were brought in to speak on behalf of others who were not their relatives and friends. Like a bribe to the judge, such paid professionals, it was feared, would skew the course of justice by their eloquence or skullduggery. But centuries before Solon first introduced professional advocates in Greece in the sixth century BC, God called prophets to be his advocates on behalf of the voiceless, the injured, and the oppressed—as when Nathan confronted King David for murdering Uriah and stealing his wife, and Elijah confronted King Ahab for murdering Naboth and stealing his vineyard.

Naturally, this meant that the Hebrew prophets were God's advocates and champions on behalf of the poor. It also meant that by definition they were viewed by those in power as meddlers and interferers. Yet always and ultimately the supreme champion of the poor, the wounded, and the oppressed is God himself. This means that advocacy on behalf of the voiceless and the oppressed should be central to the calling of Jews, Christians, and all who follow the Sinai way. With unmistakable stress on the active component, the prophet Isaiah says,

> Seek justice,
> Reprove the ruthless,
> Defend the orphan,
> Plead for the widow. (Is 1:17)

"Who is a Jew?" Rabbi Heschel asked his fellow Jews in America, "A person whose integrity decays when unmoved by the wrong done to other people."[16]

It is no accident that the leading social reformers in history, such as Bartolomé de las Casas, William Wilberforce, and Elizabeth Fry, have all been fired by such a biblical passion for justice on behalf of others. The full force of this Jewish and Christian passion for justice and outrage against injustice needs to be recovered today. It stands in sharp contrast, as Rabbi Heschel notes, to the limited way justice is usually defined. Judges are "judicious," "calm," and "balanced," and justice is a matter of "giving to each no more and no less than their due." The common symbols of justice are a combination of scales (picturing balance), a sword (picturing strength and precision), and a blindfold.

Justice as equity, deserts, and balance is of course foundational. But the Hebrew prophets add an additional dimension that is essential to fighting injustice. "Let justice roll down like waters," the prophet Amos thunders, "righteousness like an ever-flowing stream" (Amos 5:24). What it suggests, Heschel says, is a side that is quite different from balance, precision, and calmness. "A mighty stream expressive of the vehemence of a never-ending, surging, fighting movement—as if obstacles had to be washed away for justice to be done."[17] Why the passion and the force? "Balancing is possible when the scales are unimpaired and the judge's eyes sound. When the eyes are dim and the scales unsure, what is required is a power that will strike and change, heal and restore, like a mighty stream bringing life to the parched land."[18]

Seventh and crucially, full biblical justice is messianic. Full and final justice will prevail one day, but only when and not before the Day of the Lord comes and God's Messiah steps in. "We shall overcome one day," as the anthem of the civil rights movement affirms. But such is the malignancy of evil, the subtlety of the human heart, the defects of moral conscience, and the impotence of the highest human ingenuity that humanity will never redeem itself by itself. Thus the Bible stands in sharp contrast to the secularist revolutionary faiths of Paris. Sinai is not utopian like Paris. Utopianism, with its fundamental lack of realism about human nature, is always forced to bridge the gap between the ideal and the real through coercion and violence. If humans are not what utopians think they should be, they must be forced to be what the revolution requires them to be—through reeducation and social engineering today and bio- and psycho-engineering tomorrow. The slide from utopianism to cruelty and wickedness is inevitable.

In the Bible, by contrast, the peaceable kingdom is coming. Swords will be beaten into plowshares, and the lion will lie down with the lamb, but only when and not a moment before the Messiah steps in. In the meantime, change and growth, as in nature, are slow and incremental but significant and never to be despised. In the meantime, in the interim in which we are living and fighting for justice, there is a counterweight to human injustice. With the truly awesome advance of science and technology, the human capacity to manipulate, violate, and exterminate our fellow humans is unprecedented. But over all the vagaries of history, the mighty justice of God and the grand dignity of human worth deliver a mighty *no* to human wickedness. The justice of God stands higher and stronger than history, and justice will prevail.

HOMECOMING

The third component in the Sinai way of righting wrongs is *repentance*, which is *teshuva* in the Hebrew Scriptures and *metanoia* in the Christian Scriptures. The Greek term refers to an "about-turn of heart, mind and spirit" that is truly radical and comprehensive. But the Hebrew is stronger still. Repentance is an inner attitude that issues in an outer action: verbal confession. And it includes not only a spiritual act (the change of heart and mind) but a physical act (a return or homecoming). The reason, as we saw earlier in discussing the great alienation, lies in the nature of sin as wrongdoing.

On the one hand sin refuses to take responsibility for its actions and passes the buck. The buck is then passed around until more and more people are drawn into the spiraling whirl of guilt and evasion—which is only stopped when someone stops the music and takes responsibility. "I did it. I am responsible. I was wrong." Repentance, then, is truth acknowledged, responsibility restored, and freedom healed and free to be itself. In the spiritual act of turning around, being sorry, and shouldering the responsibility for what was done wrong, freedom has become itself and free again. It is no longer rationalizing and on the run.

On the other hand sin is also an act that transgresses a boundary and is *out of line*. As Rabbi Sacks describes, it is "an act in the wrong place. The result, *galut* [exile], is that the agent finds himself in the wrong place. Sin disturbs the moral harmony of the universe."[19] A fourfold turning is in play. Sin has turned from God and the true, the good, and the beautiful and turned toward something false or wrong. Repentance must therefore turn from the false and the wrong and turn back to God and the true, the good, and the beautiful. Repentance is therefore the physical act of coming home—epitomized forever by the return of the Jews from exile in Babylon, the homecoming of the prodigal son in the story of Jesus, and the heart-stopping tenderness of Rembrandt's famous painting of the prodigal's welcome by his father—which hangs in the Hermitage in Saint Petersburg.

Repentance has nothing to do with contrition chic or reputational damage control. It is a challenge to make moral amends, and such an about-turn is rare today because moral accountability is so weak. For those with moral convictions, repentance is a matter of integrity even before public accountability. Such repentance is demanding. First, it requires *confession*, the open acknowledgment of responsibility for wrongdoing. Second, it requires *commitment*, a commitment not to repeat the offense. And third, it requires a *condition*—the test that if the opportunity to repeat the offense came around again, the offender would refrain from doing so this time. All three elements together made for complete repentance—"*complete repentance*, namely when circumstances repeat themselves and you have an opportunity to repeat the same offense again, but you refrain from doing so because you have changed."[20]

Repentance can come with a heavy price for nations. It currently confronts America with a painful decision that touches on American identity, and once again pits Sinai against Paris. Are the sins of slavery and racism the ultimate contradiction of America's founding mission or the ultimate expression of America's founding? The difference is the difference between night and day. If slavery is viewed as evil and a contradiction, as John Woolman, John Leland, Samuel Hopkins, and other early Americans protested vociferously, then confession can lead to the homecoming of the American experiment, cleansed of its most terrible sin. But if slavery is seen as the very expression of the American founding, as the progressive left and the 1619 Project claim, then confession must lead to the repudiation of the American experiment as it has understood itself. The land of the free would have been unmasked as nothing but naked hypocrisy, and disqualified forever through the sin of slavery.

There is no question that from the moment when the first African slaves were landed and sold in Virginia in August 1619, the sufferings and experiences of their descendants have shaped America in a myriad of ways ever since—from economics to law to music and entertainment and sports. But was slavery the country's "original sin" or was it the country's very origin? Is America a slavocracy? The *New York Times Magazine*'s 1619 Project argued openly for the latter. Its stated goal was to replace 1776 with 1619 as the founding year of America, and already it has been adopted for thousands of classrooms across the country. The objective is to "reframe American history by considering what it would mean to regard 1619 as our nation's birth year."[21] Later, in an admission that supported George Orwell's warning about the abuse of history, the creator Nikole Hannah-Jones admitted that the project was more journalism than history. The project, she said, had always been as much about the present as the past.

The sins of slavery and racism are no less sinful in either case, but the standing and the future of the "sinner" is quite different in the two views. For Paris the sins of slavery and racism shame America forever, disqualify the American experiment in freedom completely, and call for moral and political surrender before the "liberation" of the progressive left. ("The political left," critics said, "is already in the process of turning our K-12 schools into social-justice boot camps.")[22] For Sinai (and Calvary) America must make amends, and the very real sins must be confessed with very real repentance. But if this happens, the American experiment in freedom may be given a second chance and can then go forward both wiser and more humbly.

After all, abolition is the novelty in history, not slavery. Slavery goes back thousands of years, an almost constant in human history. It was Sinai in the form of Quakers, Evangelicals, and radical Republicans who were the abolitionists, and it was the party that was the ancestors of today's progressive left that resisted them in the name of slavery, segregation, the Ku Klux Klan and the Jim Crow laws. Genuine repentance can lead America to moral restoration and genuine peace making. Culture-war shaming, in contrast, is nothing other than applying today's ideologies to yesterday's injustices, and it leads only to the moral disarmament and the suicide of a nation.

From slavery to Vietnam, all America's evils were egregiously evil, but they were contradictions of America's ideals rather than contradictions of America. Again, the difference is night and day. The ideals could and should be cited to attack the evils, and the ideals could and should be lifted high so that succeeding generations could aspire to achieve them more faithfully than their ancestors did when they fell short. It is always better for America to lose face and to admit that a course of action is wrong than for America to lose its soul by insisting that the wrong is right and that injustice itself is justified and just. As Rabbi Sacks says of his fellow Jews, "We are a self-critical people. The Hebrew Bible is the most self-critical of all national literatures. We know our failings."[23] But with such an ideal of justice, along with the possibility of repentance and forgiveness, such prophetic self-criticism can lead to a change of heart, to reform, and to the reinvigoration of hope.

DISMISSED AND GONE FOR GOOD

Mention of an about-turn and a homecoming is incomplete without the fourth component of the Sinai view of restoration, the one that makes repentance not only possible but worthwhile and makes life tolerable: forgiveness. Expressed positively, it can be said that the deepest form of freedom stems from a good conscience and a forgiven heart. Expressed negatively, it has to be said that without forgiveness, wrongs would fester unhealed and go from bad to worse. They would mount and mount and mount—from slights and insults to rape, murder, and genocide—until communities are addicted to the cycle of recrimination, the blood-soaked ground cries out, and the swirl of unresolved guilt makes human life itself unbearable. Rabbi Sacks again becomes lyrical: "There are rare moments," he writes,

> when the world changes, and new possibility is born. . . . The birth of
> forgiveness is one such moment. It is one of the most radical ideas ever to
> have been introduced into the moral imagination of humankind. For-
> giveness is an action that is not a reaction. It breaks the cycle of stimulus-
> response, harm and retaliation, wrong and revenge, which has led whole
> cultures to their destruction and still threatens the future of the world. It
> frees individuals from the burden of their past and humanity from the
> irreversibility of history. It tells us the enemies can become friends.[24]

Without forgiveness and its liberation from the past, there can be no change, no
growth, and no fruitful maturity—as thinkers, as individuals, as citizens, and
as nations.

How can that happen? How can forgiveness deal with the emotion of revenge
as well as the ethic of revenge? The Bible's resolution to this tension is so radical,
Sacks writes, that it transformed the moral horizons of humankind. We can and
must forgive because God has forgiven us, so we forgive as we have been forgiven
and as we forgive.

> It says that the God of love and forgiveness created us in love and forgiveness,
> asking that we love and forgive others. God does not ask us not to fail.
> Rather, he asks us to acknowledge our failures, repair what we have harmed,
> and move on, learning from our failures and growing thereby. . . . Therefore
> at its heart [at the heart of life] there had to be an institution capable of
> transmuting guilt into moral growth, and estrangement from God or our
> fellow humans into reconciliation. That institution is Yom Kippur.[25]

Yom Kippur, of course, is the Day of Atonement—and for Christians, the great
atonement of the death of Jesus on the cross. Atonement can cover the worst.
Terrible, truly terrible though slavery was, it no more nullifies the American
experiment than the terrible sin of the Golden Calf nullified the Israelites after
their liberation from Egypt. To be sure, the confession and forgiveness have to
be genuine. But when they are, they show that forgiveness is linked inseparably
to freedom. To retaliate or to seek revenge against someone is a reaction that is
caused by an action. It is merely part of a chain of determined events and is
therefore neither free nor freeing. But in choosing to forgive, freedom breaks the
chain and wins twice over. Forgiveness is an act of freedom by the one who for-
gives, which in turn frees the one who is forgiven. The past no longer perpetuates

itself as fate, and the future is free because it is no longer weighed down by the burden of the past. This freedom, Viktor Frankl discovered at Auschwitz and Rabbi Sacks draws out fruitfully, was the "one freedom left in Auschwitz"—"everything can be taken from a man but one thing: the last of the human freedoms—to choose one's attitude in any given circumstances, to choose one's own way."[26]

We have all sinned, and we have all been sinned against, in smaller or greater ways. The question is how we respond. Will we continue the chain of cause and effect, or will we break it? Let contrast once again be the mother of clarity. Repentance and forgiveness are not a tactic with an eye to appeasement. They are not designed to sidestep responsibility in an attempt to defuse the anger against what was wrong. Nor are they a form of social abasement that seeks to deflect the justice of the reprisal. Repentance owns up and takes full responsibility, and forgiveness dismisses all charges. To forgive is to *forth-give* and so to dismiss all possible claims of the past on the future. Forgiveness thus completes what repentance begins: the transformation of the past. We humans may transcend space, and we do so every day, but time transcends humanity. "In the dimension of time there is no going back," Rabbi Heschel says, "But the power of repentance [and forgiveness] causes time to be created backward and allows re-creation of the past to take place. Through the forgiving hand of God, harm and blemish which we have committed against the world and against ourselves will be extinguished, transformed into salvation."[27]

Every citizen of the West should reflect on this momentous point. Forgiveness must never be cheapened. Forgiveness is free, but it is costly. It is freely given, but it cannot be demanded and must never be taken for granted. The black book of the sins of the West, both Europe's and America's, is long and damning. But are Western citizens then fated, as the Greeks believed and many modern determinists believe too? Is it all over for the West, necessarily? The double freedom of forgiveness, the freedom of the forgiver and the freedom of the forgiven, says otherwise. Defenseless against the sins of history, there must be no cheap grace. "The earth will reveal her bloodshed" (Is 26:21) as the Hebrew prophet warns. But the way of Sinai and Galilee is neither fated nor tragic. As Rabbi Heschel declares majestically, writing in the personal shadow of America's Selma as well as Germany's Auschwitz, "Sin is not a *cul de sac*, nor is guilt a final trap. Sin may be washed away by repentance and return, and beyond guilt is the dawn of forgiveness. The door is never locked, the threat of doom is not the last word."[28] The miracle of forgiveness at Mother Emanuel showed the way once again.

FROM ENEMY TO FRIEND

Together, the combination of repentance, confession, and forgiveness can lead to reconciliation and so to genuine peacemaking and restoration. This fifth component of the Sinai way—reconciliation and restoration—is monumental for the human story and the present crises in America and the West. All too often people forget that peace, as a positive state and an achievable condition, is nonutopian and the extraordinary gift of the Jews. Forgiveness is crucial to peace because forgiveness and freedom together mean that the future need not be the past. There is always choice. Tomorrow can always be different.

After some wrongdoings (because of the great alienation), freedom would be a liability if there were no repentance and forgiveness. It would be the prologue to a catalog of mounting disasters with no escape. Life on the earth would degenerate into a cosmic vendetta of violence and vengeance. Wrong would breed wrong, violence would compound violence, tensions and hostilities would have no resolution, and unhealed wounds would fester and grow foul. What the Allies' resentment, retaliation, and reparations did to Germany after World War I, making Hitler all but inevitable, would be written across all the myriad sins of America and the West. Can the long-poisoned fruits of racism, colonialism, militarism, and imperialism be healed through resentment and government-imposed reparations? The outcome would be a horrific and unthinkable failure. Some cancers have grown so deadly that only the remedy of forgiveness and reconciliation can hope to offer a cure.

In Dostoevsky's novel *Demons,* it is not clear at first who the demons are. Are they the revolutionaries who form the radical cell? Are they the nihilistic ideas that come in when God is forgotten? ("Ruined altars are the breeding ground for demons.") Only at the end does Dostoevsky throw light on the title when he cites the incident from Luke's Gospel. "These demons who come out of a sick man and enter into swine—it's all the sores, all the miasmas, all the uncleanness, all the big and little demons accumulated in our great and dear sick man, in our Russia, for centuries, for centuries!"[29] One translator of the novel described them as the legion of isms that came into Russia from the West—including rationalism, materialism, socialism, anarchism, nihilism, and atheism. But then, the speaker Stepan Trofimovich comments, the sum total of all Russia's evils in history will enter the desperate hearts and minds of the revolutionaries themselves and drive them over the cliff like the Gadarene swine—leaving Russia, like the demon-possessed Legion, free of its sufferings and restored to its right mind. Are the

European and American evils of the centuries any less evil? How are they to be cured? Are Europe and America at a place where they are willing to confess the evils, repent of their past, and seek the remedy of the only way to restore them to freedom and their right minds?

Genuine repentance and genuine forgiveness contribute to peace by effecting three incomparably important things. First, they cut off the burdens of the past. Second, they open up the future as the world of another chance. And third, they break down the walls of hostility between humans and God and between humans and each other so that enemies can become friends. (Rabbi Nathan: "Who is strong? One who turns an enemy into a friend.")[30] Is there any comparable remedy for the crimes and sins that have built up to the present crisis? Nowhere is the difference between Sinai (and Galilee) and Paris starker, and nowhere is the choice more consequential. Rabbi Sacks concludes, "Forgiveness is not just one idea among many. It transformed the human situation. . . . Forgiveness breaks the irreversibility of the past. It is the undoing of what has been done. Repentance and forgiveness—the two great gifts of human freedom—redeem the human condition from tragedy."[31]

All this matters supremely because without forgiveness and reconciliation, we as modern people are being schooled in conflict and callousness. We know the monstrous crimes against humanity, we have staggered under the horrendous statistics, we have been spectators of countless disasters as they happened, we have watched and rewatched the films, we have joined the solemn litanies of "Never again," but the very weight and repetition of it all have left us less surprised, less shocked, and less shockable than when we started. Are we any nearer to making such crimes and such evil impossible? Little wonder it is said that "Never again" has become "Again and again." Insulated against suffering, we have become indifferent to evil.

The modern person, Rabbi Heschel writes, with their close experience of the Nazi death camps, is "a victim of enforced brutalization, his sensibility is being increasingly reduced; his sense of horror is on the wane. The distinction between right and wrong is becoming blurred. All that is left to us is our being horrified at the loss of our sense of horror."[32] If ever a generation and a world needed atonement, forgiveness, reconciliation, restoration, and a second chance, it is our own.

Some have concluded that America's sins are too deep, its divisions are too wide, and forgiveness is too weak. But let no one think that forgiveness is at best purely spiritual and private and at worst sentimental and impractical. The story of South Africa after apartheid and Rwanda after the massacre shows otherwise. Again, Lord Sacks is blunt:

> Forgiveness is not merely *personal*, it is also *political*. It is essential to the life of a nation if it is to maintain its independence for long. . . . When people lack the ability to forgive, they are unable to resolve conflict. The result is division, factionalism, and the fragmentation of a nation into competing groups and sects.[33]

After more than fifty years of culture warring in America, his conclusion speaks to the heart of a deeply divided America: "The message could not be clearer. *Those who seek freedom must learn to forgive.*"[34]

SPYING ON THE SOUL

Let me be content in this chapter with a single implication. All the great themes concerning freedom need to carry a public warning, and few are greater than repentance, confession, and forgiveness. Without them, freedom would be short-lived and irreparable. But their very importance means that they are liable to be distorted and sometimes devilishly so. Take the notion of confession. Rightly understood, a confession that is sincere and voluntary is a vital, precious, and rare moral act. Beginning internally with an attitude of repentance, it issues externally in a statement of voluntary confession. *A person who confesses literally goes on record against himself or herself, with no ifs, buts, excuses, or evasions.*

The *I* word is for once appropriate and not proud. "I have done this or that. I was responsible. I was wrong. I am ashamed. I will endeavor never to do it again." In shouldering the responsibility for their wrongs and making a clean breast of them, such a confession is a key step in the process of forgiveness, reconciliation, and restoration. But naturally, there is more to the story than that. Confession contains information, knowledge is power, and power is corruptible, so confessional knowledge is open to abuse in various ways.

One obvious way to twist confession is to coerce the admission. Coerced confession is a form of coercive groupthink and a flagrant abuse of power. The person confessing is simply rehearsing what they think the group would like to hear, whether the pressure applied is mild and a form of social conformism or severe as with the threat of torture. Either way, any confession that is coerced is at once inauthentic, abusive, and wrong. In a freedom-loving and rights-affirming age, such coerced confessions are rarer, mercifully, except in extreme circumstances such as war.

The greater danger today is the subtler form of false confession: using the information gained in confession to exert control. This tactic was once called *Seelenspionage* or "spying on the soul." It goes back to Adam Weishaupt, the Bavarian professor who was the pioneer of Illuminism and had such a brief but significant influence on the revolutionary faith of the left.[35] Educated by the Jesuits until he was fifteen, he vehemently rejected their Christian faith but based his secular revolutionary thinking on a key part of Jesuit spirituality—confession. Put simply, he used the knowledge gained through confession to build a chain of command based on control exercised through manipulation of the passions revealed in confession.

Choosing the code name "Spartacus," Weishaupt used his "spying on the soul" to build revolutionary cells that would follow the directions of their leaders with the blind loyalty he had seen in the Jesuits. The rigorous soul baring and examination of conscience was twisted into a form of intelligence gathering that gave him enormous power over his followers because he knew their secrets. As a disciple of Weishaupt's wrote later in alarm, "From a comparison of all these characteristics, even those which seem the smallest and least significant, one can draw conclusions which have enormous significance for knowledge of human beings and gradually draw out of that a reliable semiotics of the soul."[36]

From such a small beginning, the idea of "spying on the soul" has branched out in numerous directions over the last two centuries, so that it has become a major human problem in the advanced modern world. Its influence is obvious and most pernicious in communist and police state spying (the KGB and Stasi reports). In his 1930 play *The Measures Taken*, Berthold Brecht has the line, "The party has a thousand eyes, but we have only two."[37] Today, millions of eyes go far beyond the eyes of the communist party or the religious cult (which together created the popularity of the term *brainwashing* in the 1950s and 1960s). The information gathering is no less clear in Alfred Kinsey's use of sexual histories and the influence of psychology on the rise of advertising. Today, it flourishes not only in the blatant evils of China's face recognition and social credit system but in the closer and subtler dangers of surveillance capitalism—the growth of data gathering typified by Google, Amazon, and Facebook.

To be sure, the implications may be either benign or malign. Jeremy Bentham's "panopticon" and Orwell's "Big Brother" may have become Amazon's little sister

Alexa or Facebook's likes. The information gathered may be used to play music, sell jeans, restock fridges, market political candidates, arrest sexual deviants, or catch terrorists. But the process of *datafying* us all is the same: "You click and they collect" (data). Or as a common saying goes, "Every mouse click is a commodity." "If there is no charge for the service, you are the product." The result is a mini-you and a mini-me that is a datafied double used by advertisers to help persuade us to buy or to vote as they recommend.

Data equals precision, precision equals prediction, prediction equals power, and power equals control. "Confession" or massive data gathering, whether voluntary or involuntary, provides information, knowledge enables control, and the more comprehensive the knowledge the greater the control. The goal of total control may be political in China or commercial in the West, but the totalizing (totalitarian) tendency of the scientific, commercial, and political use of knowledge in the digital age is unmistakable. And as always, there is an elite. ("This narrow priesthood of data scientists and their bosses sits at the pinnacle of a new society.")[38] Hence the danger of the unaccountable power of the technology companies.

Once again the irony must be pondered. Through confession, whether crude and coerced or the subtle confessional of data gathering, and through the almighty algorithm, the Enlightenment assault on the bonds of tradition is morphing into the even stronger bonds of totalitarianism. Set free from spiritual and moral control, human passions are now subject to the mechanisms of scientific and social control. St. Augustine saw the dynamics clearly in the City of Man in Rome. The city (or nation or corporation or individual) that "lusts to dominate the world" will find itself "dominated by its passion for domination."[39] And that is why, as Dostoevsky warned, "unlimited freedom ends in unlimited despotism."[40]

America cannot endure permanently half 1776 and half 1789. The compromises, contradictions, hypocrisies, inequities, and evils have built up unaddressed. The grapes of wrath have ripened again, and the choice before America is plain. Either America goes forward best by going back first, or America is about to reap a future in which the worst will once again be the corruption of the best.

CONCLUSION

A NEW, NEW BIRTH OF FREEDOM?

IN ABRAHAM LINCOLN'S celebrated Gettysburg Address on November 19, 1863, he famously called for "a new birth of freedom."[1] America had been "conceived in liberty," but through the ruinous evil and contradiction of slavery, it had lost its way and required a clean slate and a fresh start. Following Lincoln's assassination, the results of the post-Civil War century were mixed, until Dr. Martin Luther King Jr. and the civil rights movement addressed the still-festering wrongs. But now, after the enfeebling of traditional liberalism and the deepening progressive radicalism of the fifty years after King's own assassination and "the long march through the institutions," the very notion of the American Revolution and the American experiment in freedom has been called into question more fundamentally than ever before. Karl Kraus described *fin de siècle* Vienna as a "research laboratory for world destruction," and unless Americans wake up, America will fast become the same for a historic betrayal of freedom.[2]

What America needs today is a massive and decisive about-turn, a return, and a new, new birth of freedom. The self-professed "land of the free" now stands at a crossroads, as almost every day's events demonstrate in one way or another. The beneficiary of its stirring heroism and monumental victory in World War II, America has succumbed to the seductions and illusions of its unprecedented power and prosperity. Over the best part of the century since then, America has come to mistake freedom with the pursuit of unappeased appetites, it has trifled with its ideals and bartered truth for power, heroism for celebrity, goodness, and beauty for entertainment and diversion, self-discipline for comfort and convenience, and self-reliance for welfare and dependency. In the process America has scaled unimaginable heights in the worlds of economics, science, technology, and medicine, but lost its soul and inner strength.

Dig deep into the philosophical cynicism, the moral corruption, and the social collapse that is now afflicting America at the height of its power. America is even losing touch with the revolution that once lifted it to be history's great experiment in freedom. Public life is now degenerating into a grand stage for the powerful and a parade ground for the hypocrite, and power-ravenous men and women across the land are sowing seeds of venom and resentment in the hearts of the young, the wounded, and the left behind. There is a reason why free societies are rare. Call it folly, call it irony, or call it hubris, but those who think that humans are the master of history and the authors of their own destiny do not end with freedom and continuing mastery. They end in self-defeating frustration, failure, and fate. There is no final exceptionalism in history and no immunity from the common condition of humanity.

In some ways America's present crisis is its equivalent of what Douglas Murray chronicled as "the strange death of Europe."[3] In other ways it is worse or at least less excusable. America is a country and not a continent, and more united than Europe. America has a clearer and more recent understanding of the ideas and ideals that made it the land of the free. America had all the answers to its present ills but has discarded them. And worst of all, America is in danger of betraying a vision of freedom that is richer, deeper, more realistic, and more comprehensive than Europe has ever achieved—the gift of the Jews and the Reformation to America, which could still be America's privilege to hand on to the world and the future.

The choice before America now is simple but stark: Revolution? Oligarchy? Or homecoming? Will there be an about-turn and an American homecoming, or will we soon see the harvest of America's spiritual and civic disaster? Will the hurricane force of history be ignored until too late? Will America, its political leaders and parties, its colleges and universities, its press and media, its entertainment world and Hollywood, and above all its more than three hundred million citizens choose to return to 1776 or give themselves over to 1789? Could there be such a restoration that addresses the wrongs and renewing America in terms of the better angels of its origins and ideals? Or are we soon to see the complete abandonment of 1776 and a final shift to 1789—a shift that has long been completed in many universities, in certain elite circles, and among the younger generation and a significant number of American political leaders?

There is no question that, though the stakes are high, the odds against a successful American renewal are long—for all the empty toasts to exceptionalism, the hollow claims of an American comeback, or the foolish pretense that the problems are only due to an error in policy so that America's best is yet to be. No one should fool themselves. The future for freedom and humanity is in the balance, as Sinai spells freedom for the future whereas Paris has so far spelled out freedom betrayed and the coming of a long night of expanding statism, surveillance, and repression. But the renewal of a new, new birth of freedom would not be easy. The progressive left, the postmodern aficionados of critical theory, and the advocates of the anti-American view of American history would all become instant naysayers. They would dismiss any recommitment to the ideals of 1776 as White privilege, as diehard and reactionary, as being on the wrong side of history, or a futile exercise in nostalgia.

Against all such opposition, a new, new birth of American freedom would require a visionary leader or leaders who understand and believe in the American experiment, who can describe the present crisis in light of the drift from America's roots, who can counter the criticisms and the alternative visions of Paris and show where they lead, and who can set out the originality of the American experiment with a freshness for our times—*and who can do all this not as a weapon to attack their political opponents but as a call that will resonate with the better angels of all Americans and even draw in many of their opponents.* Above all, national renewal would require that "we the people" throw off the mental shackles of the disdain of the elites and recover their voice and collective responsibility, not as angry populists but as free and responsible citizens. They could then respond to the call to national renewal with sufficient strength to represent a genuine new, new birth of freedom. And later, the nation as a whole would need to address the institutional rebuilding that must accompany genuine renewal—such as the restoration of civic education in American schooling.

Might it be that instead of celebrating the Fourth of July with a military-style parade to celebrate the strength of the armed forces, Americans could commemorate the Fourth with a Hebrew-style national rededication on the National Mall, acknowledging the sins and failures of the past and present, reaffirming the first principles of the American experiment, and recommitting themselves to the uniting first principles of the American *Unum* to balance the American *Pluribus*?

America restored could still be freedom's masterpiece society in history. Such a new, new birth of freedom would be helped immeasurably by a surging Jewish and Christian renaissance throughout the West. Indeed, it is unimaginable without it. Jews will always be Jews and Christians Christians, so no false ecumenism is in mind. But there can be no doubt that together the Hebrew and Christian Scriptures offer an account of the sanctity of life, the dignity of the individual person, equality before the law, and words, love, freedom, conscience, justice, truth, trust, politics, community, and peace that is incomparable.

Such a renaissance would firmly repudiate not only the vile, vile evil of anti-Semitism but its crass stupidity too, for it would demonstrate that many of the noblest roots of the West are in the Hebrew and Christian Scriptures. John Adams had no doubts about the irreplaceable contribution of the Jews. In a letter in 1808 he wrote that, in spite of Voltaire and other Enlightenment thinkers,

> I will insist that the Hebrews have contributed more to civilize men than any other nation. If I were an atheist, and believed in blind eternal fate, I should still believe that fate had ordained the Jews to be the most essential instrument for civilizing the nations. . . . They are the most glorious nation that ever inhabited this earth. The Romans and their empire were but a bubble in comparison with the Jews.[4]

Such a new, new birth is needed and is possible, but is it likely? Recent trends would suggest that drift, disarray, and decline are the likelier outcome. But once again, freedom means that the future is never fated. It is always open. Who dares still wins.

AMERICA'S HOUR

Do Americans realize what time it is? Are they going to keep on boasting about exceptionalism and pretend that their day will last forever? "Those who cannot remember the past are condemned to repeat it." Philosopher George Santayana's much-quoted remark is a healthy challenge but it is also misleading. Or perhaps it is commonly misunderstood today. History is vital, as we have seen again and again, and the exodus is one of the great events of history. But the modern tendency is to reduce history to modern ways of thinking and so to miss the element of uniqueness and singularity. In its drive to be supreme and to have supreme control, Enlightenment reason has a passion for the "theory of everything." But like the cunning innkeeper Procrustes, it cuts off and stretches, it flattens and homogenizes according to the length of the bed of what it knows now. The result is a bias for timeless truths, general laws, and abstract principles. The scientific method, for example, requires processes that are repeatable and verifiable and applicable in all situations. Thus neither reason nor science is the way to appreciate the uniqueness and singular character of history and revelation, the uniqueness of events such as the exodus—and the meaning of the present moment, which is far, far more than can be seen on the surface or understood as the repeat of an old cycle.

In the same way, the typical modern response to this argument will be to blur and blunt its challenge by asserting that the present crisis is merely one part of a cycle or another swing of a pendulum. History, however, including the exodus, turns on the unique, the singular, the one time, and the unrepeatable. The Jewish and Christian faiths, as we have seen, put a premium on time and history, and they both turn on unique and unprecedented events—on the *one time* of divine and human action rather than the *all the time* of nature. As Rabbi Heschel insists, "The term 'God of Abraham, Isaac, and Jacob' is quite different from a term such as 'God of truth, goodness, and beauty.'" It differs too from "the God of Kant, Hegel, and Schelling," and the whole difference between the first phrase and the other two lies in the uniqueness of one-time events in history.[5]

That point applies to the present as well as the past. There are days that divide history for centuries—*"if not for that day,"* the day when the Israelites crossed the Red Sea, when Julius Caesar was murdered, when Jesus of Nazareth was crucified and then was raised from the dead, when Sultan Mehmet overran Constantinople, when King John was forced to sign the Magna Carta at Runnymede, when the first shots were fired at Lexington and Concord, when the crumbling fortress of the Bastille was stormed, when the sealed train carrying Lenin arrived at Finland Station in Saint Petersburg, and the day when the Berlin wall fell. There are far longer periods too when the accumulated weight of millions of small decisions casts the die and shapes the centuries. Whether the choice between 1776 and 1789 will depend on the former or the latter or both, only God knows. But that day will come. The choice between Sinai and Paris is too consequential to leave no mark on history.

There is a striking singularity in the present moment. Right here and now the Americans in the present generation are the heirs and the carriers of a unique vision of freedom, even if many appear to neither understand nor appreciate that fact. But while the singularity is limited, the stakes are not. The stakes are far wider and almost incalculable. Such is the character of the freedom at issue between Sinai and Paris that to sustain or forfeit that Sinai freedom will have historic consequences for the rest of the world and the foreseeable human future. Quite simply, there never has been, and there is not now, any vision of freedom like that of Sinai, so for Americans to renew it or discard it will make a world of difference forever.

Success for a prophet such as Amos, Isaiah, and Jeremiah, or Fyodor Dostoevsky and Alexander Solzhenitsyn did not lie in whether they were listened to but simply in whether they were faithful to their message and the hour. Some must have felt at times like the Greek prophetess Cassandra who was fated not to be believed. When Solzhenitsyn delivered his great *Warning to the West* in the 1970s, he knew well that many were applauding but few were hearing. "My friends," he said in one speech, "I'm not going to give you sugary words. The situation in the world is not just dangerous, it isn't just threatening, it is catastrophic."[6] But nothing came close enough to make Americans care. "Just let us live in peace and quiet. Let us drive our big cars on our splendid highways; let us play tennis and golf unperturbed; let us mix our cocktails as we are accustomed to doing; let us see the beautiful smile and a glass of wine on every page of our magazines."[7]

Solzhenitsyn's challenge to Western complacency was eerily prophetic of what was to come out of the clear blue skies a quarter of a century later, on Tuesday, September 11, 2001. Twenty-five years earlier, people were not listening. Why should they? They were confident and assured. As Solzhenitsyn admitted, "But the proud skyscrapers stand on, jut into the sky, and say: It will never happen here. This will never come to us. It is not possible here."[8]

It will never happen here? Solzhenitsyn had probably never heard of Osama bin Laden, but his response to the false peace was blunt. "It can happen. It is possible. As a Russian proverb says, 'When it happens to you, you'll know it's true.'"[9]

When it happens to you, you'll know it's true. That word confronts America and the West today. We are deep into the American and the Western hour, the time that is bristling with crisis and opportunity. But most people dream on or only stir uneasily. Like love at first sight, some people don't believe in decline until it happens to them. Yes, there are problems, they admit, but decline and decadence in our time? Surely not. Complacency is still possible. The sunny illusions created by power and prosperity have not yet faded. Choices are being made, but the consequences are not yet clear. Responsibility has not yet caught up with freedom. Doesn't God take special care of babies, drunks, and the United States? Leadership can edge its way forward for a while longer, or so it seems. Haven't both Democrats and Republicans promised us that the best is yet to be?

There is no choice facing America and the West that is more urgent and more consequential than the choice between Sinai and Paris. Will the coming generation return to faith in God and to humility or continue to trust in the all-sufficiency of reason, punditry, and technocracy and the transformative power of politics? Will its politics be led by principles or by power? By right or might? Will the claim prove true or false that with no fear of God, there will soon be no justice, that without justice there will be no equality, that without equality there will be no freedom, and that without freedom there will soon be no future for America and the West? In short, will the classical Latin maxim be written over America, as it has been for so many great nations in history, including educated, civilized, sophisticated Reformation Germany, "The worst is the corruption of the best" (*Corruptio optimi pessima*)?

I make no predictions. I offer no speculations on the unthinkable consequences that the maelstrom of history will bring down on the children of the men and women responsible for rejecting the way of Sinai and Galilee. I only issue a warning and a strong plea: first, that while there is still time to change, Americans define reality and recognize the real crisis of our time; second, that Americans debate the issues in a fair and open manner that is worthy of their urgency and the immensity of the stakes; and third, that those who disagree with this vision stop carping at minor details and recognize that they must engage with an entire way of seeing the world and living life—an entire view of the world and way of life that has helped shape the best of the Western heritage and answers the present crises better than any alternative. This is not a plea for some special protection or exemption for faith. It is time and past time to set out the debate in its fullest terms and to recognize that the sequel to this generation's choices will be consequential and historic.

Two revolutionary faiths are bidding to take the world forward, not just one. Contrast is the mother of clarity. Sinai and Paris are entirely different, and the differences will make a difference, and this time not just for a generation or so but for the very future of humanity. Exodus—and not 1789, 1917, 1949, or 1968— truly stands as the Magna Carta of humanity. Sinai and not Paris offers the vision of a free and responsible republic that champions and protects ordered freedom, justice, peace, and stability. It is time to choose between the revolutions—between faith in God and faith in reason alone, between freedom and despotism, and between life and death.

This book is an open appeal to America and Americans by a lifelong admirer of the American experiment in freedom. It is written with hope as well as sorrow and anger. It is also a tribute to Rabbi Lord Jonathan Sacks and his magnificent exposition of Exodus as a vision of freedom and justice. It is therefore fitting to end with Rabbi Sacks's summary of our human task.

> Just as God created order in the universe, so are we called to create order in our personal lives and in society as a whole. We are God's image; we are God's children; we are God's partners. Within us is the breath of God. Around us is the presence of God. Near us is the home we build for God. Ahead of us is the task set by God: to be his agents of justice and compassion. Never has a nobler account been given of the human condition, and it challenges us still.[10]

Dignity, love, freedom, justice, forgiveness, reconciliation, peace, stability, and shalom as human flourishing—is there a brighter vision, and are there deeper longings for humanity than these? If these truths and these ideals are to inspire hope, thrust us forward again, and become realities and not just a mirage of words, then the way to find them must itself be found. There is no better way and no surer road than the great journey set out in Exodus (and completed in the rest of the Hebrew and Christian Scriptures). There, as nowhere else, is the Magna Carta of humanity and the once and future key to our human freedom.

America, the choice is clear, and so too will be the consequences. "Eternal vigilance is the price of liberty," but the deepest vigilance is not to watch out for your enemies but to watch out for yourself. The nation that has grown careless in defending its rich and distinctive heritage and is now being transformed beyond recognition is the nation that could still be renewed if only it awakens to reality and chooses wisely. It is time once again to weigh all the differences between life and death, and choose life.

L'Chaim!

ACKNOWLEDGMENTS

BLAISE PASCAL, WE ARE TOLD, used to say that authors should speak of "our book" rather than "my book," as "there is usually more of other people's property in it than their own."[1] That is more true of this book than of any I have written before. For a start, this one has been the most unbidden. As I was setting out to write a completely different book, the idea and content of this book came almost complete and as if by dictation. But beyond that, this book owes everything to Rabbi Lord Jonathan Sacks, as reading the book will have made clear. (Rabbi Sacks' untimely death in November 2020, as this book was being finalized, was profoundly sad. I am glad that he saw a draft of the book before the illness struck, so that he could see how I and others regard his contribution to freedom to be immense.) For these very reasons I am especially grateful for those who encouraged me in what seemed to be an almost presumptuous task. In particular, I owe a special debt of gratitude to the following:

To Dan and Lori Frost, Troy and Angelique Griepp, Ann Holladay, Bob and Diane Kramer, Stuart and Celia McAlpine, Dick and Becky Molenhouse, Dick and Mary Ohman, Dean and Linda Overman, Ryon and Jan Paton, David and Suzy Young for their friendship and constant encouragement.

To Seamus Merrigan, my invaluable assistant, for his immense help with a thousand tasks, especially when bailing out a technological dummy.

To Dennis Clarke, Kevin and Bonnie McKernan, Steve Moore, and Dick Ohman for their willingness to read the first draft of this book and offer immensely helpful criticisms. Needless to say, I remain responsible for the final outcome, particularly where some of them might still disagree with me strongly.

To Erik Wolgemuth, my friendly, skilled, and tireless agent, for all his enthusiasm and hard work on behalf of the book.

To Al Hsu, Jeff Crosby, Drew Blankman, Justin Paul Lawrence, Lori Neff, David Fassett, Ellen Hsu, Krista Clayton, and all your team at InterVarsity Press. I am indebted to you forever for your combined skills, wisdom, and friendly encouragement.

And most of all, to Jenny and CJ, my wife and son, for their unflagging loyalty, support, suggestions, criticisms, and love in my speaking and writing endeavors as in all of life. This book's dedication to Jenny, along with Rabbi Sacks, is the merest hint of all that I owe to her for our half-century of life and love together.

NOTES

INTRODUCTION: UPSIDE DOWN OR RIGHT WAY UP?

[1]Abraham Lincoln, quoted in Allen C. Guelzo, *The Crisis of the American Republic: A History of the Civil War and Reconstruction Era* (New York: St. Martin's Press, 1995), 78.

[2]Christopher Hill, *The World Turned Upside Down: Radical Ideas During the English Revolution* (London: Penguin, 1991), 107.

[3]Hill, *World Turned Upside Down*, 107.

[4]Matthew Stewart, *Nature's God: The Heretical Origins of the American Republic* (New York: W. W. Norton, 2014), 6.

[5]Stewart, *Nature's God*, 80.

[6]Thomas Jefferson, quoted in Stewart, *Nature's God*, 79.

[7]Stewart, *Nature's God*, 435.

[8]Eric Nelson, *The Hebrew Republic: Jewish Sources and the Transformation of European Political Thought* (Cambridge, MA: Harvard University Press, 2010).

[9]Nelson, *Hebrew Republic*, 139.

[10]William F. Buckley Jr., preface to Erik von Kuehnelt-Leddihn, *Leftism Revisited: From de Sade and Marx to Hitler and Pol Pot* (Washington, DC: Regnery Gateway, 1993), x.

[11]David Andress, *The Terror: The Merciless War for Freedom in Revolutionary France* (New York: Farrar, Straus and Giroux, 2005), 3.

[12]Hannah Arendt, *On Revolution* (London: Collins, 1973), 55.

[13]George Steiner, quoted in William Doyle, *The French Revolution: A Very Short Introduction* (Oxford: Oxford University Press, 2001), 108.

[14]Heinrich Heine, quoted in Paul Johnson, *A History of the Jews* (New York: Harper Perennial, 1988), 346.

[15]James H. Billington, *Fire in the Minds of Men: Origins of the Revolutionary Faith* (London: Routledge, 2017), 1.

[16]Billington, *Fire in the Minds*, 6.

[17]Billington, *Fire in the Minds*, 8.

[18]Billington, *Fire in the Minds*, 443.

[19]Jonathan Sacks, *The Jonathan Sacks Haggada* (New Milford, CT: Maggid, 2013), 30.

[20]Tacitus, *The Histories* 5:4, trans. W. H. Fyfe (Oxford: Oxford World's Classics, 1997), 234.

[21]Julian, quoted in Robert Hughes, *Rome: A Cultural, Visual and Personal History* (New York: Alfred A. Knopf, 2011), 160.

[22]Friedrich Nietzsche, *Twilight of the Idols and the Anti-Christ* (London: Penguin, 1990), 199.

[23]Billington, *Fire in the Minds*, 166; and Harry Redner, *Totalitarianism, Globalization, Colonialism: The Destruction of Civilization Since 1914* (New Brunswick, NJ: Transaction, 2014), 69.

[24]Hitler, quoted in Erik von Kuehnelt-Leddihn, *Liberty or Equality* (Front Royal, VA: Christendom Press, 1993), 247.

[25]Klemens von Metternich, quoted in Kuehnelt-Leddihn, *Leftism Revisited*, 75.

[26]Jonathan Sacks, *Morality: Restoring the Common Ground in Divided Times* (London: Hodder & Stoughton, 2020), 1.

[27]Kevin Belmonte, *Hero for Humanity: A Biography of William Wilberforce* (Colorado Springs, CO: NavPress, 2002), 198.

[28]David M. Rubenstein, *The American Story: Conversations with Master Historians* (New York: Simon & Schuster, 2019), 26.

[29]Nelson, *Hebrew Republic*.

[30]Jonathan Sacks, *Ceremony & Celebration: Introduction to the Holidays* (New Milford, CT: Maggid, 2017), 66.

[31]Abraham J. Heschel, *What Is Man?* (New York: Farrar, Straus and Giroux, 1965), 100.

1. I WILL BE WHO I WILL BE: THE GREAT REVELATION

[1]Percy Bysshe Shelley, quoted in E. Michael Jones, *Libido Dominandi: Sexual Liberation and Political Control* (South Bend, IN: St. Augustine's Press, 2000), 75.

[2]Philipp Blom, *A Wicked Company* (New York: Basic Books, 2001), 293.

[3]Harry Redner, *The Triumph and Tragedy of the Intellectuals* (New Brunswick, NJ: Transaction, 2016), 32.

[4]William Doyle, *The French Revolution: A Very Short Introduction* (Oxford: Oxford University Press, 2001), 86.

[5]Alexander Solzhenitsyn, quoted in Robert Cardinal Sarah, *The Day Is Now Far Spent* (San Francisco: Ignatius Press, 2019), 239.

[6]Friedrich Nietzsche, *The Will to Power*, trans. Anthony Ludovici (Overland Park, KS: Digireads, 2019), 22.

[7]Hilaire Belloc, *Europe and the Faith* (West Valley City, UT: Waking Lion, 2006), 2.

[8]Rodney Stark, *For the Glory of God: How Monotheism Led to Reformations, Science, Witch-Hunts and the End of Slavery* (Princeton, NJ: Princeton University Press, 2013), 387.

[9]Abraham Joshua Heschel, introduction to *Man's Quest for God* (Santa Fe, NM: Aurora Press, 1996).

[10]Stark, *For the Glory of God*, 1.

[11]Stark, *For the Glory of God*, 1.

[12]Stark, *For the Glory of God,* 1.

[13]Donovan Slack, "Bible Display at Veteran Affairs Facility in New Hampshire Triggers Lawsuit," *USA Today,* May 7, 2019.

[14]Gore Vidal, "The Great Unmentionable: Monotheism and Its Discontents," Lowell Lecture, Harvard University, April 20, 1992.

[15]Richard Dawkins, *The God Delusion* (New York: Bantam, 2006), 51.

[16]Thomas Jefferson, quoted in David M. Rubenstein, *The American Story: Conversations with Master Historians* (New York: Simon & Schuster, 2019), 65.

[17]Blaise Pascal, *Pensées 913,* trans. A. J. Krailsheimer (London: Penguin, 1995), 285.

[18]Jonathan Sacks, *Genesis: The Book of Beginnings,* Covenant & Conversation (New Milford, CT: Maggid, 2009), 288.

[19]Abraham Joshua Heschel, *Moral Grandeur and Spiritual Audacity* (New York: Farrar, Straus and Giroux, 1996), 162.

[20]Jonathan Sacks, *Ceremony & Celebration: Introduction to the Holidays* (New Milford, CT: Maggid, 2017), 284.

[21]Abraham Joshua Heschel, *The Prophets* (New York: Harper Perennial, 2001), 625.

[22]James H. Billington, *Fire in the Minds of Men: Origins of the Revolutionary Faith* (London: Routledge, 2017), 46.

[23]B. F. Skinner, *Beyond Freedom and Dignity* (New York: Penguin/Pelican, 1973), 196.

[24]Sam Harris, *Free Will* (New York: Free Press, 2012), 5.

[25]Yuval Noah Harari, *Homo Deus: A Brief History of Tomorrow* (New York: Harper, 2017), 285, 293.

[26]Jonathan Sacks, "Faith in the Future (Shemot 5780)," *Covenant & Conversation,* January 13, 2020, https://rabbisacks.org/shemot-5780.

[27]Sacks, "Faith in the Future."

[28]Martin P. Seligman, Peter Railton, Roy F. Baumeister, and Chandra Sipada, *Homo Prospectus* (New York: Oxford University Press, 2016), x.

[29]Herman Cohen, quoted in Jonathan Sacks, *Deuteronomy: Renewal of the Sinai Covenant,* Covenant & Conversation (New Milford, CT: Maggid, 2019), 384.

[30]Harold Fisch, quoted in Sacks, *Deuteronomy,* 385.

[31]Sacks, *Deuteronomy,* 287.

[32]Jonathan Sacks, *Exodus: The Book of Redemption,* Covenant & Conversation (New Milford, CT: Maggid, 2010), 140.

[33]Mendel of Kotzk, quoted in Jonathan Sacks, *The Jonathan Sacks Haggada* (New Milford, CT: Maggid, 2013), 40.

[34]Sacks, *Ceremony & Celebration,* 95; emphasis added.

[35]Jonathan Sacks, *Leviticus: The Book of Holiness,* Covenant & Conversation (New Milford, CT: Maggid, 2015), 371.

[36]Heschel, *Man's Quest for God,* 25.

[37]Sacks, *Ceremony & Celebration,* 18.

[38]Sacks, *Deuteronomy*, 248.

[39]Sacks, *Ceremony & Celebration*, 285.

[40]Jonathan Sacks, *Numbers: The Wilderness Years,* Covenant & Conversation (New Milford, CT: Maggid, 2017), 50.

[41]Jonathan Sacks, *Exodus: The Book of Redemption,* Covenant & Conversation (New Milford, CT: Maggid, 2010), 12.332.

[42]Sacks, *Numbers*, 54, 52.

[43]Sacks, *Deuteronomy*, 49.

[44]Sacks, *Deuteronomy*, 72.

[45]Sacks, *Deuteronomy*, 73.

[46]Sacks, *Deuteronomy*, 71.

[47]Sacks, *Deuteronomy*, 72.

[48]Sacks, *Deuteronomy*, 74.

[49]Sacks, *Leviticus*, 207.

[50]Abraham J. Heschel, *The Insecurity of Freedom: Essays on Human Existence* (New York: Farrar, Straus and Giroux, 1967), 88.

[51]Jonathan Sacks, *Lessons in Leadership* (New Milford, CT: Maggid, 2015), 141.

[52]Sacks, *Lessons in Leadership,* 142.

[53]Sacks, *Lessons in Leadership,* 143.

[54]Sacks, *Deuteronomy*, 181.

[55]Sacks, *Deuteronomy*, 181.

[56]Heschel, *Insecurity of Freedom*, 42.

[57]Sacks, *Lessons in Leadership*, 76.

[58]Sacks, *Lessons in Leadership*, 102.

[59]Michael Walzer, *In God's Shadow: Politics in the Hebrew Bible* (New Haven, CT: Yale University Press, 2012), 13.

[60]Walzer, *God's Shadow*, 86.

[61]Sacks, *Exodus*, 310.

[62]Sacks, *Numbers*, 222.

[63]Walzer, *God's Shadow*, 15.

[64]Walzer, *God's Shadow*, 82.

[65]Wolfgang Palaver, *René Girard's Mimetic Theory*, trans. Gabriel Borrud (East Lansing: Michigan State University, 2013), 27.

[66]Abraham J. Heschel, *What Is Man?* (New York: Farrar, Straus and Giroux, 1965), 101.

[67]Fyodor Dostoevsky, *Demons,* trans. Richard Pevear and Larissa Volokhonsky (New York: Vintage Books, 1991), 252.

[68]Fyodor Dostoevsky, *The Brothers Karamazov,* trans. Richard Pevear and Larissa Kolokhonsky (New York: Vintage Books, 1991), 254.

[69]Albert Camus, *The Rebel,* trans. Anthony Bower (London: Penguin Classics, 2000), 11, 66, 115.

[70]Palaver, *René Girard's Mimetic Theory*, 24.

[71]Ludwig Feuerbach, *The Essence of Christianity*, trans. George Eliot (New York: Harper, 1957), 251.

[72]Alexis de Tocqueville, quoted in Erik von Kuehnelt-Leddihn, *Liberty or Equality* (Front Royal, VA: Christendom Press, 1993), 20.

[73]Alexis de Tocqueville, *Democracy in America*, trans. Henry Reeves, Francis Bowen, and Phillips Bradley (New York: Vintage Books, 1990), 1:310.

[74]Fyodor Dostoevsky, *The Adolescent*, trans. Andrew R. MacAndrew (Garden City, NY: Doubleday, 1971), 389.

[75]Sacks, *Ceremony & Celebration*, 242.

2. LIKE THE ABSOLUTELY UNLIKE: THE GREAT DECLARATION

[1]Primo Levi, *If This Is a Man*, *The Complete Works of Primo Levi*, ed. Anne Goldstein (New York: Liveright, 2015), 100.

[2]Abraham J. Heschel, *What Is Man?* (Stanford, CA: Stanford University Press, 1965), 24.

[3]Steven Pinker, "The Stupidity of Dignity," *New Republic*, May 28, 2008.

[4]David Berlinski, *Human Nature* (Seattle: Discovery Institute Press, 2019), 41.

[5]Albert Einstein, Letter, 1917.

[6]Stefan Zweig, *Messages from a Lost World: Europe on the Brink*, trans. Will Stone (London: Pushkin Press, 2016), 58-59.

[7]Frantz Fanon, *The Wretched of the Earth*, trans. Constance Farrington (London: Penguin, 1967), 21.

[8]Mario Savio, "Sit-in Address on the Steps of Sproul Hall," *American Rhetoric*, December 2, 1964, https://americanrhetoric.com/speeches/mariosaviosproulhallsitin.htm.

[9]C. S. Lewis, *The Abolition of Man* (San Francisco: HarperOne, 1974), 68.

[10]Abraham Joshua Heschel, *Moral Grandeur and Spiritual Audacity* (New York: Farrar, Straus and Giroux, 1996), 275.

[11]Mark O'Connell, *To Be a Machine* (London: Penguin, 2016), 158.

[12]O'Connell, *To Be a Machine*, 39, 50.

[13]Hannah Arendt, *The Human Condition* (New York: Knopf, 1958).

[14]John Gray, *Seven Types of Atheism* (London: Penguin, 2018), 62.

[15]James H. Billington, *The Icon and the Axe* (New York: Vintage Books, 1966), 479.

[16]Paul Johnson, *A History of the Jews* (New York: Harper Perennial, 1988), 347.

[17]Johnson, *History of the Jews*, 67-68.

[18]Yuval Noah Harari, *Homo Deus: A Brief History of Tomorrow* (New York: Harper, 2017), 21, 43, 44, 47-48.

[19]Abraham J. Heschel, quoted in S. Radhakrishnan and P. T. Raju, ed., *The Concept of Man: A Study in Comparative Philosophy* (Lincoln, NE: Johnsen Publishing, 1960), 124.

[20]Cathy O'Neill, *Weapons of Math Destruction: How Big Data Increases Inequality and Threatens Democracy* (New York: Broadway Books, 2017).

[21]Heschel, *Moral Grandeur and Spiritual Audacity*, 4.

[22]Ray Monk, *Ludwig Wittgenstein: The Duty of Genius* (New York: Free Press, 1990), 140.

[23]Heschel, *Insecurity of Freedom*, 182.

[24]Heschel, *Insecurity of Freedom*, 76.

[25]Jonathan Sacks, *Exodus: The Book of Redemption,* Covenant & Conversation (New Milford, CT: Maggid, 2010), 177.

[26]Heschel, *Insecurity of Freedom,* 25.

[27]Heschel, *Insecurity of Freedom,* 27.

[28]Paul Johnson, *A History of the Jews* (New York: Harper Perennial, 1988), 155.

[29]Jonathan Sacks, *Genesis: The Book of Beginnings,* Covenant & Conversation (New Milford, CT: Maggid, 2009), 21.

[30]Abraham Joshua Heschel, *Man Is Not Alone: A Philosophy of Religion* (New York: Farrar, Straus and Giroux, 1979), 197.

[31]Abraham Joshua Heschel, "The Concept of Man in Jewish Thought," in Radhakrishnan and Raju, *Concept of Man*, 141.

[32]Heschel, *Man Is Not Alone*, 115.

[33]"Satoshi Uematsu: Japanese Man Who Killed 19 Disabled People Sentenced to Death," BBC News, March 16, 2020, www.bbc.com/news/world-asia-51903289.

[34]Heschel, *Man Is Not Alone*, 130.

[35]Blaise Pascal, *Pensées,* trans. A. J. Krailsheimer (London: Penguin, 1995), 34-35.

[36]Jonathan Sacks, *Leviticus: The Book of Holiness,* Covenant & Conversation (New Milford, CT: Maggid, 2015), 81.

[37]William Shakespeare, *Hamlet*, act 2, scene 2.

[38]Pascal, *Pensées,* 34-35.

[39]Pascal, *Pensées,* 215.

[40]Sacks, *Leviticus*, 83.

[41]Jonathan Sacks, *Ceremony & Celebration: Introduction to the Holidays* (New Milford, CT: Maggid, 2017), 85.

[42]See Os Guinness, *Unspeakable: Facing Up to Evil in an Age of Genocide and Terror* (San Francisco: HarperOne, 2005).

[43]Joseph Heller, *Good as Gold* (New York: Simon & Schuster, 1997), 72.

[44]Abraham Joshua Heschel, *The Prophets* (New York: Harper Perennial, 2001), xviii.

[45]Aristotle, *Magna Moralia,* 1208b, 29-32.

[46]Jonathan Sacks, *Deuteronomy: Renewal of the Sinai Covenant,* Covenant & Conversation (New Milford, CT: Maggid, 2019), 147.

[47]Jonathan Sacks, *Genesis: The Book of Beginnings,* Covenant & Conversation (New Milford, CT: Maggid,), 150

[48]Radhakrishnan and Raju, *Concept of Man*, 153.

[49]Sacks, *Genesis*, 153.

[50]Hilary Putnam, quoted in Sacks, *Genesis*, 153.

[51]Sacks, *Genesis*, 153.

[52]Jonathan Sacks, *Numbers: The Wilderness Years,* Covenant & Conversation (New Milford, CT: Maggid, 2017), 230.

[53]Sacks, *Deuteronomy*, xxi.

[54]Sacks, *Deuteronomy*, 151; emphasis added.

[55]Heschel, *What Is Man?*, 38.

[56]C. S. Lewis, *The Weight of Glory and Other Addresses* (Grand Rapids, MI: Eerdmans, 1949), 14-15.

[57]Nicholas Wolterstorff, *Justice: Rights and Wrongs* (Princeton, NJ: Princeton University Press, 2008), 393.

[58]Friedrich Nietzsche, *The Will to Power,* trans. Anthony Ludovici (np: nd), 20-21.

[59]Nietzsche, *Will to Power*, 23.

[60]Sacks, *Numbers*, 229.

[61]Sacks, *Exodus*, 136.

[62]David M. Rubenstein, *The American Story: Conversations with Master Historians* (New York: Simon & Schuster, 2019), 47.

[63]Sacks, *Exodus*, 209.

[64]Sacks, *Exodus*, 209.

[65]A. C. Grayling, *Towards the Light* (London: Bloomsbury, 2007), 261.

[66]Sacks, *Exodus*, 210.

[67]Sacks, *Deuteronomy*, 270.

[68]Sacks, *Deuteronomy*, 270.

[69]Sacks, *Deuteronomy*, 357.

[70]Bartolomé de Las Casas, quoted in Lawrence A. Clayton, *Bartolomé De Las Casas: A Biography* (Cambridge: Cambridge University Press, 2012), 81, 100.

[71]Sacks, *Exodus*, 244.

[72]Sacks, *Exodus*, 244; emphasis added.

[73]Sacks, *Exodus*, 2.

[74]Sacks, *Exodus*, 167.

[75]Jonathan Sacks, *The Jonathan Sacks Haggada* (New Milford, CT: Maggid, 2013), 125.

[76]Sacks, *Exodus*, 88.

[77]John Milton, *Paradise Lost*, bk. 12: 64-71.

[78]Heschel, *Insecurity of Freedom*, 16.

[79]Sacks, *Jonathan Sacks Haggada*, 125.

[80]Sacks, *Ceremony & Celebration*, 174-75.

[81]Berlinski, *Human Nature*, 47.

[82]Heschel, *Prophets*, 202.

[83]Fyodor Dostoevsky, *Demons,* trans. Richard Pevear and Larissa Volokhonsky (New York: Vintage Books, 1991), 664.

[84]Heschel, *Prophets*, 212.

[85]Sacks, *Exodus*, 268.

[86]Milton Himmelfarb, quoted in Sacks, *Jonathan Sacks Haggada*, 50.

[87]Sacks, *Exodus*, 269.

[88]Joseph Stalin, quoted in Harry Redner, *Totalitarianism, Globalization, Colonialism: The Destruction of Civilization Since 1914* (New Brunswick, NJ: Transaction, 2014), 90.

[89]Heinrich Himmler, quoted in Redner, *Totalitarianism,* 35-36.

[90]Sacks, *Deuteronomy,* 4.

[91]Sacks, *Leviticus,* 173; emphasis added.

[92]James H. Billington, *Fire in the Minds of Men: Origins of the Revolutionary Faith* (London: Routledge, 2017), 26.

[93]Billington, *Fire in the Minds,* 29.

3. EAST OF EDEN: THE GREAT ALIENATION

[1]Christopher Hill, *The World Turned Upside Down: Radical Ideas During the English Revolution* (London: Penguin, 1991), 134.

[2]Thomas Paine, quoted in James H. Billington, *Fire in the Minds of Men: Origins of the Revolutionary Faith* (London: Routledge, 2017), 56.

[3]Francis Crick, quoted in Robert Sarah, *The Day Is Now Far Spent* (San Francisco: Ignatius Press, 2019), 280.

[4]George Orwell, quoted in John Rodden, *Becoming George Orwell* (Princeton, NJ: Princeton University Press, 2020), 265.

[5]Alexander Solzhenitsyn, *The Gulag Archipelago.*

[6]Solzhenitsyn, *Gulag Archipelago.*

[7]Jonathan Sacks, *Ceremony & Celebration: Introduction to the Holidays* (New Milford, CT: Maggid, 2017), 27.

[8]Abraham Joshua Heschel, *The Prophets* (New York: Harper Perennial, 2001), 219.

[9]Abraham Joshua Heschel, *Man's Quest for God* (Santa Fe, NM: Aurora Press, 1996), 56.

[10]Jonathan Sacks, *Exodus: The Book of Redemption,* Covenant & Conversation (New Milford, CT: Maggid, 2010), 313.

[11]William Wordsworth, "The Prelude," *Poems,* vol. 22, 77.

[12]Fyodor Dostoevsky, *Demons,* trans. Richard Pevear and Larissa Volokhonsky (New York: Everyman's Library, 2000), 16.

[13]Kenneth Lantz, *The Dostoevsky Encyclopedia* (Westport, CT: Greenwood Press, 2004), 146.

[14]Lantz, *Dostoevsky Encyclopedia,* 146.

[15]Sacks, *Exodus,* 12.

[16]Sacks, *Exodus,* 203.

[17]Dostoevsky, quoted in Lantz, *Dostoevsky Encyclopedia,* 148.

[18]Simone de Beauvoir, *The Second Sex,* bk. 2, 1949, 1.

[19]Jean-Jacques Rousseau, quoted in Yuval Noah Harari, *Homo Deus: A Brief History of Tomorrow* (New York: Harper, 2017), 225.

[20]Jean-Paul Sartre, *No Exit.*

[21]Louis Antoine de Saint-Just, quoted in James H. Billington, *Fire in the Minds of Men: Origins of the Revolutionary Faith* (London: Routledge, 2017), 64.

[22]Billington, *Fire in the Minds,* 49.

[23]Ayn Rand, *Atlas Shrugged* (New York: Penguin, 1985), 572-73.

[24]Paul W. Kahn, *Putting Liberalism in Its Place* (Princeton, NJ: Princeton University Press, 2005), 205.

[25]Kahn, *Putting Liberalism in Its Place,* 205.

[26]Paul Simon and Art Garfunkel, "I Am a Rock," *Sounds of Silence¸* Universal Music, 1966.

[27]Robert D. Putnam, *Bowling Alone* (New York: Simon & Schuster, 2000); and Sherry Turkle, *Alone Together* (New York: Basic Books, 2011).

[28]Dostoevsky, quoted in Lantz, *Dostoevsky Encyclopedia,* 149.

[29]Dostoevsky, *Demons,* 617.

[30]Dostoevsky, *Demons,* 617.

[31]James Bryce, *The American Commonwealth* (Indianapolis: Liberty Fund, 1995), 2:563; emphasis added.

[32]Heinrich Heine, quoted in Mark H. Gelber, *The Jewish Reception of Heinrich Heine* (Berlin: De Gruyter, 2013), 34.

[33]Friedrich Nietzsche, *Thus Spoke Zarathustra,* trans. Graham Parkes (New York: Oxford University Press, 2008), 74.

[34]Dostoevsky, *Demons.*

[35]Yuval Noah Harari, *Homo Deus: A Brief History of Tomorrow* (New York: Harper, 2017), 43, 44, 48.

[36]Jonathan Sacks, *Ceremony & Celebration: Introduction to the Holidays* (New Milford, CT: Maggid, 2017), 188.

[37]Jonathan Sacks, *Deuteronomy: Renewal of the Sinai Covenant,* Covenant & Conversation (New Milford, CT: Maggid, 2019), 259.

[38]Dietrich Bonhoeffer, *Ethics (*New York: Simon & Schuster, 1995), 219.

[39]Sacks, *Ceremony & Celebration,* 11.

[40]Sacks, *Ceremony & Celebration,* 11.

[41]David Andress, *The Terror: The Merciless War for Freedom in Revolutionary France* (New York: Farrar, Straus and Giroux, 2005), 7.

[42]See Os Guinness, *Unspeakable: Facing Up to the Challenge of Evil* (San Francisco: HarperOne, 2006).

[43]Steiner, quoted in Guinness, *Unspeakable,* 142.

[44]Guinness, *Unspeakable,* 136-52.

[45]Friedrich Nietzsche, *Beyond Good and Evil,* aphorism 146, trans. Walter Kaufmann (New York: Vintage Books, 1989), 89.

[46]Tom Paine, *Common Sense* (Alexandria, VA: Capitol.Net, 2011), 68.

[47]Douwe Fokkema, *Perfect Worlds: Utopian Fiction in China and the West* (Amsterdam: University of Amsterdam Press, 2011), 321.

[48]Karl Marx and Friedrich Engels, quoted in Alexander Solzhenitsyn, *Warning to the West* (New York: Farrar, Straus and Giroux, 1976), 57.

[49]Robespierre, quoted in Harry Redner, *The Triumph and Tragedy of the Intellectuals: Evil, Enlightenment and Death* (New Brunswick, NJ: Transaction, 2016), 32.

[50]Harry Redner, *Totalitarianism, Globalization, Colonialism: The Destruction of Civilization Since 1914* (New Brunswick, NJ: Transaction, 2014), 56.

[51]Michael Walzer, *In God's Shadow: Politics in the Hebrew Bible* (New Haven, CT: Yale University Press, 2012), 46.

[52]Billington, *Fire in the Minds*, 14.

[53]Sacks, *Ceremony & Celebration*, 188.

[54]For a fuller discussion see Os Guinness, *Last Call for Liberty: How America's Genius for Freedom Has Become Its Greatest Threat* (Downers Grove, IL: InterVarsity Press, 2018), 99-111.

[55]Edmund Burke, *Reflections on the Revolution in France* (Oxford: Oxford University Press, 1993), 289; and John Fletcher Moulton, "Law and Manners," *Atlantic*, July 1924.

[56]Sacks, *Exodus*, 49.

[57]Sacks, *Exodus*, 50.

[58]Sacks, *Exodus*, 50.

[59]Sacks, *Exodus*, 197.

[60]Sacks, *Exodus*, 197.

[61]Sacks, *Ceremony & Celebration*, 139.

[62]Sacks, *Exodus*, 145.

4. LET MY PEOPLE GO: THE GREAT LIBERATION

[1]Samuel Johnson, *Taxation No Tyranny: An Answer to the Resolutions and Address of the American Congress*, Works of Samuel Johnson 14 (Troy, NY: Pafraets, 1913), 93-144.

[2]Henry David Thoreau, February 15, 1851, entry in *The Journal of Henry David Thoreau*, ed. Bradford Torrey and Francis H. Allen (Boston: Houghton Mifflin, 1949), 2:162.

[3]Henry David Thoreau, *Walden and On the Duty of Civil Disobedience*, ed. Charles R. Anderson (New York: Signet Classics, 2012), 51.

[4]Jonathan Sacks, *Lessons in Leadership* (New Milford, CT: Maggid, 2015), 75.

[5]Jonathan Sacks, *Exodus: The Book of Redemption,* Covenant & Conversation (New Milford, CT: Maggid, 2010), 2.

[6]Jonathan Sacks, *The Jonathan Sacks Haggada* (New Milford, CT: Maggid, 2013), 3.

[7]John Bright says, "There can really be little doubt that ancestors of Israel had been slaves in Egypt and had escaped in some marvelous way. Almost no one today would question it." John Bright, *A History of Israel* (Philadelphia: Westminster Press, 1981), 120. See also K. A. Kitchen, *On the Reliability of the Old Testament* (Grand Rapids, MI: Eerdmans, 2003); and James K. Hoffmeier, *Israel in Egypt: The Evidence for the Authenticity of the Exodus Tradition* (New York: Oxford University Press, 1996).

[8]Friedrich Nietzsche, *On the Genealogy of Morals,* trans. Douglas Smith (Oxford: Oxford University Press, 1996), 20.

[9]Hoffmeier, *Israel in Egypt,* 7.

[10]Sacks, *Exodus*, 53.

[11]Sacks, *Exodus*, 55.

[12]Sacks, *Exodus*, 56-57.

[13]Hoffmeier, *Israel in Egypt*, 14-15.

[14]Sacks, *Exodus*, 15.

[15]Sacks, *Exodus*, 16.

[16]Sacks, *Jonathan Sacks Haggada*, 15.

[17]Sacks, *Jonathan Sacks Haggada*, 15.

[18]Sacks, *Exodus*, 99.

[19]Sacks, *Exodus*, 98.

[20]Sacks, *Exodus*, 99.

[21]Sacks, *Exodus*, 99.

[22]Sacks, *Exodus*, 100.

5. SET FREE TO LIVE FREE TOGETHER:
THE GREAT CONSTITUTION

[1]Martin Buber, quoted in Paul Mendes-Flohr, *Martin Buber: A Life of Faith and Dissent* (New Haven, CT: Yale University Press, 2019), 182.

[2]Buber, quoted in Mendes-Flohr, *Martin Buber,* 183-84.

[3]Katherine Hawley, *Trust: A Very Short Introduction* (Oxford: Oxford University Press, 2012), 17.

[4]Tim Harford, "How Worried Should We Be About 'Big Brother' Technology?" BBC News, January 29, 2020, www.bbc.com/news/business-50673770.

[5]Jonathan Sacks, *The Jonathan Sacks Haggada: Collected Essays on Pesah* (New Milford, CT: Maggid, 2013), 5.

[6]Abraham Joshua Heschel, *Moral Grandeur and Spiritual Audacity* (New York: Farrar, Straus and Giroux, 1996), 246.

[7]Michael Walzer, *In God's Shadow: Politics in the Hebrew Bible* (New Haven, CT: Yale University Press, 2012), 1.

[8]Jonathan Sacks, *Exodus: The Book of Redemption,* Covenant & Conversation (New Milford, CT: Maggid, 2010), 150.

[9]Sacks, *Exodus,* 150.

[10]Sacks, *Exodus,* 155.

[11]Jonathan Sacks, *Deuteronomy: Renewal of the Sinai Covenant,* Covenant & Conversation (New Milford, CT: Maggid, 2019), 123.

[12]Sacks, *Deuteronomy,* 123.

[13]Sacks, *Exodus,* 10.

[14]Walzer, *God's Shadow,* 200.

[15]Abraham Joshua Heschel, *God in Search of Man: A Philosophy of Judaism* (New York: Farrar, Straus and Giroux, 1955), 423.

[16]Isaiah Berlin, *Four Essays on Liberty* (New York: Oxford University Press, 1969), 118.

[17]Jonathan Sacks, *Leviticus: The Book of Holiness,* Covenant & Conversation (New Milford, CT: Maggid, 2015), 180.

[18]Os Guinness, *Last Call for Liberty: How America's Genius for Freedom Has Become Its Greatest Threat* (Downers Grove, IL: InterVarsity Press, 2018).

[19]Jonathan Sacks, *To Heal a Fractured World: The Ethics of Responsibility* (New York: Schocken, 2005), 154.

[20]Sacks, *Deuteronomy*, 256.

[21]Michael Walzer, *Exodus and Revolution* (New York: Basic Books, 1985), 97.

[22]Jonathan Sacks, *Ceremony & Celebration: Introduction to the Holidays* (New Milford, CT: Maggid, 2017), 278.

[23]Sacks, *Deuteronomy*, xxix.

[24]Abraham Joshua Heschel, *Israel: An Echo of Eternity* (New York: Farrar, Straus and Giroux, 1969), 96.

[25]*The Koren Shalem Siddur*, intro. Jonathan Sacks (Jerusalem: Koren, 2009), 98.

[26]Sacks, *Deuteronomy*, 250-51.

[27]Sacks, *Exodus*, 116.

[28]Abraham Lincoln, "First Inaugural Address," Avalon Project, March 4, 1861, https://avalon.law.yale.edu/19th_century/lincoln1.asp.

[29]Sacks, *Deuteronomy*, 9; Sacks, *Ceremony & Celebration*, 239.

[30]Jonathan Sacks, *Essays on Ethics* (New Milford, CT: Maggid, 2016), xxviii.

[31]See Os Guinness, *A Free People's Suicide* (Downers Grove, IL: InterVarsity Press, 2012), chap. 4.

[32]Alexis de Tocqueville, *Democracy in America* (New York: Vintage Books, 1954), 1:247; Friedrich Nietzsche, *Beyond Good and Evil* (New York: Vintage Books, 1969), 101; and Nelson Mandela, *Long Walk to Freedom* (New York: Little, Brown, 1994).

[33]Jonathan Sacks, *Numbers: The Wilderness Years* (New Milford, CT: Maggid, 2017), 2.

[34]Sacks, *Numbers*, 12.

[35]Sacks, *Numbers*, 3.

[36]Sacks, *Jonathan Sacks Haggada*, 38.

[37]See William Holman Hunt, "Light of the World," Keble College, www.keble.ox.ac.uk/about/chapel/light-of-the-world.

[38]Sacks, *Exodus*, 175.

[39]Walzer, *God's Shadow*, 210.

[40]Shimon bar Yohai, quoted in Sacks, *Jonathan Sacks Haggada*, 21.

[41]Sacks, *Ceremony & Celebration*, 294.

[42]Sacks, *Ceremony & Celebration*, 110.

[43]Sacks, *Ceremony & Celebration*, 157.

[44]Sacks, *Exodus*, 14.

[45]Sacks, *Jonathan Sacks Haggada*, 6.

[46]Jonathan Sacks, *Lessons in Leadership* (New Milford, CT: Maggid, 2015), 85.

[47]Sacks, *Lessons in Leadership*, 86.

[48]Sacks, *Ceremony & Celebration*, 303.

[49]Oliver Goldsmith, "The Traveller," in *Oxford Essential Quotations* (Oxford: Oxford University Press, 2017), 1:429.

[50]Sacks, *Ceremony & Celebration*, 304.

[51]Sacks, *Ceremony & Celebration*, 192.

[52]Sacks, *Numbers*, 3.

[53]Abraham Joshua Heschel, *The Prophets* (New York: Harper Perennial, 2001), 609.

[54]Sacks, *Deuteronomy*, 164.

[55]Sacks, *Deuteronomy*, 165.

[56]Sacks, *Deuteronomy*, 65.

[57]Heschel, *Prophets*, 188.

[58]Sacks, *Jonathan Sacks Hagga*da, 37.

[59]Sacks, *Lessons in Leadership*, 156.

[60]Dennis Prager, *Exodus: God, Slavery and Freedom* (Washington, DC: Regnery Faith, 2018), 7.

[61]Prager, *Exodus*, 8.

[62]Jonathan Sacks, *Genesis: The Book of Beginnings,* Covenant & Conversation (New Milford, CT: Maggid, 2009), 103.

[63]Sacks, *Genesis*, 105.

[64]Norman Lebrecht, *Genius and Anxiety: How Jews Changed the World, 1847-1947* (London: OneWorld Books, 2019), 342.

[65]Sacks, *Genesis*, 103.

[66]Sacks, *Genesis*, 106.

[67]Sacks, *Lessons in Leadership*, 160.

[68]Sacks, *Ceremony & Celebration*, 227.

[69]Sacks, *Ceremony & Celebration*, 227.

[70]Sacks, *Ceremony & Celebration*, 227.

[71]Sacks, *Ceremony & Celebration*, 229.

6. PASSING IT ON: THE GREAT TRANSMISSION

[1]Mark Twain, "Concerning the Jews," *Harper's*, September 1899.

[2]Jonathan Sacks, *Deuteronomy: The Renewal of the Sinai Covenant,* Covenant & Conversation (New Milford, CT: Maggid, 2019), 99.

[3]Sacks, *Deuteronomy*, 83.

[4]Sacks, *Deuteronomy*, 104.

[5]Jonathan Sacks, *Numbers: The Wilderness Years,* Covenant & Conversation (New Milford, CT: Maggid, 2017), 240.

[6]Sacks, *Deuteronomy*, 101.

[7]Abraham Joshua Heschel, *Man's Quest for God* (Santa Fe, NM: Aurora Press, 1996), 54.

[8]Heschel, *Man's Quest for God*, 65.

[9]Jonathan Sacks, *Exodus: The Book of Redemption,* Covenant & Conversation (New Milford, CT: Maggid, 2010), 78.

[10]Jonathan Sacks, "The Story We Tell About Ourselves (Bo 5780)," *Covenant & Conversation*, January 2020, https://rabbisacks.org/bo-5780.

[11]Sacks, *Exodus*, 78.

[12]Sacks, *Exodus*, 79.

[13]Sacks, *Exodus*, 135.

[14]John Man, quoted in Sacks, *Exodus*, 135.

[15]Sacks, *Exodus*, 136.

[16]Sacks, *Exodus*, 137.

[17]Sacks, *Exodus*, 135.

[18]Sacks, *Exodus*, 135.

[19]Sacks, *Exodus*, 135; emphasis added.

[20]Jonathan Sacks, *The Jonathan Sacks Haggada: Collected Essays on Pesah* (New Milford, CT: Maggid, 2013), 160

[21]Sacks, *Exodus*, 80.

[22]Peter Abelard, quoted in Paul Johnson, *A History of the Jews* (New York: Harper Perennial, 1988), 193.

[23]Sacks, *Exodus*, 80.

[24]Andrew Cunningham McLaughlin, *The Foundations of American Constitutionalism* (Greenwich, CT: Fawcett, 1961), 159.

[25]Learned Hand, "The Spirit of Liberty," *Digital History*, May 21, 1944, http://www.digital-history.uh.edu/disp_textbook.cfm?smtID=3&psid=1199.

[26]Jonathan Sacks, *Ceremony & Celebration: Introduction to the Holidays* (New Milford, CT: Maggid, 2017), 168.

[27]Abraham J. Heschel, *The Insecurity of Freedom: Essays on Human Existence* (New York: Farrar, Straus and Giroux, 1967), 237.

[28]Sacks, *Deuteronomy,* 256.

[29]Roger Williams, "The Bloudy Tenent of Persecution," in John M. Barry, *Roger Williams and the Creation of the American Soul: Church, State and the Birth of Liberty* (New York: Viking, 2012), 336.

[30]Os Guinness, *The Global Public Square: Religious Freedom and the Making of a World Safe for Diversity* (Downers Grove, IL: InterVarsity Press, 2016).

[31]Edmund Burke, *Reflections on the Revolution in France* (Oxford: Oxford University Press, 1993), 289.

[32]Fyodor Dostoevsky, *Demons,* trans. Richard Pevear and Larissa Volokhonsky (New York: Everyman's Library, 2000), 123.

[33]Sacks, *Deuteronomy*, 296.

[34]Friedrich Nietzsche, *The Will to Power,* trans. Anthony Ludovici (Overland Park, KS: Digireads, 2019), 15.

[35]Abraham Joshua Heschel, *Moral Grandeur and Spiritual Audacity* (New York: Farrar, Straus and Giroux, 1996), 47.

[36]Abraham Joshua Heschel, *The Sabbath: Its Meaning for Modern Man* (New York: Farrar, Straus and Giroux, 1951), 98.

[37]Sacks, *Jonathan Sacks Haggada*, 88.

[38]Hugh Brogan, *Alexis de Tocqueville: A Life* (New Haven, CT: Yale University Press, 2008), 93.

[39]Ted Hughes, "Hear It Again," 1997.

[40]Jonathan Sacks, *Lessons in Leadership* (New Milford, CT: Maggid, 2015), 278.

[41]Sacks, *Exodus*, 65.

[42]Heschel, *Sabbath*, 7.

[43]Sacks, *Ceremony & Celebration*, 169.

[44]Sacks, *Ceremony & Celebration*, 178.

[45]Sacks, *Deuteronomy*, 225.

[46]Sacks, *Ceremony & Celebration*, 178.

[47]Sacks, *Ceremony & Celebration*, 253.

[48]Jean-Jacques Rousseau, *The Social Contract,* trans. Maurice Cranston (London: Penguin Classics, 1968), 89.

[49]Sacks, *Ceremony & Celebration*, 100.

[50]Sacks, *Ceremony & Celebration*, 101.

[51]Sacks, *Numbers*, 375.

[52]Sacks, *Ceremony & Celebration*, 102.

[53]Sacks, *Ceremony & Celebration*, 246.

[54]Sacks, *Ceremony & Celebration*, 246.

[55]Sacks, *Ceremony & Celebration*, 178.

[56]Sacks, *Deuteronomy*, 88.

[57]Sacks, *Deuteronomy*, 88.

[58]Abraham J. Heschel, *What Is Man?* (New York: Farrar, Straus and Giroux, 1965), 86.

[59]Oscar Wilde, quoted in Heschel, *What Is Man*, 87.

[60]Sacks, *Deuteronomy*, 91.

[61]Dostoevsky, *Demons*, 402.

[62]Dostoevsky, *Demons*, 402.

[63]Sacks, *Ceremony & Celebration*, 191.

7. PUTTING WRONG RIGHT: THE GREAT RESTORATION, PART 1

[1]Simon Wiesenthal, *The Sunflower: On the Possibilities and Limits of Forgiveness* (New York: Schocken, 1998), 35.

[2]Mary Crawford, *Shantung Revival* (St. Louis, MO: Global Awakening, 1999), 59.

[3]Patrisse Cullors, "A Short History of Black Lives Matter," YouTube, July 22, 2015, www.youtube.com/watch?v=kCghDx5qN4s.

[4]Ernesto Laclau and Chantal Mouffe, *Hegemony and Socialist Strategy: Towards a Radical Democratic Politics* (London: Verso Books, 2014), xxiv.

[5]Stephen Eric Bronner, *Critical Theory: A Very Short Introduction* (Oxford: Oxford University Press, 2017), 114.

[6]Laclau and Mouffe, *Hegemony and Socialist Strategy,* x.

[7]Helen Pluckrose and James Lindsay, *Cynical Theories* (Durham, NC: Pitchstone, 2020), 31.

[8]Pluckrose and Lindsay, *Cynical Theories*, 31.

[9]Pluckrose and Lindsay, *Cynical Theories*, 36.

[10]Abraham Joshua Heschel, *The Prophets* (Peabody, MA: Hendrickson, 2017), 159.

[11]Laclau and Mouffe, *Hegemony and Socialist Strategy*, xix.

[12]Marina Watts, "In Smithsonian Race Guidelines, Rational Thinking and Hard Work Are White Values," *Newsweek*, July 7, 2020, www.newsweek.com/smithsonian-race-guidelines-rational-thinking-hard-work-are-white-values-1518333.

[13]"BLM Leader Yusra Khogali: 'White People Are Genetic Defects,'" Clarion Project, July 7, 2020, https://clarionproject.org/blm-leader-yusra-khogali-white-people-are-genetic-defects.

[14]Helen Pluckrose and James Lindsay, *Cynical Theories: How Activist Scholarship Made Everything About Race, Gender, and Identity—and Why This Harms Everybody* (Durham, NC: Pitchstone, 2020), 134.

[15]Pluckrose and Lindsay, *Cynical Theories*, 134.

[16]G. K. Chesterton, "On Modern Controversy," *Illustrated London News*, August 14, 1926.

[17]Seneca, quoted in Tom Holland, *Rubicon: The Last Years of the Roman Republic* (New York: Anchor Books, 2003), 364.

[18]Tacitus, *Agricola* (Oxford: Oxford University Press), chap. 30.

[19]Laclau and Mouffe, *Hegemony and Socialist Strategy*, xvii.

[20]Jonathan Sacks, "How Not to Argue," *Covenant & Conversation,* June 16, 2020, https://rabbisacks.org/korach-5780.

[21]Sacks, "How Not to Argue."

[22]Michael Ignatieff, *The Warrior's Honour: Ethnic War and the Modern Conscience* (Toronto: Penguin, 2006), 188-90; and Jonathan Sacks, *Leviticus: The Book of Holiness,* Covenant & Conversation (New Milford, CT: Maggid, 2015), 107.

[23]Sacks, *Leviticus*, 105.

[24]Sigmund Freud, quoted in Paul Johnson, *A History of the Jews* (New York: Harper Perennial, 1988), 417.

[25]Johnson, *History of the Jews*, 417.

[26]Abraham Joshua Heschel, *Moral Grandeur and Spiritual Audacity* (New York: Farrar, Straus and Giroux, 1996), 6.

[27]Tacitus, *The Histories*, trans. W. H. Fyfe (Oxford: Oxford University Press, 1997), 1:7.

[28]Jonathan Sacks, *Lessons in Leadership* (New Milford, CT: Maggid, 2015), 271.

[29]James H. Billington, *Fire in the Minds of Men: Origins of the Revolutionary Faith* (London: Routledge, 2017), 409.

[30]Leon Trotsky, quoted in Norman Lebrecht, *Genius and Anxiety* (London: OneWorld Books, 2019), 266.

[31]Jonathan Sacks, *Ceremony & Celebration: Introduction to the Holidays* (New Milford, CT: Maggid, 2017), 257.

[32]Martin Luther King Jr., *Strength to Love* (Minneapolis: Fortress Press, 2010), 47.

[33]Jonathan Sacks, *Deuteronomy: Renewal of the Sinai Covenant*, Covenant & Conversation (New Milford, CT: Maggid, 2019), 202.

[34]Sacks, *Deuteronomy*, 205.

[35]Lucan *Pharsalia* I, 670, in Ronald Syme, *The Roman Revolution* (Oxford: Oxford University Press, 1939), 9.

[36]Billington, *Fire in the Minds*, 22.

8. PUTTING WRONG RIGHT: THE GREAT RESTORATION, PART 2

[1]Tacitus, "Histories," *Oxford Essential Quotations* (Oxford: Oxford University Press, 2017), 4:17.

[2]Mao Zedong, "Problems of War and Strategy," *Selected Works of Mao Tse-tung*, November 6, 1938, www.marxists.org/reference/archive/mao/selected-works/volume-2/mswv2_12.htm.

[3]Abraham Joshua Heschel, *The Prophets* (Peabody, MA: Hendrickson, 2017), 166.

[4]Jonathan Sacks, *Leviticus: The Book of Holiness*, Covenant & Conversation (New Milford, CT: Maggid, 2015), 91.

[5]Thucydides, The Melian Conference 431 BC, *The History of the Peloponnesian War* 5, 89.

[6]Abraham J. Heschel, *The Insecurity of Freedom: Essays on Human Existence* (New York: Farrar, Straus and Giroux, 1967), 254.

[7]Jonathan Sacks, *Ceremony & Celebration: Introduction to the Holidays* (New Milford, CT: Maggid, 2017), 2.

[8]Jonathan Sacks, *Numbers: The Wilderness Years*, Covenant & Conversation (New Milford, CT: Maggid, 2017), 305.

[9]Sacks, *Numbers*, 3.

[10]Heschel, *Prophets*, 172.

[11]David Hume, quoted in Nicholas Wolterstorff, *Justice: Rights and Wrongs* (Princeton, NJ: Princeton University Press, 2008), 2.

[12]Bruno Roche and Jay Jakub, *Completing Capitalism* (New York: Berrett-Koehler, 2017).

[13]Jonathan Sacks, *Exodus: The Book of Redemption*, Covenant & Conversation (New Milford, CT: Maggid, 2010), 183.

[14]Sacks, *Exodus*, 184.

[15]Sacks, *Exodus*, 185.

[16]Abraham Joshua Heschel, *Moral Grandeur and Spiritual Audacity* (New York: Farrar, Straus and Giroux, 1996), 32.

[17]Heschel, *Prophets*, 212.

[18]Heschel, *Prophets*, 212.

[19]Sacks, *Ceremony & Celebration*, 11.

[20]Sacks, *Ceremony & Celebration*, 42.

[21]Jake Silverstein, "Why We Published the 1619 Project," *New York Times*, December 20, 2019, www.nytimes.com/interactive/2019/12/20/magazine/1619-intro.html.

[22]Jason L. Riley, "A Bid to Revise the New York Times's Bad History," *Wall Street Journal*, February 18, 2020, www.wsj.com/articles/a-bid-to-revise-the-new-york-timess-bad-history-11582071646.

[23]Jonathan Sacks, *Deuteronomy: Renewal of the Sinai Covenant*, Covenant & Conversation (New Milford, CT: Maggid, 2019), 36.

[24]Heschel, *Man's Quest for God*, 34.

[25]Sacks, *Ceremony & Celebration*, 28.

[26]Jonathan Sacks, *The Jonathan Sacks Haggada* (New Milford, CT: Maggid, 2013), 154.

[27]Heschel, *Moral Grandeur and Spiritual Audacity*, 69.

[28]Heschel, *Prophets*, 174.

[29]Fyodor Dostoevsky, *Demons,* trans. Richard Pevear and Larissa Volokhonsky (New York: Vintage Books, 1991), 655.

[30]Rabbi Nathan, quoted in *The Koren Shalem Siddur* (Jerusalem: Koren, 2009), 661.

[31]Sacks, *Ceremony & Celebration*, 43.

[32]Abraham Joshua Heschel, *God in Search of Man: A Philosophy of Judaism* (New York: Farrar, Straus and Giroux, 1955), 369.

[33]Jonathan Sacks, *Genesis: The Book of Beginnings,* Covenant & Conversation (New Milford, CT: Maggid, 2009), 327.

[34]Sacks, *Genesis,* 327; emphasis added.

[35]See E. Michael Jones, *Libido Dominandi: Sexual Liberation and Political Control* (South Bend, IN: St. Augustine's Press, 2000), pt. 1, chap. 1.

[36]Jones, *Libido Dominandi*, 14.

[37]Berthold Brecht, quoted in Stephen Eric Bronner, *Critical Theory: A Very Short Introduction* (Oxford: Oxford University Press, 2017), 96.

[38]Kelion, "Why Amazon Knows So Much About You."

[39]Augustine, *City of God*, preface, bk. 1.

[40]Fyodor Dostoevsky, *Demons* (New York: Everyman's Library, 1994), 401.

CONCLUSION: A NEW, NEW BIRTH OF FREEDOM?

[1]Abraham Lincoln, "The Gettysburg Address," Soldiers National Cemetery, Gettysburg, PA, November 19, 1863.

[2]Ray Monk, *Ludwig Wittgenstein: The Duty of Genius* (New York: Free Press, 1990), 9.

[3]Douglas Murray, *The Strange Death of Europe: Immigration, Identity, Islam* (London: Bloomsbury Continuum, 2018).

[4]John Adams, letter to F. A. Van der Kemp, February 16, 1808 (Pennsylvania Historical Society).

[5]Abraham Joshua Heschel, *God in Search of Man: A Philosophy of Judaism* (New York: Farrar, Straus and Giroux, 1955), 201.

[6]Alexander Solzhenitsyn, *Warning to the West* (New York: Farrar, Straus and Giroux, 1976), 22.

[7]Solzhenitsyn, *Warning to the West*, 26.

[8]Solzhenitsyn, *Warning to the West*, 53.

[9]Solzhenitsyn, *Warning to the West*, 53.

[10]Jonathan Sacks, *Exodus: The Book of Redemption*, Covenant & Conversation (New Milford, CT: Maggid, 2010), 337.

ACKNOWLEDGMENTS

[1]Blaise Pascal, *Pensées* 913, trans. A. J. Krailsheimer (London: Penguin, 1995), 330.

NAME INDEX

ALSO BY OS GUINNESS

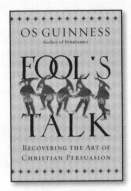

Fool's Talk
978-0-8308-4448-7

A Free People's Suicide
978-0-8308-3465-5

Carpe Diem Redeemed
978-0-8308-4581-1

Renaissance
978-0-8308-3671-0

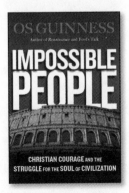

Impossible People
978-0-8308-4465-4

Last Call for Liberty
978-0-8308-4559-3